DEPRESSION IN LATER LIFE

DEPRESSION IN LATER LIFE

An Essential Guide

Deborah Serani

ROWMAN & LITTLEFIELD
Lanham • Boulder • New York • London

Published by Rowman & Littlefield
A wholly owned subsidiary of The Rowman & Littlefield Publishing Group, Inc.
4501 Forbes Boulevard, Suite 200, Lanham, Maryland 20706
www.rowman.com

Unit A, Whitacre Mews, 26-34 Stannary Street, London SE11 4AB

British Library Cataloguing in Publication Information Available

Library of Congress Cataloging-in-Publication Data
The hardback edition of this book was previously cataloged by the Library of Congress as follows:

Names: Serani, Deborah, 1961- author.
Title: Depression in later life : an essential guide / Deborah Serani.
Description: Lanham : Rowman & Littlefield, 2016. | Includes bibliographical references and index.
Identifiers: LCCN 2015045280 (print) | LCCN 2015046981 (ebook)
Subjects: LCSH: Depression in old age--Popular works.
Classification: LCC RC537.5 .S47 2016 (print) | LCC RC537.5 (ebook) | DDC 618.97/68527--dc23
LC record available at http://lccn.loc.gov/2015045280

ISBN: 978-1-4422-5582-1 (cloth : alk. paper)
ISBN: 978-1-5381-1043-0 (pbk. : alk. paper)
ISBN: 978-1-4422-5583-8 (electronic)

Printed in the United States of America

For my sisters, Karen and Paula.
May we grow old together and live deeply.

CONTENTS

Introduction   ix

1 What Is Late-Life Depression?   1
2 Geriatric Mood Disorders   15
3 Diagnosis for Depression in Later Life   31
4 Traditional Treatments for Depression in Later Life   49
5 Holistic Approaches to Depression in Later Life   65
6 How to Maintain Success in Treatment   89
7 Suicide in Later Life   107
8 What to Expect Should You Need Hospitalization   127
9 Conscious Aging with Depression in Later Life   143
10 Long-Term Care and Late-Life Depression   161
11 15 Late-Life Depression Myths Everyone Should Know   181

Appendix A: Depression Screening Questionnaire   193
Appendix B: Current Medications and Supplements   197
Appendix C: Healthcare Team Contact Information   201
Appendix D: Side Effects Checklists for Seniors   205
Appendix E : Resources   209
Appendix F: High-Profile People with Mood Disorders   219
Notes   237
Glossary   259

Index 263

About the Author 273

INTRODUCTION

I've lived with depression all my life. I experienced it as a young girl, slipped deeper into its dark abyss as a teenager, and emerged from a suicide attempt as a young adult knowing that I wanted to study mood disorders and to help others who struggled with them. As a person who's lived with this disorder and as a professional trained to diagnose and treat it, I know I have a great deal to offer readers about this devastating illness. In *Depression in Later Life: An Essential Guide*, I take you through the experience of depression when it occurs at age sixty-five and older.

The prospect of reading a book on aging might feel daunting—and the subject of depression lessens the odds that it'll be a laugh-out-loud page-turner. But a book like this is important.

"Why?" you ask.

Well, for starters, you're going to explore many myths about aging that will bring insight, hope, and ultimately greater well-being to you. You'll learn from the chapters in this book how to set up realistic goals in your golden years and how to live a life that's filled with meaning and purpose. You'll realize how the chronic illness of depression may challenge you in later life, but you'll also discover the tools to create well-being in spite of it. Moreover, if you're a senior living with a depressive disorder or caring for a loved one who has this illness, this will be your go-to resource. As someone who has lived personally with depression and as a psychologist who clinically treats seniors diagnosed with depression, my perspective offers a most unique take not found in any other book. Furthermore, the approaches, techniques, and issues found in this book are supported by evidence-based research. As a reader, you can be assured that the facts presented here are rooted in science.

Depression in Later Life: An Essential Guide begins by showing you how distinctively different depression in later life is from depression at earlier ages, how it develops, and ways to detect the illness in its early stages. In chapter 2, we move directly into the varying types of geriatric mood disorders and also highlight the importance of diagnosing sub-clinical symptoms of depression—aspects many other books don't read-ily address. You'll discover what a geriatric assessment is and the proper way to obtain one in chapter 3, and how to distinguish if other diseases like dementia or stroke are causing depressive symptoms for you or a loved one. Also addressed in this book are the benefits of seeking sim-ple genetic testing to streamline your recovery from depression. I strongly believe in this kind of personalized medicine and have seen it positively shift the treatment and recovery of depression in later life for many of my patients.

Chapter 4 goes over traditional treatments that are generally recom-mended for adults aged sixty-five and older, while chapter 5 delves into many different kinds of alternative approaches to address depression in later life: aromatherapy, bright light therapy, massage, meditation, mu-sic therapy, and the importance of consuming superfoods, just to name a few. Perhaps the greatest wisdom I've learned personally living with depression and witnessed treating others who live with mood disorders is the importance of consistency in treatment. Living with depression—or with any chronic illness, for that matter—requires structuring your self-care needs, medication management, or psychotherapy treatment on a daily, weekly, and monthly basis. For some it's easy, but for most it's a challenge. Chapter 6 takes on this critical issue of success in treatment and offers insight, tips, and techniques to help you work your treatment plan effectively.

The topic of suicide is a difficult but necessary subject to cover when anyone struggles with depression. Of great magnitude is the fact that suicide rates are the highest for those in their senior years—more than children, more than teenagers, more than young and middle-age adults. Data reports that many elderly people aren't diagnosed with depression accurately or treated effectively, placing geriatric depression at a crisis level. In chapter 7, I outline the different characteristics of suicidality, how to interrupt suicidal thinking, and ways to create emergency plans if depression devolves into a life-threatening episode. As someone who's been in the throes of untreated depression and suicidality, I know how proper treatment saves lives—and changes lives.

Another challenging subject is how to deal with hospitalization should your late-life depression require such intervention. Hospitalization tends to occur more frequently in later life, given our advanced age, multiple medical issues, and other geriatric concerns. I cover how the hospitalization process unfolds in chapter 8 and dispel many of the misconceptions and stigma that make seniors or their loved ones feel uncomfortable about this kind of intervention. You'll learn how to create a collaborative care team for your geriatric depression and how to navigate your physical and emotional well-being when you return home or move to other settings.

The concept of conscious aging takes center stage in chapter 9, teaching you how to find wellness in spite of living with late-life depression. You'll experience how to use positive aging strategies, how to practice self-reflection, find closure for moments lost or regretted, and reach a level of healthy acceptance—all of which help reduce depression. Tapping into your new insights will allow you to better plan for long-term care for yourself or a loved one with depression with the details you'll uncover in chapter10. And as you reach chapter 11, you'll be able to spot the myths and misconceptions of depression in seniors and how your own awareness of geriatric depression has evolved from reading *Depression in Later Life: An Essential Guide*.

The glossary, screenings, checklists, and resources round out the comprehensive nature of this book, and the case studies offered at each chapter's end add color and texture to your read. By the time you turn the last page, I hope you'll agree that a book like this is, indeed, important, and that it will be a go-to resource for you or for someone you love.

And above all else, you'll discover that living with depression at any age need not be filled with darkness and despair.

I

WHAT IS LATE-LIFE DEPRESSION?

I know depression because I've endured it my entire life. I had it as a child and it worsened as I became a teenager. It still lingers in the margins of my life at age 55. For me, depression was a chronic illness that left me in despair and frighteningly unaware of its grinding misery. I didn't recognize the symptoms, and neither did any family or friends. In fact, as my depression worsened as a college student, I sank into a featureless existence, either awake in a fatigued haze or sleeping the entire day away. Gradually, the bitter brine of depression flooded my mind with hopelessness. I didn't care about the future and I couldn't find purpose in the present. It didn't occur to me that anything was out-of-sorts, short-sighted, or even peculiar as my thinking became more corrosive. When I attempted suicide at age 19 with a handgun, it felt right. It felt comforting.

Of course, looking back, I was in deep emotional and physical pain and believed I had found a way to make it stop—but it wasn't a healthy choice. I was making a decision from an incredibly distorted reality. Luckily my plan was interrupted and I immediately got help. I began intensive psychotherapy and discovered that I'd been living with **dysthymic disorder** and that it escalated into a **major depressive disorder**. Having both these disorders was called a **double depression**, and I learned how to replace the quiet agony of my illness with tools to live a more meaningful life. The experience I had with talk therapy was so life changing and life saving that it inspired me to become a psychologist. I combined my personal experiences with depression in my training as a clinician and became an expert in mood disorders. I realized that my personal experiences with depression offered enormous insight to those who sought treatment with me because "I know the talk and I walk the walk." In the 45 years of personally living with depression and the 25 years of professionally treating it as a disorder, this is what I've learned:

Depression doesn't care if you're rich or famous, poor or homeless.

It doesn't care if you're young or old.

Or if you're ordinary or superlatively gifted.

Depression cuts across socioeconomic status and is found in every culture and in every country around the world.

Depression will drape its chokehold over men, women, and children—and thinks nothing of how it decays your mind, siphons your soul, and crushes the glimpse of possibility, hope, and freedom at every turn.

Depression is not an experience that fades with the next sunrise or can be shaken off with a newfound attitude. It won't be cured by tough love or rectified by ignoring it. You can't snap out of it or will it away either. And if you try to minimize its wrenching hold on your health, it'll root itself even deeper. Depression can't be ranked alongside adjectives like *blue, sad, dejected, down, melancholy,* or *unhappy.* Those words just won't do . . . because they don't even come close to describing what depression feels like.

Depression demands you to see it for what it truly is—an illness. And although it's a serious illness, it *is* treatable. The key to success in living with depression is early identification, consistent treatment, and planning to manage your illness. Appendix A has a short depression questionnaire to help you evaluate your symptoms.

DEFINING DEPRESSION

The heart of human experience beats with moments of joy, eruptions of sorrow, and the textures of many different emotions in between. These variations are considered to be a healthy range of emotions. To put it another way, everyone has good days and bad days. Sometimes the good outweighs the bad, while at other times the bad sidelines us for a bit. The experiences come and go and don't upset the quality of life. But depression is another experience altogether. The bad features strongly and the good rarely lingers long enough to ease the symptoms of this illness. Depression has a chronic element to it, meaning it persists for a long time—for weeks, months, and years on end, not for just a day or two. And it carries an intensity that is more profound than normal reactions to loss, change, or trauma.

Depression is a complex illness that significantly impacts the way you *feel*, *think*, and *behave*.[1] According to the World Health Organization, depression involves feelings of worthlessness, decreased energy, hopelessness, poor concentration, negative thinking, and disrupted sleeping and eating patterns, just to name a few.[2] The most predominant of these symptoms is a depressed mood, and because of this, depression is classified as a **mood disorder**.[3] Sometimes called **affective disorders**, mood disorders are the most common mental illness, touching over a hundred million people worldwide. Mood disorders aren't the result of a weakness of character, laziness, or a person's inability to buck up and be strong. Mood disorders are a real medical condition. Table 1.1 summarizes the most common symptoms of depression.

THE GERIATRIC POPULATION

It's important to know that depression can occur at any age, but in this book we're looking at depression in later life—specifically, the **geriatric** population, which includes all individuals 65 years of age and older. Sometimes referred to as *seniors* or *the elderly*, geriatric citizens are the fastest-growing population in the world.[4] In America alone, the baby boomer generation now makes up over 50 million of the senior population.[5] With people living longer and the combination of medical advances and technology improving the state of healthcare, the senior population is expected to soar to 72 million by the year 2030.[6] More specifically, the U.S. Census Bureau reports that in the next 45 years, people over the age of 65 will double, and people over the age of 85 will triple.[7] And now more than ever, **centenarians**—people 100 years of age and older—are not just reaching these amazing ages but living richly textured lives. While **gerontology**, the study of the aging process in human beings, has brought insights about the physical, emotional, and social needs of this population, little has been done to train geriatric

Table 1.1.   Symptoms of Depression

SYMPTOMS OF DEPRESSION
- Changes in appetite — too much or too little
- Despairing thoughts and feelings
- Fatigue, lack of motivation
- Feelings of worthlessness or guilt
- Frequent thoughts of death
- Hopelessness and despair
- Irritability
- Loss of interest or pleasure or hope
- Negative problem solving
- Neglecting personal self-care
- Restlessness agitation
- Sleep disturbances, including insomnia or sleeping too much
- Slowed decision making
- Slowed thinking, speaking, and difficulty concentrating
- Suicidal ideation
- Unexplained physical aches and pains

health professionals. In fact, 97 percent of medical school students have no training in geriatrics, and the rate of doctors graduating with a **geriatrician** degree are lower now than 10 years ago.[8] Even geriatric psychology, or **geropsychology**, the specialty that focuses on the mental health of the elderly, isn't gaining the kind of traction needed to help those living in their golden years. This makes identifying and treating depression in later life difficult.

AGE OF ONSET

There are several different kinds of mood disorders, each one ranging from mild occurrences to severe episodes. We go over these in depth in chapter 2, but of interest here is that there are different kinds of onset for depression: **early onset** and **late onset**. According to research, most mental illnesses emerge prior to 25 years of age.[9] This means for most people, disorders of mental health have an early onset, with occurrences in infancy, childhood, adolescence, or young adulthood. For example, my experience with depression is categorized as early onset because the illness of depression presented in my childhood.

When it comes to early onset, depressive symptoms can resolve on their own, especially if they're mild—and might never present again in a person's life. An example of this is a child who has a mild depression that moves into remission, and the child never has another episode. In other instances, the depressive illness continues and evolves, remaining present throughout one's life; this type of early-onset depression endures. I have this kind of depression—where an early onset happened but then, at several times throughout my life, I experienced a recurrence, falling into another depressive episode.

And then there's late-onset depression, clinically called **geriatric depression** or **late-life depression** (LLD), which is defined as depression that occurs in men and women 65 years and older.[10] What makes late-onset distinctly different from early-onset depression is that depression has never before been an issue for the senior up to this point.

Table 1.2 illustrates why age of onset is a very important facet in understanding depression. Late-onset depression tends to have a different **etiology** than early-onset depression.[11] For example, studies suggest early onset is caused more by a strong genetic link while structural changes in the brain and vascular issues are more associated with late onset.[12] Children and young adults who experience early-onset depression tend to have more personality disorders, abuse drugs and alcohol, react with less resiliency to stress, and experience a more severe course of depression over their lifetime. Seniors suffering from late-onset depression endure more physical illnesses, encounter cognitive difficulties, and endure losses related to end of life more than their younger counterparts.[13] Age of onset also impacts how seniors experience depression. For example, studies show that individuals with geriatric depression aren't always in touch with their depressive symptoms, instead reporting more physical complaints than younger depressed individuals.[14] Seniors are also likely to display cognitive and neurological changes like memory loss or slowed speech and movement, and to appear confused or lost. Although people with both early- and late-onset depression have a serious risk of suicidal thinking, research notes that late-onset depression is associated with a significantly higher rate of suicide.[15]

STATISTICS FOR LATE-LIFE DEPRESSION

Depression affects an estimated 15 percent of Americans ages 65 and older.[16] The World Health Organization estimates that late-life depression affects 7 percent of older people worldwide.[17] Given their advanced age, many mistake this mood disorder for other conditions associated with getting older, such as memory loss, muscle/joint weakness, or side effects from medications. As a result, upwards of 90 percent of seniors with depression don't receive adequate care, with 78 percent not receiving any treatment at all.[18] The elderly who live on their own are diagnosed with depression at a rate of about 3 percent. However, the statistics for depression in seniors who lose their self-care and independence via hospitalization, assisted living, or skilled nursing home care dramatically increased to 50 percent.[19] Rates of depression appear to be higher in older women than in older men, with women having more episodes of depression than their male counterparts.[20] When it comes to late-onset depression in other cultures, studies report people of African American, Caucasian, and Hispanic ancestry have the highest rates, while Asian countries experience the lowest.[21]

Statistics for late-onset depression also point to specific issues that can increase the likelihood of developing depression.[22] These are called **risk factors** and include:

- Bereavement
- Chronic pain
- Disability
- Family history of depression

Table 1.2.   Early- versus Late-Onset Depression

Early-Onset Depression	Late-Onset Depression
Genetic family history of depression	Structural changes in brain
Higher rate of personality disorders	Higher rate of vascular risk factors
More severe course for the disorder	More cognitive/neurological issues
Psychological vulnerability	Severe life stress
Greater drug alcohol abuse	Greater comorbid physical illnesses
Express depressive symptoms	More somatic than depressive symptoms
Second highest rate for suicide	Highest rate for suicide

- Fear of death
- Female
- Lack of a supportive social network
- Living alone, social isolation
- Multiple medications
- Multiple physical illnesses
- Neurological illness
- New medical illness
- Skilled nursing home or assisted living
- Onset of vascular issues
- Recent fall or injury
- Recent loss of a loved one
- Single, unmarried, divorced, or widowed
- Sleep disturbance
- Stressful life event
- Untreated subclinical depression

SUBCLINICAL DEPRESSION

Another important facet in understanding depression is to know that seniors can experience symptoms of depression but not meet the clinical diagnosis. Those who fall into this category have **subclinical symptoms**—which can get better on their own or worsen to the point where a clinical depression diagnosis emerges. Subclinical depression is sometimes referred to by different names like *subthreshold*, *subsyndromal*, *nonmajor*, or *minor depression*. All of these terms indicate that a person is experiencing many but not all symptoms necessary to diagnose a mood disorder.

Statistics for those 65 years or older who have subclinical depression approximates 25 percent of the geriatric population.[23] This is a particularly startling number that carries with it an equally startling fallout because there are more seniors with subclinical depression than those with a diagnosed depressive disorder.[24] And what's even more alarming is that seniors who have subclinical symptoms are not identified early—and therefore not treated appropriately. Studies show that a long untreated subclinical depression of up to three years will lead to a major depressive episode.[25] The single cause for this oversight is that many people, some health professionals included, believe that depression is a normal part of aging. *It is not.* In fact, this is one of the greatest myths about aging found the world over.[26]

THE COST OF DEPRESSION

The illness of depression is costly—and not just on a personal level where it taxes your mind, body, and soul. The price tag of depression is immense for the economy, for healthcare, and for families. According to the World Health Organization, depression is the leading cause of disability worldwide.[27] The 2010 Global Burden of Disease Study agrees and further identifies depression as producing the highest economic burden in countries around the globe.[28]

On the employment front, depression is associated with less productivity at work and causes the highest rates of short-term disability. Perhaps the most stunning statistic is that depression is responsible for upwards of 200 million lost days on the job.[29] To put this in dollars and cents, in the United States alone, the cost of depression from lost productivity, absenteeism, and related services for treatment is around $80 billion annually.[30]

Depression for those in late life specifically overloads the healthcare system in ways that nondepressed seniors don't. For instance, research reports individuals who have geriatric depression consult more often with primary care doctors, see more specialists, and undertake lab and medical testing more than nondepressed peers. They also have higher rates of emergency room visits and are hospitalized more frequently, and longer, than nondepressed seniors. We know that geriatric depression diminishes a person's ability to function well, and as a result, some seniors prematurely retire from the workforce or question their own ability to care for themselves. The cost of these emotional decisions and missed opportunities to get mental health treatment places depressed seniors at an enormous risk for increased mortality and suicide.[31]

The negative consequences of late-life depression extend to family members of the elderly. Studies show that over 42 million adults take on the role of full-time caregiver for their loved ones, with an additional 61 million people providing part-time care at some time during the year. In 2009, the National Alliance on Caregiving estimated the economic value of the work that caregivers provide, which is unpaid, approximates $450 billion a year.[32] It should be no surprise that family caregivers adjust their own lives to provide elder care. Be it arriving late/leaving early from work, taking time off, cutting back on work hours, changing jobs, or stopping work altogether, caregivers make less money and experience more physical health problems than noncaregivers. Perhaps one of the most distressing consequences is that family caregivers are themselves at risk for depression, with upward of 15 percent meeting the criteria for a depressive disorder.[33]

DIATHESIS–STRESS MODEL

I'd like to write that it's easy to detect why someone develops depression, but all bubbles here will burst because there's no cookie-cutter formula for why some people are prone to it while others never experience it at all. The best way to describe the onset of illness comes from the **Diathesis–Stress model**, which states that seniors have, in varying degrees, predispositions for developing mental illness. These hard-wired vulnerabilities are called *diatheses* and include genetics, neurobiology, and cognitive and physical changes. The other part of this model looks at the overwhelming feature of life events, social experiences, and environmental changes, otherwise known as *stress*.

The Diathesis–Stress model is a whole-person approach, looking at the interaction of dimensions in a person's life and their influence on that individual. These dimensions are biological, psychological, and social. Biology involves a person's unique genetics, his or her body's functioning and biological structure. Psychology factors include personality, intellect, thoughts, feelings, and perceptions. Finally, social experiences—where a person lives, his or her culture, ethnicity, religion, economic status, and social connections—have a tremendous impact on that person's life. Figure 1.1 depicts how these dimensions influence the Diathesis–Stress model. When a person understands his own genetics, the styles and patterns of how he thinks and feels, and the environment he grew up in, he becomes more insightful about how stress affects his life.

The Diathesis–Stress model can be used as both a philosophy and a practical guide toward understanding depression.[34] As a philosophy, it

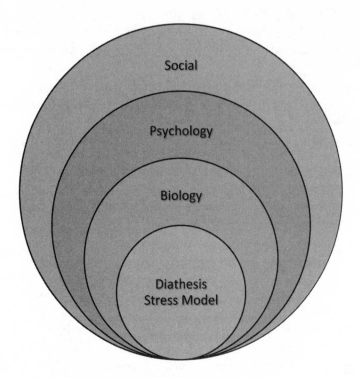

Figure 1.1.   Diathesis–Stress model.

helps identify how the interplay of trauma, illness, genetics, and culture may set the stage for depression to emerge. On the practical level, it offers a powerful way to understand how subjective life experiences can worsen or enhance depressive symptoms.[35]

When it comes to geriatric depression, research tells us that biological factors like genetics can bring about a late onset of depression but so can changes in brain structure, shifting neurochemistry, and cardiovascular disease—as do psychological factors, like negative patterns of thinking and difficulties with reasoning, judgment, and cognition. Also pressing down on the elderly can be social and cultural issues like financial troubles, loss of purpose due to retirement, stigma about seeking help for depression, or coming to terms with end of life. The Diathesis–Stress model explains that late-life depression arises from a complex interaction of these dimensions. Said another way, your mind, body, and environment uniquely influence each other,[36] and this is why some seniors are more prone to mood disorders than others.

SUMMARY

Geriatric depression, sometimes referred to as late-life depression (LDD), is a mood disorder that affects men and women 65 years of age and older. In this chapter, you've discovered that depression is not a normal part of aging. You've also been clued into the concept that unique biological, psychological, and social stressors are responsible for disease onset. Late-life depression has a unique set of symptoms, making the elderly vulnerable to cognitive and vascular impairments, the worsening of coexisting physical illnesses, increased mortality and suicide, just to name a few. Statistics show that more seniors suffer with subclinical depression, which if left untreated will evolve into a full clinical depressive disorder. Geriatric depression takes an enormous toll on those who live with it as well as on the caregivers who look out for their **well-being**. It is a serious but treatable disorder.

CASE STUDY: SULLY

Sully, 68 years old, was referred to me for psychotherapy from his general practitioner. He was a tall man, well over six feet, with a slender build. His pepper-gray hair almost touched his shoulders and fell in fine, straight planks.

"Last hold-out of my hippie days," he said when I took notice of it.

Sully had been having trouble sleeping for several months now, being unable to fall asleep and stay asleep. He also reported having occasional chest pain and feeling more forgetful than usual. Sully told me that his doctor sent him through every test imaginable, with every specialist imaginable.

"They couldn't find anything," he recounted.

When I went over reports from his internist, cardiologist, and neurologist, I confirmed Sully had gone through the testing mill. Aside from a recent knee replacement, he was in terrific physical shape for a man his age.

"My doctor thinks I'm depressed, but I don't see that going on. I mean, I'm not sad," Sully stated.

Sully had been in the restaurant business all of his life. Starting first as an errand boy in his grandfather's restaurant, graduating to bus boy, eventually waiter, and then to maître d', finally he had been anointed to run the family landmark. Sully described himself as a hard worker, never too good to work the back of the house, tend to the coatroom, or cook in the kitchen—even in his suit. Sully shared that he loved the restaurant life: getting up early, working with vendors, keeping track of staff hours, tweaking the menu, and making sure service and customers were never out of synch. He never worked the books, leaving that and other aspects to his brother—but said he always knew what money was coming in, where it was spent, and how to bankroll his life.

"Seems to me you really enjoyed the social aspects of running the business," I said.

"That's true," Sully said, nodding.

Sully had retired almost two years earlier at the urging of his wife, who had done the same from a long-standing clerical job in the local county offices. They planned to extensively travel Europe and relax, and they were also awaiting the birth of their first grandchild with great excitement. A series of events, though, delayed the traveling and the relaxing, one of which was Sully's knee replacement. The other was a decision to sell the house because Social Security and the limited return on other investments made keeping their rather lavish home impractical.

"We didn't do our homework before calling it quits," Sully declared.

"But nothing's set in stone. You can do things to supplement your retirement income," I said encouragingly.

"Yeah, I guess." Sully frowned and shrugged his shoulders.

"Tell me what you're thinking," I said, after he got quiet for a while.

Sully shared that his new home, a condo, was very small and he didn't really like it there. He missed his garage, winced at the "over 55 aspect" of the community, and rarely socialized without his wife at community events.

"Makes me feel old," he said.

Sully said that his surgery and rehab weren't too big a deal for him, but it took time away from planning their long-awaited trip to Europe. Then the grandson arrived, and his wife had been over there every free minute. Sully told me that she'd been watching the baby every day since their daughter-in-law had gone back to work.

"Don't get me wrong, I love the kid," he said. "But no way I'm gonna be there every damn day."

"What do you do with your time?"

"Not a helluva lot."

"Hmmm. This really wasn't in your plan, the waiting, the changing," I said.

"No." He tightened his lips.

Sully and I begin to trace the stressors piling up one after another in his life. In our sessions, he realized he felt lonely, resenting the time his wife left to spend with their grandson. And he recognized that all the decades he had spent at work left him little time to develop hobbies or friends outside the business. I administered the Geriatric Scale of Depression, and Sully was right: He didn't meet the criteria for a formal depressive disorder.

"But," I said with an arched eyebrow, "you have many symptoms that concern me."

Sully was irritable, impatient, and bored—experiences he had rarely felt in his life before retirement. He also felt helpless to change his situation and wondered if things were ever going to get better. Sully certainly had subclinical depressive symptoms that placed him at risk. And like so many seniors, he wasn't aware of the symptoms. Therapists are teachers at heart, and I happily helped him learn how his aches, pains, and sleeplessness were part of the subsyndrome of depression. Our work in psychotherapy allowed him to restructure the next chapter of his life by redefining his goals and dreams.

With the help of his wife, Sully returned to the restaurant, working three days a week while she cared for their grandson. He tended bar, told stories—all the while letting his younger brother have his "day in the sun" running the restaurant. Sully's negative attitudes about his senior housing shifted as he gradually put himself out there. He found a few men who liked to play cards, fish, and putter in the parking lot with their cars. Feeling less lonely and finding purpose again, Sully's focus and energy returned. Psychotherapy assisted him in discovering what he needed and wanted in life, which lifted many of his subclinical symptoms.

"So, where are we with getting you to Europe?" I asked, learning that his chest pains and insomnia were gone.

Sully let out a hearty laugh. "The wife ain't gonna leave that kid."

"Well, what about a family trip?" I suggested. "Rent a house in the Tuscany region like you want and invite your family to visit. Maybe during a school break. The summer. Or Christmas."

"I see what you're doing, Doc."

"Oh yeah, you do?" I replied.

"Okay, I'll talk it over with the wife tonight," Sully said.

"Don't oversell it though," I reminded him. "Just be open and honest about how you feel. And let compromise be your goal."

Sully couldn't seal the deal of a rental in Tuscany, but he was able to make a reservation for a seven-day family cruise to the Caribbean.

"It's a start," he said, pleased.

After a few more sessions, Sully and I decided to end sessions because he was in a great place. At our last session, I told him to send me a postcard from Tuscany when he finally gets there.

2

GERIATRIC MOOD DISORDERS

It's not unusual for people to use the words *feeling* and *emotion* interchangeably or substitute the word *mood* for the word *affect*.[1] In casual speak, they mean the same thing. But in truth, they are all very different words, with very specific experiences. It's important to understand these psychological terms because late-life depression affects all of them.

A *feeling* is defined as a personal sensation—one that has been checked against previous similar experiences, catalogued and labeled for your sense of self to call upon. It is an internal, subjective experience that is genuine and real.[2] For example, if you witness something inspiring, like a baby taking her first steps, you may feel joy, happiness, or surprise. Your feeling is your distinctive sense of the experience.

An emotion is the expression of a feeling outward to yourself or others. Emotions are the "verb" to the "adjective" of your feeling. So if we go back to the baby and her first steps, you may feel joy witnessing it, which will be emotionally expressed outwardly as pleasure. Feelings aren't often detected by others because they are internal experiences, but emotions are observed because they are expressed. A good way to remember this is that feelings are personal and emotions are social.

Now let's look at mood and affect. They, too, are very different in how they occur. An affect is a short-lived, momentary expression that occurs nanoseconds before we realize what we're feeling.[3] Affects are direct expressions of emotions that are observable in our body, speech, and gestures. So, if we go back to the baby and her first steps, affect can be seen when your eyes widen as you watch her totter forward, or in how you hold your breath, clutch your chest in anticipation, and perhaps smile and laugh in delight as she makes it successfully across the room. After the feeling and emotion are expressed, these affects disappear. They're gone because you're processing other things in your environment.

Mood is a longer, more enduring feeling state, one that generally has a good or bad quality. Mood can sometimes change easily, shifting rapidly from one extreme to another, or can remain in a fixed manner for a long period of time. Mood has the ability to greatly impact how you react, respond, and live within the world. Sometimes a good mood can make it easy to experience things and people, while a bad mood impacts negatively in that regard. Your mood can allow you to experience feelings and convey them emotionally, while other times your mood dulls or prevents this from happening.

Let's go back to our baby and her first steps: If you're in a good mood, you can experience the array of feelings, emotions, and affects positively. This moment feels good for you, for the baby, and for anyone else taking part. This progression makes sense, right? A good mood generally leads to good experiences all around. But mood can take on a depressed or euphoric quality, and this can lead to difficulties. If your mood is depressed and you're watching the baby walk, your affect may show your delight and pleasure, and the feeling of joy may bubble up too, leading to an emotional expression of laughter and delight . . . but after the moment, the depressed mood returns. The happiness you felt was momentary—and you've returned back to the depressed mood.

Another possibility when your mood is depressed is that it's so severe it blurs your awareness and you can't register this great moment in any way, shape, or form, so there's no affect, feeling, or emotion about the event. If your mood is elevated or manic, you may be too distracted to take in the milestone, or maybe your affect is overbearing, your gestures too over the top, and your emotional overreactions spoil the moment, stopping the baby midstep or causing her to flop in a puddle of tears.

Affects, feelings, emotions, and moods are vital ingredients to emotional well-being and can serve as diagnostic tools in evaluating geriatric depression and other mental health issues. Generally speaking, the *Diagnostic and Statistical Manual of Mental Disorders* (DSM) or the

International Statistical Classification of Diseases (ICD) are used by mental health professionals to diagnose mood disorders.[4]

CATEGORIES OF GERIATRIC DEPRESSION

A good way to understand mood disorders in the senior population is to view them in four categories. Table 2.1 shows an overview of these different categories.

1. *Unipolar*—in which mood roots itself in a depressive state
2. *Bipolar*—where mood fluctuates between the lows of depression and highs of mania
3. *Other*—where mood is affected by other disorders or conditions
4. *Neurobiological*—in which mood is a result of brain and/or cardiovascular issues

Unipolar Depression

Statistics reveal that 2 percent of the geriatric population experiences **unipolar** depression.[5] Various studies of depression in elderly adults find that mood is more often irritable than depressive and that seniors aren't aware they are depressed. Studies show that upward of 60 percent of elderly men and women experience at least another depressive

Table 2.1. Types of Depression in Later Life

Unipolar	*Bipolar*	*Other*	*Neurobiological*
Major Depression	Bipolar I	Adjustment Disorder with Depressed Mood	Catatonic Depression
Dysthymic Disorder	Bipolar II	Mood Disorder Due to Medical Condition	Depression-Executive Dysfunction Syndrome
Depressive Disorder Not Otherwise Specified	Cyclothymic Disorder	Substance-Induced Mood Disorder	Post-Stroke Depression
	Bipolar Disorder Not Otherwise Specified	Mood Disorder Not Otherwise Specified	Vascular Depression

recurrence in the future, making geriatric depression a chronic illness.[6] A unipolar depression in an elderly adult ebbs and flows in the margins of an irritable, depressed mood, as illustrated in table 2.1. Geriatric unipolar depression may include the following:

- *Agitation*: Verbally aggressive, physically aggressive, or physically nonaggressive behavior that is socially unacceptable. Of these three aspects of agitated behavior, verbal aggressiveness is considered to relate to depressed seniors.
- *Anhedonia*: A word of Greek origin that literally translates to *without pleasure*. Unipolar depression often withers a person's ability to experience normal reactions to things in life; as such, a loss of interest in experiences that were once pleasurable or satisfying occurs.
- *Anxiety*: In elderly patients, anxiety is often present along with depression. Seniors may experience tension, unrest, or feelings of insecurity or fear.
- *Appetite loss*: Neurological changes from depression disrupt brain structures that often blunt the sense of smell and taste, which can leave the elderly with a decreased enjoyment of food. Sometimes depressed seniors lose interest or forget to eat, which can lead to malnutrition.
- *Cognitive difficulties*: Depression affects cognitive function in all age groups, but the executive tasks of thinking, reasoning, memory, and sustained effort are more frequently impaired in geriatric depression.
- *Fatigue*: Tiredness, lack of energy, and a sense of heaviness are frequently seen in anyone who experiences depression. However, this hallmark symptom is often dismissed and blamed on old age in the geriatric population.
- *Flattening of emotions*: Often, seniors with a unipolar depression experience a dullness or numbing of feelings. The presentation of emotions can appear flat or empty. Some seniors may lose the capacity to cry.
- *Hopelessness*: For seniors, the bleakness and despair that swells in later life is one of the biggest risk factors for suicide.

- *Hyposomnia*: Another symptom overlooked and wrongly attributed to old age is the need for increased sleep, which is a hallmark sign of depression.
- *Insomnia*: Although elderly adults sometimes report having trouble sleeping as they age, not being able to sleep at all is a red flag for depression.
- *Neurocognitive disorders*: Unipolar depression in seniors can include the coexistence of other neurological or cognitive disorders, so evaluation is a vital part of the diagnostic process.
- *Pseudodementia*: This is a slowing of mental functions from depression that causes memory difficulties, disorientation, and confusion in the elderly.
- *Psychomotor sluggishness*: A slowness in motor activity or language expression can occur. It is seen as a kind of body expression inertia and is often wrongly attributed to old age.
- *Psychotic depression*: This type of depression, sometimes referred to as *delusional depression*, affects less than 0.1 percent of the elderly population. Losing touch with reality, nonrecognition of known others, an unawareness of one's own self, delusions, and hallucinations are typically present.
- *Reduced sexual libido*: Although seniors can enjoy sexual activities well into late life, unipolar depression often minimizes or even eliminates the desire for sexual contact.
- *Somatic complaints*: Aches and pains are emotionally felt in this depressive experience but are recognized as physical complaints. **Somatic complaints** are generally found more in late-onset depression than in early onset. This depressive symptom is tricky to detect because seniors do experience health problems.
- *Weight gain*: Some seniors may gain weight from the depressive symptoms of overeating and decreased activity. Again, this is another symptom that is wrongly attributed to the process of aging.

There are three unipolar disorders that comprise the geriatric depressive experience. Those who have a unipolar disorder experience varying degrees of irritability, confusion, melancholy, loss of interest, slow thinking, poor judgment, and in some cases, suicidal thinking.

1. *Major Depressive Disorder* (MDD): Major depressive disorder is the most serious of the unipolar disorders. MDD can be diagnosed after a single depressive episode that has lasted for a period of two weeks or more. Some of the hallmark symptoms of MDD include depressed mood, body aches, fatigue, slowness of thinking, changes in appetite and sleep, and a debilitating sense of hopelessness—which can lead to despair and suicide. MDD is not a result of a reaction to grief or bereavement, a medical condition, or substance abuse. MDD for seniors has a late onset, but MDD can also vary with seasonal changes for those in later life. This major depressive disorder would be diagnosed as MDD with a "seasonal onset."

2. *Dysthymic Disorder* (DD): Dysthymic disorder is characterized by depressed or irritable mood for at least two years. The depressive experience takes on a less severe form than MDD but is more chronic than major depressive disorder. Though dysthymic disorder is often described as a low-grade depression, the depressive impairment is quite significant. Fatigue, irritability, negative thinking, and melancholy can cast an imperceptibly long and elusive shadow—one that may not be detected by those in their golden years or seen by family or caregivers who tend to them. Because of the slow and subtly harmful trajectory of dysthymia, seniors who experience dysthymic disorder can find their symptoms worsening to the point of experiencing a major depressive disorder. As mentioned in chapter 1, a double depression is the clinical term used to describe this. With major depressive disorder, the significant change in mood is more readily noticeable, but dysthymic symptoms can be harder to detect. Furthermore, when dysthymic symptoms are observed, they are wrongly dismissed as being part of the aging process so treatment isn't readily sought.

3. *Depressive Disorder Not Otherwise Specified* (D-NOS): When depressive symptoms do not meet the criteria for MDD or DD, a diagnosis of "depressive disorder not otherwise specified" can be given. This diagnosis is generally offered when the reason for the presenting depressive characteristics are unclear but are of significant concern to warrant treatment.

Bipolar Depression

Statistics report that 90 percent of individuals with **bipolar** depression have an onset prior to age 50; therefore, late-onset bipolar disorder occurs in approximately 10 percent of the geriatric population.[7] The experience of bipolar disorders involves a greater fluctuation of moods than do unipolar disorders. Seniors who have a bipolar disorder move through a range of highs and lows, at its worst cycling from despair to mania. Late-onset bipolar disorders are associated with fewer genetic causes and a higher rate of medical and neurological origins.[8] Researchers suggest that geriatric symptoms associated with mania may share a common pathway caused by neurological vulnerabilities. What remains unclear, however, is whether the emergence of late-life bipolar disorder is a direct result of an independent medical reason or is an age-specific triggered mood disorder.[9]

Studies suggest that bipolar disorders are less widespread in the geriatric population than geriatric unipolar disorders. Another age-specific issue is that seniors experience more severe depressive episodes and less severe manic episodes than younger individuals who have bipolar disorder. As for recurrence, 85 percent to 100 percent of seniors with bipolar depression will experience frequent episodes.[10] Just as with bipolar disorder in younger individuals, timing, intensity, and frequency of a **mood swing** will determine which type of bipolar disorder is operating.[11] Geriatric bipolar depression includes many of the symptoms listed above in the unipolar category, as well as the following:

- *Confusion*: Another myth about aging is that it's common for seniors to be confused. But bewilderment, slip-ups, and mix-ups are a hallmark sign for bipolar depression in late life.
- *Crying jags*: Some seniors may be frequently tearful or experience bursts of crying.
- *Delirious mania*: This is a severe expression of mania that involves a sudden onset of disorientation, delusions, hallucinations, overactivity, and sleeplessness.
- *Distractibility*: Seniors with bipolar disorder can be distractible and move quickly from one thing to another, with heightened interest in each new moment. Sometimes the distractibility can lead to falls and other injuries.

- *Elevated mood*: The heightened level of mood is one of the classic symptoms of bipolar disorder and includes elation, euphoria, and extreme, unbridled excitement.
- *Emotional lability*: This refers to the rapid, unstable expressions of emotions that result in exaggerated changes of mood. Seniors who experience this aren't aware of their unstable moods and can become argumentative when confronted.
- *Flight of ideas*: Seniors may experience an accelerated kind of thinking where thoughts and associations become difficult to follow. The lightning speed of ideas can lead to confusion for caregivers, family, or friends who are trying to keep up with such expressions that often don't make sense.
- *Grandiosity*: Individuals with late-life bipolar disorder often display an inflated sense of self-importance and self-esteem.
- *High energy*: Unlike those with unipolar depression, seniors with bipolar disorder can be indefatigable; poor judgment often coincides with this extended level of energy.
- *Hypersomnia*: This symptom is different from insomnia, which is having trouble going to or staying asleep. Hypersomnia is the reluctance to want to sleep.
- *Hypervigilance*: Seniors become highly sensitive to their own physical experiences and body functions, sometimes overreacting to normal body aches as pains.
- *Impaired decision making*: Cognitive difficulties are a great concern for those who struggle with geriatric bipolar disorder; as a result, poor decisions and impaired problem solving frequently occur.
- *Impulsive behavior*: Another hallmark symptom of bipolar disorder is the inability to control one's impulses, like spending money, stealing, or gambling, to name a few. The impulsivity seniors demonstrate more than their younger counterparts includes being meddlesome, intrusive, and disinhibited.
- *Irritability*: Sometimes mania can present more as irritability or agitation for a senior with bipolar disorder.
- *Pain sensitivity*: Seniors with bipolar depression often experience an inability to tolerate physical pain, often heightened by mood elevation and impulsivity.

- *Pressured speech*: This is a rapid, thickly textured verbal expression, where an elderly person is unable to slow or soften speaking. Sometimes, there are clang associations, where words are linked together by rhyming or consonant-sounding patterns.
- *Psychomotor agitation*: Accelerated body movements and restlessness are hallmarks symptoms of bipolar disorder. This can result in falls, injuries, and accidents for elderly adults with bipolar depression.
- *Rapid cycling*: Seniors with late-onset bipolar depression are likely to be rapid cyclers more than younger adults with bipolar disorder.
- *Sexual excess*: The range of mania can cause an increased level of libido for seniors with bipolar depression, leading to sexual promiscuity and/or indiscretion.

There are four bipolar disorders that comprise the depressive and elevated mood range of experiences for elderly adults. Just like unipolar depression, late-life bipolar depression can range from mild to moderate to severe to profound levels and is sometimes referred to as **late-onset bipolar illness** (LOBI).[12]

1. *Bipolar Disorder I* (BD-I): Bipolar I disorder is the most serious of the bipolar disorders and is diagnosed after at least one episode of mania. Mania is defined as an elevated mood where euphoria, impulsivity, irritability, racing thoughts, and decreased need for sleep significantly impair judgment and daily functioning. Elderly adults with bipolar I disorder typically also have had a major depressive episode, but this is not needed for initial diagnosis.
2. *Bipolar Disorder II* (BD-II): Bipolar II disorder is characterized by at least one major depressive episode and an observable hypomanic episode. **Hypomania** is a milder form of elevated mood than is mania and does not necessarily impact daily functioning. Sometimes called **soft bipolar disorder**, the symptoms of bipolar II disorder are less intense that bipolar I but more chronic.
3. *Cyclothymic Disorder* (CD): In cyclothymic disorder, there are numerous hypomanic periods, usually of a relatively short duration, that alternate with clusters of depressive symptoms. The

sequence and experience of these symptoms do not meet the criteria of major depressive disorder or bipolar I or II. The mood fluctuations are chronic and have to be present for at least two years before a diagnosis of cyclothymia can be made.

4. *Bipolar Disorder Not Otherwise Specified* (BD-NOS): For symptoms that don't align with the above-mentioned disorders or follow a different pattern of euphoric and dysphoric symptoms, "bipolar disorder not otherwise specified" may be used as a diagnosis. Researchers and professionals believe that bipolar disorder has a spectrum of experience and expression, and that current diagnostic manuals may change as research better defines bipolar disorders. [13]

Other Mood Disorders

There are times when specific situations and/or medical conditions can alter mood in the geriatric population. In those cases, symptoms fall into the category of "other mood disorder." There are four categories in this section.

1. *Adjustment Disorder with Depressed Mood* (ADDM): When a senior moves through identifiable traumas or stressors and reports depressive symptoms, "adjustment disorder with depressed mood" is diagnosed. Criteria for ADDM are met if symptoms occur within three months of the identified trauma and do not persist longer than six months.

2. *Mood Disorder Due to Medical Condition*: Mood disturbances often accompany medical conditions. For example, hypoglycemia (low blood sugar) can spike irritability. Anemia (iron-poor blood) can cause fatigue and make a person feel listless. Hypothyroidism (hormone imbalance) can flatten or even agitate mood. There is a strong causal relationship between depression onset and age-related diseases like Parkinson's, Alzheimer's, and dementia. Mood changes may also occur from the medications used to treat medical conditions in later life. This is why it's so important to obtain a differential diagnosis—a diagnosis that evaluates all possibilities for symptoms for an elderly person.

3. *Substance-Induced Mood Disorder*: "Substance-induced mood disorder" is the diagnosis if mood changes are the direct result of substances such as drugs, alcohol, medications, or exposure to toxins.

4. *Mood Disorder Not Otherwise Specified*: This category is used when individuals have a mood disorder whose presentation does not fit the typical diagnostic categories.

Neurobiological Depression

As we covered in chapter 1, late-life depression can result from changes in brain functioning and/or neurological issues that occur later in life.[14] There are four kinds of neurobiological depression that elderly seniors can experience.

1. *Catatonic Depression*: Catatonia, a severe motor syndrome where an elderly adult can remain motionless and/or speechless for a period of time, is a neurobiological syndrome associated with unipolar and bipolar depression.[15] Psychomotor slowing may be so extreme that seniors can fall into a stupor, entirely unresponsive to the world around them. Studies suggest catatonic depression is caused by imbalances in the **dopamine**, gamma-aminobutyric acid (GABA), and glutamate neurotransmitter systems.[16] Prognosis of catatonic depression is good when recognized early and when treatment is aggressive. However, if untreated, a life-threatening situation called *lethal catatonia* can occur where fever, exhaustion, central nervous system irregularities, collapse, coma, and death result.

2. *Depression–Executive Dysfunction Syndrome*: Late-life depression is often associated with executive dysfunction, a structure in the frontal part of the brain responsible for goal-directed behaviors. When depressed elderly adults have executive dysfunction, they're more likely to have less interest in others or activities; a lack of insight; deficits in initiating, planning, and carrying out behaviors; and a slowness in their response style. Like catatonic depression, depression–executive dysfunction can improve with treatment if diagnosed early and aggressively treated.[17]

3. *Post-Stroke Depression* (PSD): Approximately one third of stroke survivors experience a late onset of depression.[18] Studies have shown approximately 19 percent of seniors in stroke rehabilitation centers had major depression disorder, while 18 percent had minor depression disorder.[19] These statistics are most concerning because one of the most influential outcomes for quality of life for elderly adult stroke survivors is a well-adjusted mood. Furthermore, seniors with post-stroke depression are 3.8 times more likely to die during a 10-year period after their stroke than post-stroke seniors who don't have depression.[20] Post-stroke depression is underdiagnosed because many believe that depression is a normal response to having a stroke.

4. *Vascular Depression* (V-Dep): The vascular depression hypothesis, proposed in 1997, believes that damage to cerebral nerve pathways, or cerebrovascular disease, can cause geriatric depression.[21] More specifically, blood vessels harden over time, reducing or blocking normal blood flow to the brain. This impaired blood flow causes vascular depression.[22] People with vascular depression may also be at risk for heart disease or stroke. Conversely, seniors with cardio or vascular issues, high blood pressure, high cholesterol, and/or diabetes are at risk for developing vascular depression. Studies looking at magnetic resonance imagings (MRIs) found that elderly adults with depression had higher rates of white matter brain hyperintensities and cerebrovascular lesions compared to individuals with early-onset depression.[23]

SUMMARY

Geriatric depression interferes with feelings, emotions, mood, and affect. Understanding the range of emotions and behaviors for well-being aids in the detection of geriatric depression. When diagnosing late-life depression, it's important to remember that illness varies in polarity (unipolar and bipolar), can be caused by genetic or neurobiological issues, may have varying cycling patterns, and ranges in intensity from mild to moderate to severe.

CASE STUDY: JOAN

Shortly after her 76th birthday, Joan received news that her long-standing immune disorder, lupus, had limited her kidney functioning and that dialysis was imminent. Joan felt ready to meet the challenges of dialysis because she already lived many years with a chronic illness. She had been diagnosed in her 40s with lupus and had made eating healthy and aiming for physical well-being a must-do for herself, and a motto for her husband and three children. Joan used her whip-smart sense of humor and sparkling intelligence to get her through tough times and never found herself impossibly overwhelmed. She worked part time while raising her sons and later cared for her grandchildren, never allowing lupus to restrict her life too much.

Joan began her dialysis treatment by going three times a week and found the experience challenging. As an active, independent woman, she bristled that she couldn't drive when dialysis started and also disliked how she needed to sit still for the many hours treatment took each day. She also cringed at the strict dietary changes that came with dialysis. Ever the fighter, Joan watched her salt intake and measured her water consumption, listened to books on tapes, watched old movies, and allowed her husband to drive her around. Joan spent her off-treatment days resting, which was not an uncommon experience for seniors on dialysis.

As weeks went by, Joan became more exhausted at the end of her dialysis treatment and even more fatigued during her off-treatment days. Her family grew concerned, but Joan's nephrologist said that routine blood work didn't note anything serious. There was a discussion about depression, but Joan dismissed it because she wasn't feeling sad or upset. She was just tired—very, very tired. Her family didn't consider depression as a possible issue either because she was still her old smart and snarky self. A decision was made to add Procrit, a protein that helped her feel a little bit stronger. But as weeks turned into months, Joan's sparkle and wit dimmed. She became irritable on the days she had to go to dialysis and once there, didn't find anything comforting to help her through the day. She didn't want to watch movies or listen to her books on tape. Furthermore, she refrained from talking to others and preferred to sleep the day away to pass the time. The nurses at the dialysis center noted Joan's behavioral and personality changes and her nephrologist, again, believed depression might be operating. A referral was made to a psychiatrist, who diagnosed Joan with unipolar depression and recommended antidepressant medication to help ease symptoms. Joan was reluctant to take the prescription and balked at the diagnosis. So her family sought me out for a second opinion.

"I'm not depressed," Joan said at our first appointment. "I'm frustrated sometimes."

I nodded, listening. "I know dialysis is a big production. I understand how tough and long the day is—and how that can be frustrating."

"How do *you* know?"

"My dad. He was on dialysis late in his life."

"I wouldn't say it's always frustrating. It's—," Joan paused and blinked her eyes for a moment. "Restricting, confining."

Joan yawned a few times before talking again. I sensed she was working with very low energy.

"How so?" I asked her, trying to engage her.

"Well, I can't really use my left arm for anything anymore."

I waited for her to tell me more. When she didn't, I engaged her again.

"What does that mean, you can't use your arm?"

Joan slowly pushed up her sweater and showed me her bruised and swollen fistula.

"Mmmm," I said, pursing my lips in concern.

"I'm so weak," Joan replied.

"I see that."

"I can't really get dressed by myself. Showering is hard. Can't cook for myself." Joan paused again for a moment. "I wish I wasn't so tired all the time."

"Must be tough to rely on others."

Joan nodded.

"Why does your nephrologist think you're depressed?" I asked.

"It's very common with dialysis patients, he says."

"Well, that's true for some people. But what is it that he sees that makes him think you're depressed?"

"That I'm so tired."

"What else?"

"That everything bothers me. Things like that. But . . . I'm not depressed."

"Or sad?"

"I don't want to kill myself." Her eyes widened for a second. "Sometimes I want to kill my husband, but that doesn't make me depressed. That makes me normal. I've been married 57 years. And that's normal, I say."

I smile and let out a soft laugh. Her sense of humor is there, but it's so muted. I wonder how I can get her to see she's confined and restricted in more ways than one.

"Well, let's do a questionnaire together and then I can go over what some of the other symptoms of depression can look like."

Joan agreed. And as we completed the Major Depression Inventory and the Geriatric Depression Scale she began to understand that depression is not just hopelessness, melancholy, or suicidal thinking. It also includes changes in energy, interests, sleeping, eating, focus, thinking, behavior, and attitude—things she was clearly experiencing.

"They want me to take medicine. The doctors."

"Well, what do you think about that?" I asked.

Joan narrowed her eyes. "If I don't think I'm depressed, why would I take medicine for it?"

"That makes sense." I leaned forward before I spoke again. "Does that mean if you believed you were depressed, you'd consider taking medication for it?"

Joan glared at me and raised her finger, shaking it. "You are a smart cookie." She remained still and reflected on what I said. "Maybe," she finally replied.

"How does your family feel about medication?"

"My kids want me to. My husband . . . I think he wants me to take it too. He just wants me to feel better."

"They love you. They're concerned."

Joan looked down and then back at me. "What do you think?"

"I think it's important, Joan," I said.

I encouraged Joan not to accept this current quality of life as being the best it could be. I told her that I believed she was dealing with something else in addition to lupus and kidney failure.

Depression.

Joan agreed to look into taking the medicine and together we told her husband, who was in the waiting room. We arranged another appointment to assess how antidepressant therapy was going.

When I finally saw her again six weeks later, Joan looked different—brighter, taller. She reported feeling better and was visibly more verbal and engaged.

"You look great, Joan. Tell me, how are you feeling these days?"

"I have so much more energy now," she said, smiling broadly.

"What a wonderful thing to hear," I replied.

"I'm doing more on my own. Not everything. But more than before," she said. "I'm still not driving—but I'm learning to enjoy that I have a chauffeur."

We spent the rest of the session talking about the Oscar awards and how she was able to see every movie up for an award during her dialysis treatments. She told me how the dialysis center has an Oscar pool and how she feels confident about winning the pot.

"So, can I visit with you again?" Joan asked. "I think it'd be good to check in with you."

"Sure," I replied. "We can meet again in another six weeks."

As Joan got up to leave, she urged me to see *The Grand Budapest Hotel* and *Birdman* because the Best Picture will go to one of the two. I promised that I would. As she walked toward her husband in the waiting room, she smiled slyly and snapped her fingers.

"Home, Jeeves," she said, and waited for him to help her on with her coat.

3

DIAGNOSIS FOR DEPRESSION IN LATER LIFE

Now that you have an understanding of depression in later life, it's time to explore how it's diagnosed and treated. Let's start off first with a quick word lesson. *Diagnosis* is a Latin reframing of the Greek word *diagignoskein*, with *dia* meaning "apart" and *gignoskein* meaning "to know, learn." So diagnosis literally translates "to know apart."

Given that many medical illnesses and emotional stressors can mimic a late-life mood disorder, a multistep approach for diagnosis is recommended. This is called a geriatric assessment.[1] This wide-ranging assessment includes a physical and mental health evaluation. Let's go into a more detailed description of what a geriatric assessment will entail.

THE GERIATRIC ASSESSMENT

Diagnosing depression will require you to make appointments with health professionals. If you cannot arrange the scheduled appointments, ask a family member, friend, or caregiver to do so. If you can make each appointment without assistance, that's terrific. But if you want someone to take you or accompany you because you have limitations, please know that health professionals are ready for such accommodations. You will also be completing a lot of paperwork, so put together a list of your past and current medications, vitamins, or supplements you take as well as previous surgery dates or emergency room visits. I have all my medical and surgery information in a file on my computer, and I update it as things change. I print it out to take with me to every doctor appointment I have. I also keep a copy of my current medications and their dosage in my wallet in case such information is needed in an emergency. If you don't already do this, I urge you to do so.

THE PHYSICIAN EVALUATION

The first stop on your diagnostic journey should begin with a physician. It's best if you can find a geriatrician, but if you cannot, your general or family practitioner is a good start. There will be three areas examined by your physician: physical health, screening for diseases, and functional abilities.[2]

- *Physical Health*: The geriatric assessment will begin with a cursory physical exam with your physician. In addition to checking blood pressure, pulse, and breathing, an inquiry into relevant geriatric issues will occur. You and your doctor will talk about your nutrition, vision, hearing, speech and language, your reflexes, coordination, and muscle tone. You will also discuss osteoporosis, balance and fall experiences, vitamin and/or mineral deficiencies, and the delicate subject of fecal and urinary incontinence. Also covered in this visit will be an exploration of all the medications you take—or what's called polypharmacy. A detailed medical history will be taken where you and your doctor discuss your current illnesses and/or diseases, your previous illnesses and/or diseases, all your previous surgeries, and your family's medical history. You and your doctor will also talk about the current symptoms you're experiencing and the treatment plan to diagnose their origin. This will likely include blood and urine testing, which may be collected at the time of your office visit or ordered to be obtained by a local laboratory.
- *Screening for Diseases*: In addition to a physical exam, your doctor will also be screening you for diseases that mimic depression, such as Alzheimer's, anemia, dementia, diabetes, **frailty**,[3] heart dis-

ease, sleep apnea, stroke, thyroid disorders, and others. It's not unusual, given your age, that your physician will refer you to a specialist like a neurologist, cardiologist, or endocrinologist where more intensive tests like a magnetic resonance imaging (MRI), computerized tomography (CT scan), blood-oxygenated-level-dependent functional resonance imaging (BOLD fMRI), or carotid ultrasound will be performed.[4]

- *Functional Ability*: A most significant part of the geriatric assessment requires an exploration of your proficiency performing simple and complex tasks required for living, clinically called functional ability. Studies show that measuring functional status of a senior helps to predict life expectancy.[5] There are two divisions of functional ability: activities of daily living (ADL) and instrumental activities of daily living (IADL). ADL skills are self-care activities that you perform daily like eating, dressing, bathing, transferring between the bed and a chair, using the toilet, and controlling bladder and bowel functions. IADL skills are activities that are needed to live independently, like doing housework, preparing meals, taking medications properly, and managing finances.[6] You answer the questions your physician asks, or your caregiver or loved one may respond if you cannot do so. Sometimes seniors downplay their need for help with daily living skills because they want to maintain a sense of integrity and independence. It's best, though, to be honest about your functional abilities, because underestimating them will greatly limit your recovery from geriatric depression (if you are so diagnosed) and impact your well-being.[7]

MENTAL HEALTH SPECIALIST

After you've seen your physician, your next stop is to be evaluated by a mental health professional. Although there are many different kinds of mental health professionals, the ones licensed to do this kind of geriatric testing tend to be psychologists, neuropsychologists, or psychiatrists. Often, your physician will recommend a mental health specialist, but you can also inquire further to find one. This can be done by contacting Medicare and your secondary insurance carrier; calling your local town, county, or state psychology or medical societies; or doing a search on-line for geriatric or depression specialists in your area. The mental health assessment will look at several areas: psychological symptoms, mental status, cognitive functioning, mood, and coexisting disorders.

- *Clinical Interview*: When you meet with your mental health pro-fessional, you'll be asked a series of questions that is called a *clinical interview*. This is where the clinician will gather informa-tion about your presenting concerns and symptoms, your previous medical history, and any results. You'll also go over your previous psychotherapy or antidepressant experiences, psychiatric treat-ment history, family history of mental illness, as well as any mental health programs or hospitalization experiences. A clinical inter-view is generally done in a casual question-and-answer format, with the clinician taking notes or a Structured Clinical Interview Form may be used.[8] You should also know that symptoms check-lists are often used during this time as well.

- *Mental Status*: After the clinical interview, a series of short skill assessments will be done. The most common is called a mental status exam, which evaluates a range of everyday mental skill abil-ities. The kinds of questions presented are likely to include ques-tions to find out if you know the day, date, time, and location of where you are at the moment, and to see if you can you recall a short list of words, follow simple commands, reproduce a drawing, and other such things. I often use the Mini-Mental State Exam (MMSE)[9] or the Geriatric Mental State Schedule (GMSS),[10] but some clinicians use a less formal mental status inquiry approach.

- *Cognition*: Diagnosing geriatric depression requires the clinician to rule out other kinds of issues that can look like depression. Much like your physician did a medical illness and disease screen-ing, the mental health professional will do a cognitive screening—assessing your thinking, reasoning, memory, attention, and pro-cessing speed. A commonly held misconception is that getting older results in an inevitable loss in cognition. Research, though, tells us that as we get older the most affected cognitive skills are attention and memory, while all of our other cognitive abilities tend to stay intact.[11] The cognitive assessment will be looking to discover if polypharmacy (many different kinds of medication) are producing side effects such as dullness in thinking or distractibility, if sensory losses (diminished hearing, eyesight) are interfering with your cognition, if medical illnesses (Parkinson's, arthritis, or poor muscle tone) slow your processing speed, or if a mood disorder (dysthymia, major depressive disorder, vascular depression) is responsible for impaired reasoning, thinking, and attention. Of great concern in the geriatric years is the detection of the neurocognitive disorders of delirium or dementia. Delirium is a syndrome characterized by inattention and acute cognitive dysfunction that is often brought on by polypharmacy, surgery, infection, malnutrition, or severe stress. Often, an elderly person with delirium will experience disorientation, distorted reality, and very poor concentration. Sometimes delirium can make a formerly passive senior appear manic or restless. An elderly person with delirium can also present in ways that appear like depression—hopelessness, slow movements, or speech and thinking impairments.[12] Delirium is not often recognized in the senior who has it, but loved ones will easily detect that something is very, very wrong. It's important to know that early detection of delirium can often lead to reversal of this condition.[13] Dementia, which is now being called *neurocognitive disorder*,[14] is a syndrome of multiple cognitive deficits in thinking, reasoning, memory, and language communication. The most common neurocognitive disorder is Alzheimer's disease, and the second most common is vascular dementia (a stroke-induced illness).[15] The cognitive assessment with your mental health specialist will likely involve the Mini-Cognition Test ("Mini Cog"), where you'll be asked to complete tasks like listening to a list of several items and asked to recall them a few minutes later, drawing a face of a clock showing all 12 numbers in the right places or, perhaps, a specific time. More formal cognitive testing might include the Behavior Rating Inventory of Executive Function (BRIEF), Clinical Dementia Rating (CDR), Dementia Rating Scale (DRS-2), or the Wechsler Memory Scales (WMS).[16] There are many different kinds of standardized testing measures for cognition, too many to detail here, but the take-away point is that your geriatric assessment should include a thorough look at your cognitive functioning. If further geriatric assessment is needed in the area of cognition, a neuropsychologist will be called in to investigate further. Otherwise, the mental health evaluation will move on to this next category.

- *Mood Assessment*: Testing in this area will specifically look at your overall mood functioning. You may be asked to fill out questionnaires or, if reading and writing are difficult, questions will be asked of you and recorded by the clinician. Symptoms of unipolar and bipolar depression in later life will be the focus, with tests measuring sadness, helplessness, hopelessness, aches and pains, mania,[17] loss of interest, and agitation. The Geriatric Depression Scale (GDS) is a most favored tool, but your clinician may administer the Adult Suicide Ideation Questionnaire (ASIQ), Apathy Evaluation Scale (AES), Beck Depression Scale (BDS), Cornell Scale for Depression in Dementia (CSDD), Geriatric Hopelessness Scale (GHS), or one of many others. Particular focus will be paid to unipolar and bipolar symptoms, time of onset, and intensity of symptoms as well as spotlighting your personal, home, and social environments for stressors. Diagnosis will also include subthreshold or subclinical symptoms.

- *Co-occurring Issues*: As mentioned in earlier chapters, depression can co-occur with other psychological illnesses. When two or more illnesses occur in the same person, it is called **comorbidity**. Depression can accompany anxiety disorders,[18] substance use disorders, and personality disorders,[19] so the geriatric assessment will broaden its scope and diagnosis. Looking for coexisting disorders is extremely important, because research reports co-occurring disorders that are not properly diagnosed result in poorer treatment in depression in later life.[20] The gold standard is the Clinical Assessment Scales for the Elderly (CASE), which will evaluate for anxiety, somatic issues, substance abuse, and other relevant points, but a mental health practitioner may use other diagnostic tools.

TIPS FOR THE GERIATRIC ASSESSMENT

Going to healthcare professionals for the geriatric assessment can be intimidating for many, it can cause anxiety in some, or it may feel altogether too overwhelming to coordinate for others. Calling to arrange appointments takes a little elbow grease. Here are some tips I recommend to seniors or their caregivers.

1. Start a file to keep all your assorted lab reports, tests, and doctor's notes and recommendations. If you cannot do this, have a family, friend, or caregiver set one up for you. Having a one-stop shop for all your health records make things easy for you.

2. Be aware that exams and assessments may take a few hours or require several days of appointments, depending on what is needed to address your health concerns. Don't overschedule yourself by making too many appointments in a row. You want to be at your best when taking these assessments or exams.

3. When you schedule your appointments, ask if the medical or mental health offices can mail forms to you at home to complete ahead of time—before your appointment date. This can save a lot of time and effort, and make the assessment move along more smoothly.

4. Try to schedule appointments early in the day and refrain from accepting late afternoon or evening appointments, as doing so can leave you feeling enormously taxed and tired.

5. If you are independent, please consider having someone go with you for the assessments. They can be long and you may be weary when all is done. It's also helpful to have another set of eyes and ears there to process what the professionals recommend.

6. If you're not independent or are limited mentally or physically, you'll still be asked to perform some tasks. But be prepared for family members and caregivers to answer many of the questions if you cannot. Many tests have self-report forms (meaning you report your symptoms and concerns) as well as caregiver forms (for friends, family, or health staff to complete).

7. Bring a list of your medications, allergies, surgeries, supplements, and other relevant information to each and every appointment. I cannot stress this enough. If you're asked once about your medications, you'll be asked a hundred times before the assessments are done. Make it easy and take a list every time. Appendix B has a sample outline for your use.

8. Also bring a list of all your doctors and their contact information (name, their specialty, address, phone, and fax). Appendix C has a chart for your use.

9. Try to be open and honest about your symptoms, thoughts, and feelings during the exams and assessments. Although many of you will do this with ease, there may be some of you who feel insecure or afraid to identify your struggles. Just remember that your health team wants you to experience well-being. The only way to achieve that is to identify issues accurately so they can be treated effectively. The goal of a geriatric assessment is to get a whole-person picture of what's going on uniquely with you—so you need to share all of who you are with your health team.

10. Make sure to ask your health professional for written instructions to review after each appointment and after your evaluation is completed. There is so much going on during these assessments that it can be easy to forget what was said. Having written instructions helps ensure that you haven't forgotten or misremembered anything. Sometimes all this takes is for the clinician or doctor to hand write instructions or recommendations on their letterhead stationery. I keep 5×8-inch letterhead stationery pads on my desk and make sure that I jot everything down, not just for the seniors I work with but for individuals of every age.

GENETIC TESTING FOR DEPRESSION IN LATER LIFE

Though not considered a part of the geriatric assessment per se, genetic testing, sometimes called pharmacogenetic testing, is something that I've been recommending for seniors for a long time now. This kind of genetic testing is called **personalized medicine** and offers a unique way of tailoring medications for you and your genetic profile. The reason to take this simple cheek-swab test is to help determine how antidepressant medication can work for you, if it's discovered that you have depression in later life. What was once thought of as science fiction, personalizing medicine uniquely for each individual, is now here—and it offers enormous potential to manage diseases, particularly depression in later life.

The genetic lab test encompasses what's known as cytochrome P450 tests. Your liver is responsible for the cytochrome P450 enzymes, but what most people don't readily know is that cytochrome P450 enzymes are among the most important metabolizers affected by individual **gene** variations. Also noteworthy is that cytochrome P450 enzymes are responsible for metabolizing more than 80 percent of the medications you take.[21] As a senior, you're likely to be on multiple kinds of medications, more so than younger adults. Additionally, your metabolism is likely to be more sluggish than it was when you were younger. The risk for adverse reactions to medicines increases as a result. Please consider using appendix D to keep track of the kinds of medications you're taking as well as the different kinds of side effects experienced.

When antidepressant medication is going to be recommended, I believe it's wise to have genetic data to help you make informed decisions. Adverse drug reactions (ADRs) cause an estimated 7,000 outpatient deaths per year. More than two million serious ADRs and 100,000 deaths occur annually in hospitals, with another 350,000 ADRs in nursing homes. Adverse drug reactions cost an estimated $177 billion each year—more than cardiovascular diseases.[22] And studies show that many seniors, given their older age status, have metabolic issues that can result in a negative experience called *age interactions antidepressant response*.[23]

The results gained from getting this type of genetic panel can minimize dangerous adverse drug interactions, sidestep side effects, and offer greater confidence taking medication. The problem, however, has been getting people to know that this test is out there . . . and finding physicians who understand what this genetic test does. Though I live in the vicinity of New York City, a mecca of progressive healthcare and research, my patients have had a tremendously difficult time finding a physician or nurse practitioner who understands the benefits of the cytochrome P450 test. There appear to be few in the medical field who utilize this genetic test, but the majority seems unfamiliar with it. Some healthcare professionals discard its potential value or believe its "out-of-pocket" expense is too much for their patients to manage. Others don't appear to know that cytochrome P450 testing is fully covered by Medicare and that many insurance companies cover the genetic panel. Through my experiences reading about why this ignorance existed, I came upon research that calls this lack of awareness *genetic illiteracy*[24]

—where many in the field of medicine, as well as healthcare insurers, have a hard time keeping up with genetic tests that are now available. Regardless of the whys, cytochrome P450 testing needs more mainstream notice. Its usefulness is enormously far reaching.

One last note before I talk about what cytochrome P450 can offer as an assessment tool. It's also important to tell you that with the practice of personalized medicine has sprung the worry about how your DNA may be used. The Genetic Information Non-Discrimination Act of 2008 (GINA) prohibits the use of genetic information by health insurance companies for determining a person's eligibility for insurance or determining insurance premiums—as well as by employers for making decisions about functions such as hiring and firing, assigning jobs, and promoting and demoting.[25] I hope knowing this law exists helps you feel more secure if you go for genetic testing.

What Cytochrome P450 Testing Provides

This genetic panel of tests helps evaluate your scientific pairing with the medication you're taking and looks at two vital issues, the first of which is to identify what kind of metabolism for medications you genetically possess. There are four metabolizing categories: poor, intermediate, extensive, and ultrarapid.[26] Discovering what kind of "metabolizer" you are will help steer your antidepressant treatment. Let's look at these in more detail.

- A *poor metabolizer* (PM) is a person whose metabolism takes in the medication very slowly, resulting in increased levels of the medicine in the bloodstream. This sluggish process causes significant side effects and poses toxicity risks such as **serotonin** syndrome—a potentially life-threatening condition caused by toxic levels of serotonin. If you're a poor metabolizer, you not only have the hardship of experiencing side effects and toxicity, you also continue to have depressive symptoms.
- An *intermediate metabolizer* (IM) is a person whose metabolism of a drug occurs at a slower rate than normal. People in this category experience side effects and mild toxicity but not as intensely as do poor metabolizers. As you might expect, medication

success is guarded in this category. You notice some symptom relief, but it won't be substantial.

- *Extensive metabolizers* (EM) have an average expected range for metabolism. Herein, you absorb medication effectively and are able to experience symptom relief with little or no side effects.
- *Ultrarapid metabolizers* (UM) quickly process medication, rendering drug treatment virtually ineffective. Because your genetic metabolism synthesizes the medication too fast, you cannot experience its therapeutic effects. If you're an ultrarapid metabolizer, you feel no symptom relief whatsoever.

The second component of this test allows you to understand how your other medications affect you, and evaluate if you are at risk for adverse drug reactions. Remember, ADRs are frequently serious, requiring admission to the hospital, and in rare instances, result in death. Your genetic panel will determine if you're at risk so that your physicians can prescribe more genetically friendly medicines.

Tips for Obtaining Cytochrome P450 Testing

All of these reasons are why I recommend seniors to get this simple genetic test. Being informed, educated, and ready is important when dealing with depression in later life. Here are tips to help you navigate the cytochrome P450 testing:

1. Call Medicare and your secondary insurance carrier and ask them what the coverage is for cytochrome P450 testing. Generally, the testing panel carries the Current Procedure Terminology (CPT) codes 81225, 81226, and 81227.
2. Be patient as you talk to the claim representative. Chances are he or she may not be aware of this genetic test. If necessary, ask to speak to a supervisor.
3. Then ask what lab Medicare or your insurer uses to provide this service. Get the name of the lab, the address, and the phone number.
4. You may be able to go out of network and choose a lab of your own. If you do this, find out what your deductible is and what the insurance company considers customary as a fee. Some out-of-

network laboratories will accept whatever your insurance company pays as reimbursement, without any additional cost to you. I have taken the cytochrome P450 panels and had this experience—where the lab accepted my insurance carrier's payment, with no additional payment for me.

5. If you choose to find a lab of your own, be sure to do a thorough checking of the lab, how long they have been providing this genetic test, and so forth. Check out their website, and take notice of their research, grants, and publications.

6. Many genetic labs like the Mayo Clinic, Genelex Labs, and GeneSight Labs are but a few of the private laboratories that can send you pamphlets and information about personalized genetic tests. Whether you choose to seek an out-of-network lab or go with one assigned by your insurance, you can give the brochures to your health professionals or family members should they not understand cytochrome P450 testing.

7. Call the lab and ask how they obtain the genetic material. Some labs will send you a prepackaged swab kit, while others will want you to come in and have the test done there. Although most labs use cheek swabs that collect DNA from the inside of mouth, some rely on blood samples.

8. When your test results arrive from the lab to your prescribing doctor's office, it's important to schedule a meeting to go over the results. This is not something that can be delivered with a cursory phone call from the doctor's office. Don't let your doctor tell you over the phone that "Everything looks good" or "Your panel indicates no problems." Those blanket statement are meaningless. Your testing will detail what kind of metabolizer you are, what kinds of medications are risky for you, and other relevant information. You need to discuss this in person with your doctor, and you must take home a copy of the report for your own records.

9. Finally, this genetic test will help in the treatment of your depression because you and your doctor will make informed decisions about your antidepressant medication, the dosage, and possible changes of your other medications based on your metabolism phenotype.

10. The genetic indicators from the cytochrome P450 test will also be used to help prescribe future medications for you. Results should be shared with all of your healthcare professionals.

SUMMARY

The geriatric assessment is a valuable tool for identifying depression in later life. Though there are two major areas that need to be fully assessed, the physical and the mental, I suggest a third part to this comprehensive assessment: genetic testing of the cytochrome P450 profile. Although it may be tempting to find a practitioner who will do a simple depression screening or sign off on a prescription for antidepressants after a 10-minute consultation, doing so may end up missing vital health issues, as the following case study shows.

CASE STUDY: DAVINA

Dennis from across the hall in my office building came in one afternoon and asked if I'd take a look at his 81-year-old mother, Davina, who had moved in with him a few months earlier. Dennis told me that she hadn't been herself the last few months. Dennis and his wife, Gail, thought she was depressed and so did her general practitioner. The reasoning behind this, they felt, was that Davina had recently stopped driving and seemed to be having some difficulties adjusting to the new living arrangements. A prescription for an antidepressant, Zoloft, was filled, but before beginning the medicine, Dennis wanted a second opinion. I agreed to see his mother but also wanted him and his wife to be part of the consultation. I sent Dennis home with some informational papers for his mother to complete ahead of time, suggesting that if she could not, that he could do so for her.

On the day of the appointment, I welcomed Davina into my office and watched as she slowly walked with her walker to a sturdy chair. Her hair was a soft puff of white and styled short. She was dressed and groomed well, wearing a black velour sweat suit and supportive black sneakers. Davina's eyes were at half mast, heavy lidded, until she placed her glasses on. Then they popped open.

Davina told me that she had been an elementary school teacher for 33 years and married for 56 years. She had four children and seven grandchildren and could name them all, but had trouble recalling their exact ages. Davina shared that her husband, Larry, had died from a stroke on May 29, but she couldn't remember the year. She took his passing very hard but managed to fill her days with reading, playing on the computer, watching television, and spending time with her grandchildren next door.

Davina disclosed that once she started having trouble walking and driving, her son thought it'd be wise to sell her home and use some of the money to build an addition to his house for her, which is what they did. She reported liking the arrangements, having her own living area far enough away but also being close enough should she need help with things.

Davina spoke well and didn't need me to repeat any questions or comments made to her during the consultation. When asked about her physical health, Davina said she takes Zocor for high cholesterol and Lopressor for her heart but couldn't remember the exact dosages. She had weakness in her legs, especially in both knees, and has been told she needs knee replacements.

"Do you know why you're here to see me today, Davina?"

"Dennis thinks I'm depressed."

"Do *you* think you're depressed?"

"Some days. I think about things and get depressed."

"Like what?"

"Oh, this and that." She paused. "Missing Larry. Feeling old."

"What else do you think about?" I asked, wanting to know more.

"Not too much else. I try not to think about things too much," Davina replied.

"Well, I'd like to talk to you today about some things. Would that be okay?"

Davina nods.

"But before we start, I want you to remember these three words: *Rabbit, pencil, bedroom.* Can you say them for me?"

"Rabbit, pencil, bedroom," Davina repeated.

Davina and I completed the Geriatric Depression Scale, the Beck Depression Inventory, the Beck Anxiety Scale, and the Mini-Mental

State Exam. At the end, I asked Davina to tell me the three words I wanted her to remember.

She couldn't.

"Rabbit, pencil, bedroom," I replied.

Davina narrowed her eyes. "Yes. I remember now."

After a brief moment to score the tests, I invited Dennis and Gail in to join us.

Dennis and Gail both agreed that Davina seemed sad and lethargic. They talked with Davina in the session about how she doesn't want to do a lot of the things she used to do. Dennis told his mother that sometimes she's irritable and snappy. Gail reminded Davina how she hasn't wanted to talk on the phone with Linda, Ken, or Greg (her other children) or interact with the grandchildren like she used to. Trying not to make Davina feel broadsided, I stopped and asked Davina how she felt about listening to all of this.

"Okay," she said, "I've heard this from them before."

Dennis and Gail continued to share their concerns, and the list was a long one. They reported that Davina doesn't like go out as much anymore, and when she does, she nervously insists on going home early. Gail said that she seems confused a lot of the time and sometimes forgets to lock up her side of the house, leaving the front door open all night. When Gail reminded her of what she needs to do, Davina would get upset and sometimes cry. Dennis shared openly and with great concern that Davina wasn't understanding how serious this is.

"I do," Davina responded. "I just don't see what they're saying. I'm fine."

I took out the Beck and the Geriatric Depression forms.

"Remember these?" I lifted them up for everyone to see. "We filled them out a little while ago."

Davina nodded.

"Well, it shows here that some of the things you think and feel suggest depression, Davina." I tried to be gentle and waited for her to process the information. "You got scores in the moderate range for depression. You have some anxiety too, but it's on the milder side."

"You can have both?" Gail asked.

"Oh, yes, it's not uncommon for depression and anxiety to buddy-up sometimes," I replied.

"Does the Zoloft take care of that?" Dennis asked.

"It does, but I have a bit more to share with you all." I paused a beat and looked at Davina. "How do you feel learning this?"

"Well, if it says so, then it must be true," she said.

Not satisfied that Davina understood me, I explained the symptoms of late-life depression and went over some of the questions we had completed. I did this in order to review her memory of the experience and to educate everyone in the room about late-onset depression. I went on further and illustrated that while simple forgetting and confusion are part of depression, there are some things that warranted further inspection. I shared that Davina obtained a score of 15 on the Mini-Mental State Exam, which suggests a moderate impairment of cognitive functioning. Davina could not identify the day or date and had trouble drawing an object, counting backward from 100 by sevens, and other recall issues. I recommended more in-depth testing by a neurologist, who would perform relevant medical and lab tests related to brain functioning, and also a neuropsychologist, who would test Davina's executive functioning and further assess her mood and anxiety states.

"You're thinking Alzheimer's?" Dennis asked, upset.

"Alzheimer's!" Davina snapped back, upset. "Oh, I don't have that. What are you talking about?"

"There are many different kinds of issues related to how the brain works. And as we age, our thinking can slow down a little. It's natural. But there are some things that concern me. Things that concern Dennis and Gail. And I'm thinking maybe you may feel confused sometimes and it makes you feel upset. Or nervous. Maybe even depressed," I said.

Davina was agitated but was listening.

"I can't say what's going on because more information is needed, but early identification and treatment can be very helpful."

We continued talking a bit more before the consultation ended. Before they left, I urged them to start making appointments and to keep me in the loop as things progressed. As I closed the door, I realized that Davina's general practitioner was right about her having depression. But it was only half the story. Davina appeared to also have some form of dementia. It was easy to Monday-morning quarterback his decision to prescribe Zoloft from the vantage point I had now, but it was also easy to miss Davina's entire diagnostic picture.

Why? Because so many of the symptoms of dementia can overlap with the symptoms of depression and vice versa.

And this is why a comprehensive, multiprofessional assessment ensures a proper diagnosis of late-life depression.

4

TRADITIONAL TREATMENTS FOR DEPRESSION IN LATER LIFE

Once your geriatric assessment is complete, a diagnosis will be made. You will discover if your late-onset depression is unipolar, bipolar, or neurobiological in nature and if the intensity is mild, moderate, or severe. Diagnosis will also uncover if your late-life depression is subclinical, meaning that you don't meet the criteria for a diagnosable depression but you have many symptoms of it. Based on your unique findings, treatment will be recommended. There are two types of traditional treatments: psychotherapy and medical. Let's begin with psychotherapy.

PSYCHOTHERAPY TREATMENTS

Psychotherapy is the treatment of emotional conflicts through the use of talking and communicating with a trained professional. Also known as **talk therapy**, psychotherapy is practiced by psychologists, psychiatrists, social workers, and psychiatric nurse practitioners.

There are many different schools of psychotherapy, each one working from a unique model of mind and behavior. Though the schools differ in approach and technique, they all share the same goal: to reduce depression in later life.

As far as evidence-based research goes, all traditional talk therapies can be effective in reducing mild to moderate depressive symptoms.[1]

However, research reports that specific kinds of short-term psychother-apies work more effectively for the senior who has depression in later life.[2] Here they are listed in alphabetical order for you:

- *Behavior Therapy for Older Adults* (BT-OA) is a psychotherapy that focuses solely on understanding the relationship between your mood and your behaviors.[3] The theory behind BT-OA is that your depression has resulted from a lack of pleasant experiences or an excess of negative interactions in your life. Treatment con-centrates on heightening your awareness of your negative behav-iors and helping you better identify positive moments. For exam-ple: Are you spending more time focusing on the negative aspects in life instead of the positive ones? Are you stuck in a loop of negative social reinforcement from other people? Do they re-spond to you with great concern when things are bad but gloss over the happier moments? Do you lack a set of skills to combat fatigue? Behavior therapy for older adults will help sharpen your observational skills, teach you about the power of consequences, and show you that well-being can come from changing your be-haviors and actions. You'll monitor your moods and behaviors, record pleasant and unpleasant events, notice the connection be-tween interactions and your mood—and ultimately increase par-ticipation in more positive experiences.
- *Cognitive-Behavioral Therapy for Older Adults* (CBT-OA) is an evidence-based treatment that works successfully for seniors who have mild to moderate depression. For severe depression, CBT-OA has been shown to be effective when paired with medication.[4] Among psychotherapies used with older adults, CBT has received the most research for late-life depression.[5] This kind of treatment expands beyond the theory of behaviorism by looking at thoughts as well as actions. CBT-OA stresses that specific thinking patterns cause depression. Does sadness leave you thinking that there's no way out? Are your thoughts an endless stream of self-critical state-ments? Do you think in all-or-nothing terms? Are your thoughts about issues truly realistic? In this therapy, you'll meet with a therapist to begin identifying the belief systems you use on a daily basis, with the end goal of correcting unrealistic beliefs by replac-

ing them with more realistic attitudes. Essentially, changing how you think will change the way you feel.

- *Cognitive Bibliotherapy* (CB) uses books and writing exercises to help seniors identify and challenge negative thinking, fight fatigue, and minimize helplessness. Cognitive bibliotherapy aligns itself with the cognitive theory of depression, which aims to help identify and challenge the maladaptive ways you think. Generally, a therapist will recommend books on the subject of depression or related writing exercises and check in via e-mail, telephone, or in person with you. It's important to know that this is a short-term approach of treatment with minimal contact with a health professional. Cognitive bibliotherapy has been shown to be effective for treating subclinical or mild levels of depression in older adults.[6]

- *Dialectical Behavior Therapy* (DBT) for late-life depression emphasizes acceptance of what can and cannot be changed. This is attained by using the DBT skill sets of mindfulness, interpersonal effectiveness, emotion regulation, and distress tolerance.[7] You and your therapist will treat your symptoms by identifying emotional experiences that lead to depression, reducing your emotional vulnerability, and decreasing your depressive symptoms. DBT will teach you to offset rigid responding styles for more flexible and adaptive responses. You'll also work on improving your social engagement, openness to new experiences, and monitoring emotional expressions.

- *Intensive Short-Term Dynamic Psychotherapy* (ISTDP) focuses on identifying conflicts and unresolved emotional issues, heightening your insight, and getting you to see issues beyond your awareness. The theory of ISTDP is that depression arises because you aren't aware of the problematic patterns or core relational themes that impact your life. The goal of this therapy is to reduce symptoms and bring about insight, so you can use your new awareness to shift decisions, change behaviors, and kick depression to the curb. Like cognitive behavior therapy for older adults, intensive short-term psychotherapy is effective for mild and moderate depression, and when paired with medication, successfully addresses severe depression in later life.[8]

- *Interpersonal Psychotherapy* (IPT) focuses on current interpersonal difficulties rather than behaviors, thoughts, or unresolved issues.[9] IPT is based on the idea that negative social interactions often precede depression and that depression can lead to further negative interpersonal conflicts. For seniors, IPT looks at four areas of conflict: 1) grief after the loss of a loved one, 2) conflict in significant relationships, 3) difficulties adapting to changes in relationships, and 4) life circumstances and difficulties stemming from social isolation.[10] With IPT, you'll learn how to identify where the glitches occur in your life, how to better address them, and how to prevent relapse of late-life depression.

- *Life Review Psychotherapy* (LRP), sometimes called *Reminiscence Therapy*, helps seniors put their life story into perspective with the goal of coming to terms with losses, failures, and missed opportunities as well as marking significant moments. Life review psychotherapy works from the long-held belief that reminiscence is a universal and naturally occurring mental process where you visit your past, your lost loved ones, unresolved conflicts, or moments of joy so you can reintegrate them into your life in a newfound way. In life review psychotherapy, you'll be encouraged by your therapist to talk openly about these thoughts, feelings, and stories so you can gain a balanced sense of perspective of your life. This approach reduces depressive symptoms, increases life satisfaction, and builds self-acceptance—even leading to catharsis for many.[11]

- *Problem-Adaptive Therapy* (PATH) is a treatment designed for depressed seniors who are physically challenged or have mild dementia.[12] This kind of treatment occurs in your home where you, your caregiver, and a therapist work together to create a home environment that will enhance your well-being, minimize your struggles by having step-by-step approaches laid out, and address any emotional depression or anxieties you may experience.[13]

- *Problem-Solving Therapy* (PST), sometime called *Solution-Focused Therapy*, is a short-term, intensive intervention for seniors who do not have any cognitive issues. In this therapy, you and your therapist will identify problems that you're facing and develop an action plan to solve the problems. The theory behind problem-solving therapy is that depression is a result of repeated and failed attempts to solve problems, which leads you to feeling hopeless, helpless, and disconnected from others. Individuals in later life may encounter difficulty solving problematic issues because they are particularly challenging. With PST, you'll learn a number of different things, including how to clarify and define the problem, how to set a realistic goal, how to generate multiple solutions, how to evaluate and compare your solutions, and then how to put your chosen solution into action.[14]

- *Problem-Solving Therapy for Executive Dysfunction* (PST-ED) is used for adults in later life who have both depression *and* cognitive functioning issues. It differs slightly from problem-solving therapy in that you and your therapist will address ways to help improve your day-to-day life living with cognitive decline, improve your coping by helping you find ways to communicate more effectively and structure your day better, and any other issues that arise.

- *Psychoeducation* (PE) is a professionally delivered treatment that can be done individually (with families and caregivers) or in a group setting to address issues of depression in later life. This kind of intervention generally uses educational materials like reading or worksheets and teaches those in attendance about symptoms, treatment, and access to care. Therapists who provide this treatment often do so in the form of workshops or lecture series—and make time for questions and answers.[15] Psychoeducation is generally something you might get involved in if you're looking to understand depression in later life. The knowledge you'll gain will take you to the next level, be it getting a diagnosis, looking for treatment, or finding resources.

- *Supportive Psychotherapy* (SP) is used to treat depression by simply getting you to talk about whatever's on your mind, without direction or judgment.[16] Different from the other psychotherapies, supportive psychotherapy is only focused on providing you with assistance, advocacy, or advice. Supportive psychotherapy also contains a strong educational component, so you and your therapist will spend time on the type of depression you're experiencing, how to treat it effectively, and how to recognize signs of overload, stress, and relapse.

MEDICAL TREATMENTS

Medical treatments are often recommended alongside psychotherapy. As with anything you choose to undertake, be an educated consumer by learning all you can about these treatments. And always seek second opinions when treatments are being recommended for your late-life depression. Become familiar with treatment risks and benefits, pros and cons, short-term versus long-term benefits, cost, and accessibility so you can make an informed decision.

Table 4.1. Depressions and Their Treatments

Type of Depression	Psychotherapy Treatments	Medical Treatments
Adjustment Disorder with Depressed Mood	PE, PST, SP	Not generally recommended
Alzheimer's Disease with Depressed Mood	PE, PATH	Pharmacotherapy
Bipolar Disorders	BT-OA, CBT-OA, DBT, IPT, ISTDP	Pharmacotherapy
Catatonic Depression	Not generally recommended	Hospitalization, Pharmacotherapy, ECT, rTMS
Dementia with Depressed Mood	PATH	Pharmacotherapy
Depression–Executive Dysfunction Syndrome	PST-ED	Pharmacotherapy
Mild Depression	BT-OA, CBT-OA, DBT, IPT, ISTDP, LRP, PE, PST, SP	Pharmacotherapy, if chronic
Mood Disorder Due to Medical Condition	PE, PST, SP	Pharmacotherapy
Post-Stroke Depression	BT-OA, PE, PST, SP	Pharmacotherapy, rTMS
Psychotic Depression	Not generally recommended	Hospitalization, Pharmacotherapy, ECT, rTMS
Subclinical Depression	BT-OA, CBT-OA, DBT, IPT, ISTDP, LRP, PE, PST, SP	Not generally recommended
Substance-Induced Mood Disorder	BT-OA, CBT-OA, DBT, IPT, ISTDP, LRP, PE, PST, SP	Pharmacotherapy
Treatment-Resistant Depression	BT-OA, CBT-OA, DBT, IPT, ISTDP, LRP, PE, PST, SP	ECT, rTMS, VNS, DBS
Unipolar Depression	BT-OA, CBT-OA, DBT, IPT, ISTDP, LRP, PE, PST, SP	Pharmacotherapy
Vascular Depression	PE, PST, SP	Pharmacotherapy, ECT, rTMS

- *Pharmacotherapy* is the most often used medical treatment for depression in later life.[17] My experience reflects this research. I'd say well over two thirds of my patients with late-onset depression use pharmacotherapy alongside psychotherapy with successful results. Pharmacotherapy treats emotional illness through the use of medication. Long ago, plants and flowers were sourced for their medicinal purposes. Nowadays, scientists in the medical field of **psychopharmacology** create bioactive compounds for medicinal purposes. Sometimes referred to as **drug therapy**, pharmacotherapy changes the neurochemistry in your brain and body to prevent illness and to treat illness. In this treatment, you'll meet for a consult with a psychiatrist or nurse practitioner, preferably one who has geriatric experience. The pharmacotherapy process involves a thorough medical history, one that will take up your entire first consult. While you're there, the specialist will match your symptoms with relevant medications and begin you on a small dose. At first, you'll have scheduled appointments within weeks of starting your medication. As time progresses, dosage may remain the same or increase based on your reported symptoms. If side effects are intolerable, a change in medication may be necessary. However, once you are stabilized on your medication, you won't need to be seen as often. It's not unusual for your medication treatment plan for unipolar or bipolar depression to include one or more different kinds of medicines. Your unique experiences will help determine in what direction pharmacotherapy will progress. I recommend that the seniors I work with fill out a side-effect questionnaire checklist before they begin pharmacotherapy and during their pharmacotherapy treatment. Appendix D can be used for this. Using these forms can help you monitor your day-to-day experiences before you begin medication and then track possible side effects. Another thing I do is encourage my senior patients to refrain from comparing their medical regime to others or placing a negative spin on the kinds of medications they're taking. Depression is not a one-size-fits-all illness. What works for one does not work for all. The important thing is to find what works for you. Generally, I recommend that seniors ask their prescribing healthcare professional for cytochrome P450 testing before starting pharmacotherapy. Remember from chapter 3, this kind of genetic testing can help streamline medication and offset adverse reactions. For depression in later life, pharmacotherapy may be recommended alone or will be utilized in addition with psychotherapy. For example, you might be taking antidepressant medication with supportive therapy for late-onset unipolar depression. Or you might be prescribed a mood stabilizer medication working together with dialectical behavior therapy for late-onset bipolar depression.

- *Electroconvulsive Therapy* (ECT) is generally the gold standard for depression in later life if there is no issue with cognitive functioning.[18] ECT is generally recommended when a senior with late-life depression doesn't experience a reduction in symptoms. Depression that isn't easily remedied is clinically called **treatment-resistant depression**. Electroconvulsive therapy is a misunderstood and fearsome intervention, portrayed as barbaric treatment in television and films, where you're strapped down, awake, and blasted with electricity. The truth is that ECT is performed while you're asleep, in a hospital suite, with a team of skilled professionals who monitor the procedure. Those involved are anesthesiologists, nurses, and medical doctors. ECT is the process by which electrical currents are passed through the brain to create a brief seizure. This seizure activates signal pathways and **neurotransmitters** in the brain and reduces the severity of depression. ECT treatments are generally given every other day for up to 12 treatments. The treatment takes about 15 minutes to perform. For seniors, neuroimaging testing prior to ECT treatment can predict if ECT will be an effective treatment.[19] Also, research suggests that the quality of the pulse and electrode placement can significantly reduce side effects, which can include confusion after the procedure, memory loss, nausea, and muscle soreness.[20] I have worked with several seniors who've experienced ECT, but it should be mentioned that none of them had significant cognitive issues (dementia, executive functioning) at the time of their treatments. Given the side effects of memory loss, short-term confusion, and forgetfulness, I'm more prone to recommending rTMS for seniors with depression and cognitive decline, as it is less invasive and has significantly fewer side effects. That being said, those who underwent ECT for their depression reported it to be very beneficial.

- *Repetitive Transcranial Magnetic Stimulation* (rTMS) is another medical treatment for late-life depression that has not improved with other traditional means. Repetitive transcranial magnetic stimulation is a medical, noninvasive procedure that has been shown to help late-life depression, especially vascular depression.[21] rTMS has been shown to produce changes in neuronal activity in regions of the brain implicated in mood regulation, such as the prefrontal cortex.[22] The procedure involves sitting in a reclining chair, awake, while a coil-like tool is positioned around your head by a specially trained physician. Short, undetectable magnetic pulses will excite target-specific areas in the brain. rTMS requires a series of four to six weeks of treatments. Sessions are generally less than an hour and you're able to drive yourself home. Side effects are said to be minimal, with brief headache being the most reported. Some of the seniors I've worked with have opted for rTMS to help alleviate their resistant depression. Several found it significantly helpful and felt immediately better after the first treatment. Others, though, informed me that once the rTMS treatment stopped, their symptoms of depression returned.

- *Inpatient Hospitalization* is recommended for severe late-life depression when psychotherapy and pharmacotherapy aren't successfully reducing your symptoms and when life-threatening symptoms emerge. For example, inpatient hospitalization may be recommended if you become suicidal or if you're in the throes of an agitated mania. Though the thought of going to a hospital causes discomfort, the safe setting of a hospital is enormously vital for stabilizing your symptoms. Sometimes inpatient hospitalization can be planned—that is, you and your health team decide to take this route because current treatment isn't yielding results. Other times, it's done on an emergency basis. Generally, I call ahead and try to get the admission process started to ease the transition. In an emergency situation, when you may be in severe crisis, there often isn't time to set up admission. In this event, getting to the nearest hospital's emergency room is the primary goal. Many inpatient hospital wards have geriatric units, specially designed to address late-life depression, dementias, and other geriatric issues. The main purpose of seeking inpatient hospitalization is to intensify all aspects of your treatment. The goal is to reduce your depressive symptoms and to improve cognition and your activities of daily living. Once you're stabilized, you will be discharged and head back home. For those of you in assisted living or nursing homes, you will return to your room there and may receive additional treatments upon your arrival.

- *Vagus Nerve Stimulation* (VNS) is another treatment-resistant depression procedure that involves the surgical implantation of a pacemaker-like device under the skin of the collar bone that sends electrical pulses through the vagus nerve, a nerve pathway that sends information to and from the brain.[23] Long used for Parkinson's disease and other motor illnesses, VNS has recently been developed to treat severe depression.[24] After implantation, your surgeon programs the device to deliver small electrical bursts every few minutes. You generally remain in the hospital overnight for monitoring. Individuals who have undergone this treatment report almost immediate reduction in depressive symptoms with no side effects in memory or thinking. Typically complaints are soreness, irritation, or infection at the surgical site.

- **Deep Brain Stimulation** (DBS), sometimes called neuromodulation, is an additional treatment-resistant surgical procedure designed to help reduce severe depression in later life. This treatment is similar to vagus nerve stimulation in that a pacemaker-like device in implanted, but it differs in that the vagus nerve is not the target specific site; rather two tiny electrodes are implanted directly into brain structures such as the **basal ganglia**, thalamus regions, Brodmann area 25, or the **medial prefrontal cortex**. You and your doctor will personalize the electrical pulse settings that will reduce your depressive symptoms.[25]

- *Magnetic Seizure Therapy* (MST) is a newer medical treatment where a high-intensity rTMS is used to induce a seizure. The main difference between MST and ECT is that MST imparts electrical energy to a limited area on the surface of the brain, while ECT causes electricity to flow throughout the entire brain. Magnetic seizure therapy has been shown not only to reduce depression but is also associated with lowered anxiety and has been recommended for older adults who have depression, dementia, or traumatic brain injury because no evidence of deterioration in cognition and memory has been noted.[26] Magnetic seizure therapy is a new form of treatment and may not be easily found in the area you live.

SUMMARY

Depression in later life is unique, more so than depression at earlier stages in life. As you've already learned from your readings in previous chapters, seniors don't readily sense that they're depressed and instead report feeling unwell in nonspecific ways. If seniors can report specific things, they fall in the category of physical symptoms like stomach pain, back pain, headache, low energy, or muscle aches. Research tells us that effective treatment of depression requires early detection, so having a geriatric assessment helps to pinpoint a diagnosis. But the other half of this picture is making sure to know what kinds of treatments can be successful for late-life depression. Psychotherapy is not always a go-to treatment, nor are medical treatments. Each and every case of depression in later life requires a thorough review. And if you're a senior with late-life depression or care for someone who does, you need to be prepared to adjust or change treatments as needed. The following case demonstrates this.

CASE STUDY: WENDY

I began working with Wendy, age 66, shortly after her husband, Bill, had a stroke. Wendy was consumed with taking care of him alone, as her children lived out of state. Keeping track of the medical bills, getting him to and from physical and speech therapy, as well as taking on Bill's share of the chores on top of her own pressed heavily on Wendy. Her blood pressure soared. She also began having trouble sleeping at night. She fell apart frequently, sharing that she'd break dishes on the floor or scream at the top of her lungs when she was alone in the house. Afterward, she'd drink or eat everything in sight, which initially seemed to make her feel better but later didn't, as she felt terrible about her binging.

Wendy reported that prior to her husband's stroke, she was just settling into retirement. Her husband, Bill, seven years older, had already been enjoying retired life, fishing and boating in the good weather on Long Island. In the winter months, he'd play cards and enjoyed bingo at the temple they regularly attended. Wendy had a son and a daughter, both married. One had settled in Florida, while the other set down roots in North Carolina; neither had children yet. Wendy shared that she and Bill planned to sell their home in New York and move down south to be closer when grandkids arrived.

Wendy reached out to me after talking to her priest, who said that he worried she was not just "under stress" but actually depressed. At our first appointment, I could tell that she was truly overwhelmed with situational issues that negatively affected her day-to-day living. Nonetheless, I administered a few depression and anxiety scales, which indicated moderate depression and mild anxiety. Though Wendy had been given a full physical several months back, I felt it was important to have another consult with her general practitioner for a cursory exam and simple blood and urine tests to ensure nothing medical was adding to the issues her life. Medical testing was all negative, but a recommendation for blood pressure medication was made if her next check-in showed it hadn't reduced. Wendy's physician and I discussed the possibility of antidepressant medications, but I suggested she hold off on that until a few sessions of psychotherapy occurred. Wendy agreed to this proposal.

Wendy and I began working using a problem-solving therapy treatment. Together we made a list of priority issues and graded them from low to high. Then we began brainstorming solutions. I saw that Wendy and Bill were not taking advantage of available augmented care such as visiting nurse services or getting mobility devices like a wheelchair, commode, and even a hospital bed, so we began there straight away. Wendy had been so crushed by stress that she had never completed an application for a handicapped tag to aid in Bill's transportation, so that was an immediate need as well. Wendy and I tackled each of the goals and before long, things were calmer. Not better, but calmer. Wendy still experienced sleeplessness, crying jags, and bouts of anger, but the management of Bill's needs in the home and out traveling improved significantly.

The next set of goals for Wendy was to break apart the chain of never-ending tasks by getting her to see that asking for help from others was vital. There were many neighbors and friends from temple who were not only asking about Bill but wanted to come by and help out. Wendy didn't like relying on others and had rejected their offers politely. Additionally, Bill was not comfortable with others seeing him so "different." Problem-solving therapy highlighted the advantages and disadvantages of certain decisions, and soon Wendy realized that doing this on her own was unrealistic. She began inviting trusted others into her home and found the company helpful and even healing for Bill. It also allowed her to take a few moments for herself to grab a long shower or tend to her garden.

Over the course of the remaining weeks of our work, problem-solving therapy helped Wendy gain a sense of assertiveness, be it requesting her children to help or come for visit, or asking doctors and rehabilitation specialists questions. Wendy reported feeling less angry, sleeping better, and feeling as if "a weight had been lifted off" her since our work began. Her blood pressure normalized. After several months of working together, Wendy's symptoms were gone and it was suggested that treatment stop. I reminded Wendy of the step-by-step goals of problem-solving therapy and encouraged her to contact me should she feel irritable or stressed.

I never heard from her again.

Until six years later.

Wendy called, saying she was deeply depressed; her voice was lower and slower than I recalled.

"Tell me what's going on," I pressed.

"I'm so down. I just don't think I can take much more."

She sounds terrible, I said to myself. "Okay, let's get you in. Can you come tomorrow? I can do either 12:15 or 4:30."

"I'm in North Carolina. Bill and I moved here about two and a half years ago," Wendy replied. "Can you help me find someone down here?"

"Of course," I said.

Wendy described how Bill had made improvements with his speech, walking, and with his fine motor coordination since we last worked together. They returned to socializing more at the temple, and when their daughter announced her pregnancy, they readied the house to be sold. Wendy and Bill rented for a time before buying and settled on a gated community about 10 minutes from their daughter. Wendy indicated that the move was exciting and full of promise at first, but things had slowed down and she found herself feeling very lonely. They joined a temple in town, but it didn't offer the kinds of activities and sense of community she was hoping for. Furthermore, Wendy reported that Bill had grown distant romantically since his stroke, and that she felt an enormous sense of loss with regard to intimacy, sexuality, and affection.

After I secured Wendy's address, I told her that I'd find a professional. I urged her to call me if she had self-destructive thoughts or if her despair worsened. She assured me that she wasn't suicidal but that she was feeling hopeless, helpless, and so very lost.

It didn't take long for me to find a great resource for Wendy, and I called back several hours later. It was a geriatric center at Duke University, about a 25-minute ride from her home. I gave her several contact names and numbers and told Wendy they were expecting her call to make an appointment. I instructed Wendy to sign releases so her new clinicians could speak with me, and I told her to touch base after she made a connection there. About three weeks later, I received a message.

"Deb, it's Wendy. Just wanted the thank you for helping me get to the Duke center," she said, her voice sounding stronger. "Call me when you get this message."

When I reached Wendy, she shared that she was working with a psychologist she liked very much as well as a psychiatrist who had prescribed Cymbalta. She learned that her current depression was different from her first experiences years earlier in that it's a more intense episode revolving around her relationship with Bill, so she's working with an interpersonal psychotherapy frame in sessions. As Wendy talked, I could see that she had adapted easily to the different treatment approaches, from problem solving to interpersonal, and had also integrated medication without difficulty in her life. She had few to no side effects.

"I'm already feeling better, but I know there's more work to do," Wendy said as we started winding down our conversation.

"One thing that always impressed me is how you roll with the changes, Wendy."

"Well, I'm still rolling," she said, laughing. "And I know it'll be worth it."

5

HOLISTIC APPROACHES TO DEPRESSION IN LATER LIFE

Depression is an experience of depletion. When the illness presented in me as a child, I distinctly remember feeling worn down, hollowed out, devoid of enthusiasm and vitality. I didn't realize back then how the biological aspects of depression were dulling my senses, draining me to a level where I took in very little around me. I lived a featureless existence—one that I understand far better today as both a clinician and a patient in remission. But as a young girl, I thought the world was just a muted place that had little to offer . . . and I had little to give back in return.

Even now as I near the age of "senior discounts" and "old lady status," my depression requires me to manage it differently than I did as a young woman. In addition to using the skills I've learned in psychotherapy and antidepressant medication, I practice a variety of alternative treatments. These are called *holistic approaches* (HA), or sometimes referred to as *complimentary alternative medicine* (CAM), and are great ways to buoy yourself when depression in later life occurs. For the most part, holistic approaches are helpful treating mild and subclinical types of late-onset depression.[1] For more moderate or severe depression, holistic approaches should be used alongside traditional psychotherapy and/or medication treatments.

There are many different kinds of holistic approaches and complementary alternatives, and the best way to understand them all is to frame them around our five senses. Let's begin.

FEEDING YOUR FIVE SENSES

Research shows that our moods are affected the most by what we take in through our senses.[2] What we see, smell, taste, touch, and hear activates our brain and every cell of our being, setting into motion a series of neural pathway causes and effects.[3] Our senses don't work in a linear way, where one-domino-touches-another-and-then-another kind of experience. Our sensory system is a collective tour de force of cell receptors, firing neurons and surging chemistry that gives way for emotions and thoughts to be born. The relationship among our senses, brain, and body is a complex physiological symphony that creates the human experience.

When depression hits in later life, the sensory system deteriorates.[4] For example, senses become dull. Neural pathways slow down. Important feel-good neurochemicals wither in production. Depression flattens the human experience. That's the bad thing. But the good thing is that research shows that feeding the senses in the right ways can help balance neurochemistry, revive sluggish neural pathways, and ease depression.[5]

Sense of Sight

The very first thing you need if you're a senior with depression is *light*. The data on sun and natural light holding powerful holistic benefits for depression is vast. It's been my professional opinion, as well as my personal experience, that in order to lift the veil of depression, one has to be able to see the light—literally and figuratively. So, open the curtains. Draw the blinds. Let the sun's light spill into your world. Make it your business, every day, to sit in a pool of sunlight, be it indoors or outdoors. If you're in assisted living or a skilled nursing home, make sure to have natural light feature strongly in your day. Research says even just a few minutes is beneficial.

Light is responsible for turning on the brain and the body. Light enters through our eyes, moves through the retina, and signals the **hypothalamus**, which regulates mood, sleep, and appetite. Light also activates the **pineal gland**, a tiny pea-shaped brain structure that essentially runs our body clock, producing the hormone **melatonin**. When we live in dim or dark settings, the pineal gland produces too much melatonin, making us sleepy, fatigued, and listless. One of the greatest benefits of being in sunlight is that it helps to even out melatonin production and keep our body clock, also known as **circadian rhythm**, running smoothly. If abundant sunlight is not available, you can create it for yourself or for your loved one with artificial light. There are two kinds of light therapy. The first is **bright light therapy**, which has been shown to suppress the brain's secretion of melatonin almost as well as natural sunlight. Studies show that an hour of bright light therapy improves sleep and mood for depressed seniors.[6] Keep in mind that the device for light therapy need not be directly in front of you, but within the room so your retinas can register the luminescence. The other kind of light that is helpful for seniors with depression is called **dawn–dusk simulation light therapy**.[7] This light therapy simulates a sunrise and helps adjust your melatonin so you can wake up feeling refreshed, not groggy. The dawn simulation setting can be set to occur at a time you wish, with low luminescence filling the room, gradually increasing in strength over a set period of time. When you're sleeping, light still enters your eyes and triggers the pineal gland to begin its wake-up cycle. The dusk setting can help your body adjust to the nighttime more readily, dimming the luminescence as if the sun has set. Bright light therapy boxes and dawn–dusk simulators can be bought online, but do some research to match what you're looking for with what each device offers. For those of you who are minding your dollars and cents, consider leaving your curtains drawn or shades open a quarter to halfway when you go to sleep. The natural dawn will slowly fill your room with light and create the same experience as a dawn simulator. I actually use this method often and find it beneficial.

Your sense of sight can help lift your listless state of depression in other ways. Once you feel the benefits of natural or artificial light therapy, invite yourself to *see*, not just *look* at things. Drink in the colors and textures of the world. Linger in nature's uplifting beauty.[8] Take notice of the budding leaves on trees, the tinted blooms of newborn flowers, or the way the sun's hue deepens its orangey glow as spring arrives. Renew your interest in observing people, animals, and things in your world: how they look and move, what makes them unique and beautiful. I know as we get older, aspects of life aren't new or novel, nor do they feel fresh. As a senior, you feel you've "been there, done that." But, in truth, you can teach yourself new ways to experience things, and research shows that it's valuable for your mind, body, and soul.[9] Speaking of color, don't forget to bring it into your world for greater health and balance. Color is a well-documented mood lifter and has been used to help arthritis, bulimia, cancer, wound healing, and, yes, depression too. If your schedule is too chaotic to manage big ways to bring color, like painting a room or installing a color-lighted shower head, ask for help. Consider buying adult coloring books, which are not only a popular trend nowadays but scientifically good for your mood.[10] If you're a caretaker to a depressed senior, find ways to bring color in with brightly colored towels, vivid clothing, decorative items, and even colored flowers from your yard or local supermarket. A little pop of color will go a long way.

The practice of using color to heal is called **chromotherapy** and has been around for thousands of years.[11] Some of the first to use this ancient healing method were Egyptians, who built large glass rooms called solariums where the sun's light would flood an ill person with color. Chromotherapy uses the visible spectrum of colors, calling on their electromagnetic properties to heal illness. Blue is calming, violet simulates imagination, red is invigorating, orange optimistic, yellow brings lightness and fun, and green summons harmony. Find what colors move you or your loved one and integrate them into living spaces. Another way sight that can enhance mood is the notion of space. Research shows that high ceilings and open spaces aid in the recovery of depression. Dwelling in rooms with low ceilings and confined environments reduces cognitive performance and memory, and dampens moods.[12] So make sure to expand the space you live in, even if it means getting out of your room if you're in assisted living or a skilled nursing home. These facilities often incorporate high ceilings, spacious light, and greenery in their architecture. If you live independently, consider decluttering rooms so the line of vision is elongated and fluid. If arranging a clutter-free, open area isn't possible, there's always the outdoors. No matter the season, get yourself to the big wide open.

A further strategy to use the sense of sight to enhance well-being is to look at photos that are colorful, cheerful, inspiring, or spirited in content. I'm always on the lookout for pictures online, in magazines, or in my personal photo collection that bring forth these emotions. I call this "antidepressant photo therapy": beach scenes, glorious landmarks, nostalgic photos of family and friends. Maybe for you it's muscle cars, the latest NASA Hubble telescope photos, or playful animals. Find photos that spark your interest, set your imagination afire, warm your heart, or tickle your funny bone. Another sight-oriented idea is to collect uplifting or motivational sayings. Fortunes from cookies, blurbs from magazines, poster quotes, or even sayings and proverbs from surfing the Internet are all great ways to get active with words of wisdom. I've been known to cut, paste, and print those that I find online and tack them around my home and in my office for when I need a motivational boost. Some are funny: *Don't let anyone rent space in your head unless they're a good tenant.* Or wise: *A problem shared is a problem halved.* Or loving: *You are treasured.* Or inspiring: *Do something today that your future self will thank you for.* I also leave them on my computer screensaver and my iPhone to keep me buoyed if my depression hits me when I'm away from home. If you're a caregiver, consider leaving inspiring quotes or motivational reminders around the home. How about some unconventional spaces, like your loved one's dresser, your pillow, a coat pocket, or the bathroom mirror? The art of living with depression in later life is not only about diagnoses, treatments, and education about this illness; it's also about using humor and inspiration wherever and whenever possible.

Perhaps one of the most important aspects of the sense of sight is to be sure that your vision is well cared for. Although it's common for seniors to have sensory losses due to age, some may encounter what's called **dual sensory loss** (combined vision and hearing loss). Dual sensory loss is scientifically linked with decreased levels of well-being.[13] Moreover, studies emphasize that adults with late-life depression suffer from a larger number of hearing and visual impairments compared to nondepressed seniors and that depressed seniors don't receive adequate care for their sensory issues.[14] That being said, make sure you have your eyes checked regularly and always, always, always wear your corrective lenses as prescribed.

Smell

Smell is the most nostalgic of all your senses. A certain aroma, scent, or fragrance can immediately remind you of an experience or a memory. This is because smell takes a direct route to the **limbic system**, where emotional memories are processed. Smells can bring forth good feelings or bad ones. So when you find depression knocking at your door, learn what kinds of scents unlock your depressed mood.

Using the sense of smell to help offset depression is called **aromatherapy**. Like chromotherapy, aromatherapy is an ancient practice that has tomes of research backing its claims. The science of scent shows that the right kinds of fragrances activate brain structures responsible for mood, focus, and thinking—specifically the **hippocampus** and the **amygdala**.[15] Scents like bergamot, basil, or peppermint have been shown to increase concentration. Want to lift your mood? Try lemon, vanilla, or lavender. If you are struggling with the sadness of a recent loss, citrus or minty scents like orange, lemon, spearmint, and grapefruit can help minimize your broken heart. For calming and relaxing, try scents like jasmine, chamomile, lemongrass, and rose.[16] Aromatherapy need not feel like something only a woman would use. Sometimes men bristle at my suggestion to incorporate aromatherapy into their life, thinking the approach is too fruity or flowery for their taste—that is, until I tell them the origin of how aromatherapy began. Aromatherapy was coined by a male French chemist named René Maurice Gattefossé, who used his creations to help heal stress. And later, in World War II, male surgeon Dr. Jean Valnet used essential oil aromatherapy to heal soldiers wounded in battle.[17] There are many mood-boosting scents that are less flowery or citrusy, like sandalwood, patchouli, cypress, cedar, ginger, and black pepper, that men find more appealing.[18] The key is to find a scent that you or your loved one likes. You can buy aromatherapy items in the form of essential oils, incense, candles, potpourri, wax melts, sachets, linen sprays, diffusers, vaporizers, and heating beads at your go-to local bed and bath stores or online at specialty shops. Spray a beloved scent on your bedsheets; dab some essential oils on your wrist, neck, or temples; or place a diffuser in a room to welcome you with its soft healing scent. On the cheap, take a pot of water and add cinnamon, vanilla, or peppermint extract. Simmer for a few minutes and then turn the stove off. The scent will travel through the house, offering a welcoming lift to all. Aromatherapy at home is an easy thing to do, but when it comes to assisted living or nursing homes, check in with the staff to make sure holistic measures are permissible. Another way to help revitalize the sense of smell and minimize depression is to use air filters and ionizers. Studies done on ambient indoor pollutants are linked to irritability, lethargy, physical illness, and decreased cognitive functioning, just to name a few.[19] We spend nearly 90 percent of our lives indoors, so cleansing with a high-efficiency particulate arrestance (HEPA) air cleaner helps not only your mental well-being but your physical health too.[20] Ionizers are small machines that produce a flow of negative ions into the air. Different from positive ions, which are produced by climate-controlled air, televisions, and computers (causing sleepiness, irritability, and weakness), negative ions balance serotonin levels, thus improving mood. Not only have negative ionizers been shown to reduce depression, they also relieve stress, improve concentration, and boost energy.[21] Such devices can be pricey, so cost may not allow for one to be in every room of your house. If so, consider placing at least one combination air filter/ionizer in your bedroom, and another in a part of the house you most spend time in. Other forms of **negative ion therapy** include wearable personal ionizers, negative ion sprays, feng shui waterfalls, and salt lamps—but do keep in mind to note negative ion output levels for best results.

Fresh air is often overlooked as a treatment. Studies have shown that seniors who experience **green space**—more specifically, fresh air and nature—have lower rates of depression and anxiety as well as better health than those who don't.[22] Additionally, stilted, unventilated air has a surplus of positive ions and, as previously mentioned, will create a sleepy and fatiguing effect. Keeping the window open for fresh air on a sunny day is always a welcoming experience but after a rain shower is the best of all. Negative ions are at their highest then. During my depressive episodes as a child, I had experiences with many of these scent-based mood-altering methods. My father, who trained as a chiropractor in the 1960s, frequently used essential oils in his practice and would also incorporate them in our home life. I can still remember how the eucalyptus my dad kept in the living areas of the house instantly awakened me from my dulled and dark moods. My mom would soak clean washcloths in a pot with either orange peel and vanilla extract, or fennel seeds and honey, wring them out and rest them on my forehead when I had crying spells. Open windows abounded in my childhood home, especially after a rainstorm. Aromatherapy has been a constant in my life. I still use essential oils, favoring lavender and sandalwood, keeping candles lit from time to time, and placing potpourri here and there. I love the fresh air, be it outside or inside from an open window, and I use air filters and ionizers in my home and office. I know all of these holistic things make me feel grounded and balanced, because if I forget them when traveling, I feel a big difference . . . and the difference *ain't* good.

Taste

Research has shown that your sense of taste diminishes as we age, but if you have late-life depression, you may experience even more taste loss due to the shift in serotonin levels.[23] For some, this may mean loss of appetite. For others, it may kick your appetite into overdrive as you crave the taste you're lacking. Whether your appetite increases or decreases, it's important to be mindful that certain foods will worsen your depression. How and what you eat has long been associated with having direct effects on mood and cognitive function.[24] There's evidence that deficiency or supplementation of nutrients can affect not only mood but also behavioral patterns.[25] With regard to depression, sugary foods and starchy carbohydrates may give you a quick feel-good rush, but in the long run will irritate your blood chemistry and digestion and ultimately worsen your mood.[26] Studies show that refueling yourself with nutrient-dense foods and healthy fluid intake is not only nourishing but also helps in the recovery of late-life depression.[27] It's important to mention that many independent seniors can change their nutritional intake on their own, while others—who may be in assisted living, skilled nursing homes, or under the supervision of a caregiver—may require a more comprehensive assessment of their nutritional needs. As with any holistic treatment, make sure you run nutrient-rich suggestions by your physician to ensure they'll work with your unique health needs.

- *Ancient grains* are called "ancient" because they've been around, unchanged in their wholesomeness, for thousands of years. These foods are high in protein content, have more calcium than milk, and are rich in vitamins and minerals. Research reports that ancient grains like quinoa, millet, teff, amaranth, spelt, barley, and kamut are complex carbohydrates, which take longer to digest, so they don't cause spikes in blood sugar that can create roller-coaster moods.[28]
- *Folate* is a water-soluble form of vitamin B9 that the body requires from food for cell growth. Folate gets its name from the

Latin word "folium," for leaf. Research has long connected folate in the synthesis of serotonin. Studies show that depressed adults, and even children, often have low levels of red-cell folate and serum folate. Folate can be found in leafy green vegetables, certain dried beans like black-eyed peas, brown rice, and lentils, as well as in fruits like oranges and bananas. Sometimes foods high in folate can cause gastrointestinal (GI) stress, so an alternative is to use folic acid supplements. Studies show that folate supplements also work to help reduce dementia and other cognitive deficits as well as depression.[29]

- *High-flavonoid foods* are prized for their deep plant pigment coloring because they offer anti-inflammatory and antioxidant benefits. Research shows that flavonoid-rich foods are associated with better performance in cognitive abilities and strengthen the immune system. Flavonoids also help improve mood, and decrease irritability and fatigue.[30] So don't be afraid to plate up foods like apples, blueberries, dark chocolate, red grapes, deep-steeped teas, and tomatoes.

- *L-theanine* is an essential amino acid derived from tea leaves that works to balance production of dopamine and serotonin. Research on L-theanine has shown that it can induce alpha waves, the brain waves one achieves when meditating. It has been shown to reduce heart rate, increase focus, and lower blood pressure, as well as improve periodontal health by reducing cavities.[31] L-theanine is found primarily in green tea and *matcha* (finely milled green tea powder that is made into cakes, cookies, and even *matcha* ice cream).

- *Magnesium* is involved in hundreds of biochemical reactions in the body. Some of them include regulating blood pressure, heart rate, sugar levels, metabolism, and keeping our immune system in tip-top shape. What's significant is that research reports magnesium is often low or deficient in seniors who experience depression. More specifically, magnesium plays an important role in the production and synthesis of serotonin, so low levels will affect well-being.[32] Magnesium can be found in foods like legumes, vegetables, whole grains, nuts, soy, and seafood, as well as cereals, milk, and chocolate. Sometimes magnesium is offered in supplement form. If you have kidney issues, don't incorporate magnesium without working alongside your physician. For those without kidney issues, side effects of magnesium supplements can include slight GI distress.

- *Omega-3 fatty acids* are called essential fats because they can't be manufactured within the human body and must be consumed through food. Essential fats make up about 60 percent of our brain—but not any fat will do. We need a special fat, called **docosahexaenoic acid** or DHA. Surveys have shown that countries that eat fish have lower rates of depression.[33] The reason why? Fish contain high amounts of omega-3 DHA, which has been shown to increase blood flow to the brain, balance dopamine and serotonin levels, and enhance mood, just to name a few. Research has found that increasing DHA consumption also boosts gray matter in the amygdala, the hippocampus, and the **cingulate gyrus**—three specific areas of the brain associated with mood. Keeping a diet rotation of superfoods rich in DHA like salmon, nuts, eggs, and olive oil will help reduce your late-life depression. Another alternative is to incorporate omega-3 supplements if you don't find such foods palatable. Omega-3 supplements have been shown to slow cognitive decline in the elderly, improve cardiovascular functioning and joint health, and reduce depression. As with any supplements you may take, make sure you work alongside a trained medical professional because there's a risk of adverse reactions if you take omega-3 supplements along with anticoagulant medication.

- *Proteins* contain amino acids that aid in the creation of **endorphins**—a family of super-feel-good neurotransmitters that influence our mood. Proteins like pork, poultry, lean meats, eggs, and fish take longer to metabolize, which stabilizes blood sugar and leads to a more satisfied feeling after eating. Remember, high sugar levels can leave you feeling irritable, fatigued, and moody—and also hungry a short while later. More importantly, eating lean proteins replaces catecholamines, a neurotransmitter that balances serotonin.

- *Vitamin B12* is involved in every cell of your body. It is significantly important for brain and neural pathway functioning, metabolism, and blood production. Studies show a connection between low levels of vitamin B12 and symptoms of depression.[34]

A blood test can help determine if you or your loved one is lacking in this important nutrient. As far as food is concerned, vitamin B12 can be found in seafood like snapper, shrimp, and scallops, and in fermented vegetables like miso and tofu. Just like omega-3 and folate, vitamin B12 dietary supplements can be useful. Injections, sublingual tablets, or sprays are also available as well, but talk with your doctor about these options.

- *Vitamin D* works along with melatonin to even out your sleep/wake cycle and regulate your immune system. Vitamin D also lowers the production of **cytokines**, which are proteins that increase inflammation. A number of studies have shown cytokines to be a possible risk factor for depression in later life.[35] Low vitamin D levels have been implicated in depression in older adults, with children and adolescents,[36] and with seasonal affective disorder.[37] Blood tests are available to determine if you have a low or deficient vitamin D level, and are usually done with your full physical exam. Vitamin D can be found in foods like shitake mushrooms, eggs, fortified milk, fortified grains, and oily fishes like salmon, cod, catfish, tuna, and mackerel. Ninety percent of vitamin D gets absorbed through sunlight, so make sure you grab some sunshine whenever possible. Remember, it doesn't have to be outside sunshine. A pool of sunshine indoors will do the job just fine.

Once you've experienced a lift from your depressive symptoms, see if you can use your sense of taste to call forth positive feelings. Studies show that even small moments of flavor sensations can lift mood. Nurse a delicious cup of tea or swirl a piece of candy slowly. Savor and take delight in what you taste, what the texture is, and how it feels in your mouth.

Touch

There are many positive effects that come from touch, being touched, and moving your body. For example, touch reduces the production of the stress hormone **cortisol**. Touch eases irritability, soothes loneliness, lowers blood pressure, calms your heartbeat, and surges the feel-good hormone **oxytocin** and natural morphine-like **opioids**.[38] Touch is a reaction to contact and is especially meaningful when it's skin-on-skin. In addition to providing health benefits, touch promotes bonding and social contact.[39] Another thing touch does is activate the **orbitofrontal cortex** (a brain structure associated with the processing of emotions), which studies show is linked to depression.[40] So you see, touch can do a lot. Let's look at several of kinds of holistic activities that incorporate touch.

- *Acupuncture* dates back about 5,000 years in China. It is based on the theory that health and wellness depend on a delicate balance of *chi* (energy) and that any blockage along meridian lines where energy flows will cause illness. Eastern medicine believes that each meridian line is associated with an organ or system of the body. With acupuncture, a certified acupuncturist inserts ultra-thin sterilized needles or uses cutaneous stimulation (a mild electrical current administered on top of the skin) at specific neuron pathways along your body. The needles remain for about 30 minutes and free the blocked energy, enhancing central nervous system functioning. Acupuncture is safe for seniors; reduces depression and age-related pain; increases endorphins, serotonin, and dopamine levels; and strengthens your immune system.[41] Side effects are minimal, but if you take blood thinners, you may develop bruising.

- *Acupressure* is a less-invasive method of acupuncture, using pressure by the practitioner's hands or fingers at meridian points. The goal of acupressure is the same as acupuncture, to unblock the flow of energy so healthy synaptic transmission can occur. Like acupuncture, acupressure can be useful in the treatment of late-onset depression.[42] Several studies have shown that not only does acupressure from a professional reduce depressive symptoms but also that success can be attained by using self-administered acupressure. Seniors can learn these acupressure techniques to use on their own.[43] Similarly, caretakers can be taught how to apply acupressure to help manage their loved one's depression. Acupressure has few to no side effects.

- **Animal-assisted therapy** (AAT), which is sometimes called **pet therapy**, is scientifically shown to have beneficial effects on the severity of depressive symptoms in older adults, particularly those residing in assisted living, nursing homes, or hospitals.[44] Animal-assisted therapy is defined as the use of trained animals to facilitate a feeling of well-being.[45] Though animals have been known to have a positive influence on human beings for centuries, animals specifically assisting in the physical or mental healing of others began to be more formally used in the nineteenth century, with many animals visiting World War II convalescence and recovery wards.[46] One of the most famous proponents of AAT was Florence Nightingale, who believed that a small animal was an excellent companion for patients who were sick or confined to their beds.[47] Nowadays, animal-assisted therapy can be found on college campuses to help students reduce anxiety and depression during final exams, at military facilities to support soldiers recovering from posttraumatic stress disorder, and in senior communities to reduce depression and loneliness.[48] Although adopting a pet will offer you companionship, the commitment and caretaking may be too involved at an advanced age. This is where animal-assisted therapy comes in. AAT can be a great alternative to owning a pet. Local senior programs and animal societies can pair you with an animal like a cat, dog, bird, bunny, or even a horse if you're so inclined. Sessions with animals can range from an hour to as long as a day. The bond you make by touching and interacting with your pet therapy animal will diminish symptoms of depression, improve mood, relieve pain, and sharpen focus. Perhaps more than anything else, playing with and caring for an animal makes many seniors feel special and loved unconditionally.

- *Exercise* has long been associated with good physical and mental health. And with regard to the geriatric population, regular physical activity increases longevity, reduces the risk of developing chronic diseases, protects the immune system, and aids in healthy sleep. Other exercise benefits include increased oxygen flow to the brain, which helps improve cognitive functioning, attention, and mood.[49] When it comes to depression in later life, exercise is a key component in keeping symptoms at bay. What's hard is to find exercise that suits your physical abilities. For some, it may be walking or running. For others it can involve strength training. Some depressed seniors with mobility issues may have to rely on chair exercises (performing movements while sitting in a chair), a recumbent bicycle, swimming, or water therapy, as these forms of exercise have low impact on bones and joints. With its breathing practices and specific postures, yoga is also a viable form of exercise for seniors.[50] It's been shown to improve concentration, inner peace, body awareness, and mood. For elderly adults who are frail, exercise may seem unrealistic or overly challenging, but just getting them up and out for a little air or change of scenery can make an enormous difference.[51] The thing is, when you experience depression in later life, getting yourself to move may feel like an impossible feat. The fatigue that comes with depression often prevents many seniors from getting out of bed, let alone exercising. Some of the things I've learned living with depression is to set small goals for exercise. The first goal I always aim for is a short burst of movement, like getting up, taking a shower, moving into a room other than my bedroom. Next up might be venturing a little further with an increase in exertion and length of time: doing some housework or chores, maybe a walk around the block, a trip to the store. If you're a caregiver, invite your loved one to join you in physical activities. "How about we go sit outside for coffee this morning?" or "I could use some company when I run errands. I'm hoping you'll join me." As you move more and more, you'll experience an opioid release that should help keep the momentum going.[52] Once your depression has lifted, consider incorporating other evidence-based complementary treatments for late-life depression like dance and movement therapies,[53] Pilates,[54] water aerobics and aquatic therapies,[55] and tai chi.[56]

- *Massage therapy* has been used for over 3,000 years to heal the elderly. Ancient Egyptians, Persians, Hindus, and Chinese applied forms of massage for many ailments, and Hippocrates wrote papers recommending the use of touch for joint and circulatory problems and physical and emotional illnesses too. Today, the benefits of massage are varied and far-reaching. For example, massage therapy decreases anxiety, loneliness, stress, and depression; improves breathing and circulation; deepens relaxation and inner peace; improves sleep; lowers blood pressure; reduces swelling and edema; and relieves joint pain.[57] Massage therapy for seniors, clinically known as **geriatric massage**, is designed to meet the specific needs of the elderly population.[58] This type of massage therapy uses gentle and light application of massage techniques and passive stretching, which is different from massage therapy for younger adults and children. If you're not comfortable with a full-body massage, a geriatric massage therapist can tailor a treatment that suits your preferences, like focusing on your hands, arms, neck, or feet. Geriatric massage therapy treatments can be arranged in your home or at a medical office. Sessions generally range from 30 minutes to an hour.

- *Reflexology* is a form of touch therapy where a therapist applies pressure to strategic areas on your feet and hands. This kind of treatment bases its approach on a system of zones and reflex sites that when touched bring physical changes to your body. Reflexology is an ancient practice dating back to 2300 BCE Egypt and has been steadily used throughout the centuries as a holistic treatment.[59] In modern reflexology, a therapist will use her thumb and fingers and gently massage these reflexive points. Stimulating these areas increases blood flow, which improves circulation and helps to eliminate toxins. Furthermore, reflexology stimulates the lymphatic system and encourages the release of endorphins, the natural feel-good hormones that relieve the symptoms of depression, high blood pressure, anxiety, and chronic pain. Reflexology sessions are generally 30 minutes to an hour and require you to sit in a specially designed reclining chair.

- *Reiki*, a Japanese word that means *universal life energy*, is a form of energy healing that uses light touch to channel energy. This ancient Japanese treatment believes disturbances in energy fields, called *chakras*, cause illness and that a "laying on of hands" by a Reiki practitioner can restore the flow and balance of energy.[60] During a session, the patient remains clothed and the practitioner's hands are placed near or lightly touching various parts of the body, including areas around the head, shoulders, stomach, legs, and feet. Most patients report feelings of relaxation, and patients often fall asleep during a session. Sessions can last from 10 minutes to more than an hour, depending upon availability. Results from Reiki treatment are so robust that the American Hospital Association reported in 2007 that over 800 American hospitals offered Reiki as part of their hospital services.[61] With respect to late-life depression, Reiki has been shown to improve depressive symptoms, increase mood and well-being, sharpen cognitive and sensory skills, and enhance self-care skills.[62]

- *Shower*—I think one of the greatest tools for helping ease depression is the basic shower. The warmth of the water will wash away fatigue as well as soothe and awaken your skin. If you are a senior with depression, make sure the shower stall is prepped for safety. Install grab bars, slip-resistant shower chairs, and nonslip shower mats. Once this space is secure, see if you can find scented soaps or scrubs to invigorate your muscles—and sense of smell too. Make sure these products are gentle enough for your delicate skin. If you can, invest in a good handheld showerhead—one that offers different kinds of sprays, pulses, and pressure—and of course, lots of clean, fluffy towels. For caregivers tending to older seniors with late-life depression, in addition to grab bars, shower chair, and a nonslip mat, be mindful to test the water temperature and water pressure. Another tip is to buy a long-handled sponge to help with washing and use towels large enough to provide a sense of security and privacy. For severely depressed elderly adults, the routine of a daily shower or a sponge bath is essential—even if it's the only task that gets accomplished in the entire day.[63] The shower was singularly curative for me when I was depressed and continues to be my go-to healing tool. The numbness of my own depression can't stand up against the warm streams of water. Though it's hard some days to get myself *to* the shower, I know that once I'm there, I'm better.

I've involved myself in virtually all the touch therapies mentioned above. Each of these holistic treatments offered me significant relief from my depression and also gave me a feeling of inner peace. When it comes to your sense of touch, discover what feels good to you. Just remember that there are less-formal kinds of touch that are healing when you're depressed: a hug, a kiss, sexual activity, or simply holding someone's hand. Don't be afraid to ask for these physical exchanges. They are genuinely healing.

Sound

As previously noted, the senses of sight and hearing often diminish with age. If they occur simultaneously, it's known as a dual sensory loss. You, however, may be an older adult whose vision is excellent but whose hearing is a problem. If so, you need to consider augmenting your hearing. Some seniors I work with don't mind that their hearing "isn't what it used to be" and refuse to modify their sense of sound with hearing aids. This is a mistake. Studies show that uncorrected hearing loss leads to cognitive decline.[64] Hearing loss also leads to feelings of loneliness, sadness, anxiety, irritability, and frustration.[65] Because depression can dull your sense of sound, and as a senior you're at risk for hearing loss, make sure you get your hearing checked regularly. If you need hearing aids, try your best to wear them. At first it will feel challenging, but the gains are worth the effort. Sound is an enormous tool to treat depression.

One of the best ways to utilize sound is to listen to music. Research shows that music activates the brain's reward system that releases dopamine.[66] Studies also show that listening to music decreases pain, bolsters the immune system, increases feelings of power, decreases fatigue, and reduces depressive symptoms in older adults.[67] Music has a profound effect on your memory and can revive feelings of nostalgia. This kind of musical awakening is called a **reminiscence bump**.[68] When you listen to music from particular decades, the songs bring you back to memories, stories, and experiences from that time. When considering music, keep in mind that research shows certain kinds of music are better than others for lifting mood. For example, certain tonal tensions and changes in chords induce physical shivers, prickles on the back of the neck, sadness, and a lump in the throat in some people.[69] This musical ornamentation is called an **appoggiatura**, a note that clashes with the melody just enough to create a dissonance and can lead to feelings of "moved to tears."[70] British singer Adele's 2011 song "Someone Like You" was noted to have numerous appoggiaturas, which explained why so many people cried when hearing that song. Take into consideration that Yo-Yo Ma's cello weeps in the wallows of appoggiaturas, as does a lot of opera. So try to stay away from music that sounds sad. Research on emotions and music suggests that upbeat songs lead to feel-good sensations.[71] Music with be-bop beats, power chords, major scales, dynamic chord shifting, and inspirational messages can serve you well. Consider trying meditative music that uses **binaural beats** (rhythms the brain mimics to produce meditative theta waves) to bring you into a deep state of relaxation and improve your mood.[72] Find what music you fancy and listen to it often. Create playlists on your iPod, iPad, cellphone, or computer devices to play anywhere, anytime. If you're a caregiver, make sure to stock your loved one's music library with tunes that appeal to him or her. And if you wish to listen to music with earphones, invest in a good set that offers soft ear cushions and is sturdy yet lightweight for your head.

Another way to invite sound is to listen to audio books (books on tape, CDs, or digital recordings of books read by another). Being read to is a very special experience. We loved it as kids and research shows that audio books help you rest, refuel, or learn as you relax. More specifically, audio books reduce loneliness, lift mood, and prevent cognitive decline in seniors.[73] Find a book where the story is an inspiring one, comical, or empowering in content. Audio books can be experienced anywhere: at a park, while walking, sitting in a chair, reclining on the couch, in bed, and even in the car. And with phones and small computer devices offering apps for audio books, it's easier than ever to plug in and enjoy being read to.

To help ease the heaviness of depression, consider adding soundscapes to your environment. Sometimes called **acoustic sound therapy**, the pleasant background or ambient sounds of birds singing, a soft rain shower, a babbling brook, or the tides of the ocean activates neurons in the cortex of the brain, increase dopamine and serotonin production, and lift mood.[74] You can find soundscapes to purchase on CDs or tapes online and in stores, or download albums of these environment sounds on your phone or computer devices. Satellite radio stations offer programs that exclusively broadcast soundscapes. There are even convenient travel soundscape machines that you can pack along on trips to reproduce soothing sounds. And remember, an open window provides an instant soundscape so long as it's free from traffic and chaos.

Another form of sound that is healing for late-life depression is **vibroacoustic therapy** (VBT). It was first developed in 1980 by Olav Skille, who discovered that the physical vibrations of music soothed his special-needs students.[75] He placed bean-bag chairs on top of audio speakers and played music loud enough to transfer vibrations through the chairs. Skille found his students enjoyed both the sensation of sound as well as the sensation of vibration. Adapted since then as a treatment for the elderly, vibroacoustic therapy is designed to blend low-frequency music and vibrations that can be experienced in pillows, body mats, beds, and chairs. VBT is offered by specially trained speech/language therapists, physical therapists, rehabilitation therapists, and vibrational therapists. Sessions last about 20 minutes to an hour. VBT may be hard to find in your community if you live in a rural area, so an option is to purchase vibroacoustic therapy supplies online. But be forewarned, they are pricey. What I recommend, instead, is to buy sound therapy pillows or similar supplies—what I like to call "vibroacoustic therapy-lite." I purchased a sound pillow for under $40 online and find it soothing and relaxing. I plug my iPod in the specially designed pillow and adjust the volume to suit my needs. I generally play *Deep Theta Music* by my favorite musician, Steve Halpern, which relaxes and softens my mood.

Don't forget the power of the voice of a loved one, friend, or child in your life. I don't mean the strength or loudness of it, I mean the significance it carries for you. When you listen—not hear but listen—to someone who speaks to you with love, support, delight, or enthusiasm, dopamine and oxytocin levels surge. The human voice holds tremendous medicinal powers, so enjoy your grandchildren's stories. Relish the sound of their voices, their laughs, the words they choose. Notice the tone and timbre of voices of your friends. Pay attention to your emotional responses and physical reactions when you hear the voice of someone you love. If you're a caretaker, the simple act of varying the register of your own voice or adding a distinctive melodic shape to your words is known to deeply affect others.[76] For example, "I am so happy to see you, Mom" is experienced more poignantly if you shift your intonation to "I am soooo happy to see you, Mom." Consider leaving voicemails with messages of love and encouragement. Or simply call a senior who is struggling with depression just to talk. Studies show that communications that are heard surge the feel-good hormone oxytocin.[77]

One last thought about the sense of sound that I believe doesn't get its rightful due is silence. Though research papers, books, and theories indicate that silence can be a sign of depression, it shouldn't preclude you from wanting to dwell in its margins. Solitude can be therapeutic. Being quiet allows you to invite relaxation and self-reflection.[78] Just don't spend too much of your time in silence. Consider this: Healthy silence has a quietness to its texture and energy whereas unhealthy silence feels secluded and isolating.

SUMMARY

Most traditional methods to treat depression in later life include talk therapy and medication. The uses of complementary and holistic approaches have been presented here through the framework of using your five senses. Although there are many more kinds of holistic approaches than covered here, I'd like you to be mindful of a few things. Remember that depression is an illness of depletion and can often result in a dulling of your senses. When using holistic measures, science reports success with mild depression. Holistic approaches are generally not recommended solely as a treatment for moderate or severe late-life depression. Take time to read about the holistic measures that pique your interest. Discover scents, sounds, touches, tastes, and colors you like.

CASE STUDY: UNCLE REY

"I'd like to talk to you about my uncle Rey," Vanessa said. "I think he's very depressed."

Vanessa was a young graduate student in supervision with me. Though the subject of her uncle was a detour from the case she was seeking counsel on—a young girl with oppositional disorder—I felt there'd be a teachable moment in this segue and invited her to continue.

"What's doing with him?" I asked.

"Well, my uncle Rey hasn't left the house in almost three weeks now. I know the winter was really tough on him, but all the snow's gone and he just doesn't want to do anything. The family is super worried."

Vanessa told me that Uncle Rey, who was really her great uncle, was 91 years old and resided in the same Brooklyn apartment he lived in for over 60 years. He was a decorated police officer and retired only because he aged out. Never married and a self-proclaimed happy bachelor, Uncle Rey was well known and regarded in the neighborhood. He was a fixture in the corner coffee shop and often strolled the avenue wearing his unmistakable black and gray fedora. Vanessa said her large family of aunts, uncles, and cousins who lived nearby took turns looking in on Uncle Rey as he got older. He was fairly independent, able to shop, cook simple meals, and care for himself.

"What makes you think he's depressed?" I asked.

"Well, for starters, he doesn't go out, which is a big deal. My aunt Maria says he sits all day in the apartment, watches television, orders in food if he's hungry."

"Is he taking care of himself, like showering, grooming?"

"I think that's okay, but my aunt says the place is really messy."

"Has he had any falls or illnesses that you know about?"

"I don't think so."

"What about taking him to his doctor for a visit? Get things checked out?"

"My mom says my aunt Maria took him a few days ago and that there's nothing physically wrong." Vanessa used her fingers to air quote the word physical.

"So, you think he might be depressed."

"Yeah."

"Well, you may be right."

Vanessa paused and crinkled her brow. "I was thinking about, you know, that I'm becoming a psychologist and I could help him feel better."

"Tell me what you have in mind."

"Well, he won't go to therapy, so that's out. In fact, my entire family thinks what I want to do for a career is ridiculous."

I nodded. "Yeah, I get that. There are people who find talking to a stranger about personal things objectionable."

"Anyway, the doctor didn't suggest medication for him. But even if he had, I wonder if my uncle would take it."

"There are some other things you could do," I said. "Think about what you told me about how he's living: the dark apartment, the clutter."

Vanessa grew quiet and I watched as she shifted her ideas.

"I guess we could clean things up at his place, have people spend more time with him so he's not alone."

I nodded.

Vanessa smiled as her thoughts expanded. "Hmmm. Maybe we can do a little extreme makeover, Brooklyn style—paint the place, take him to the stores to pick things out."

"That would be very helpful, I think."

Vanessa and I talked about holistic treatments for a short while: how it can be a stepping stone to see if someone's depression is subclinical, mild, or moderate. When utilizing complementary therapies, you can see if your loved one's mood improves. If irritability decreases and if isolation and withdrawal recede, that means the psychological issues were not deeply rooted. If positive changes don't occur—and Uncle Rey remains sad and withdrawn—Vanessa and her family can move forward more assuredly toward traditional treatment for a geriatric mood disorder.

Vanessa and I eventually returned back to focus on her willful and defiant student. And supervision continued for many weeks on that case until one session when Vanessa wanted to update me on her uncle Rey.

"Okay. I gotta show you what we ended doing for my uncle," she said, skooching her chair closer to mine.

She prepped her cellphone and swiped it to pictures of a darkish, cluttered room. There, in a dingy plaid-colored wingback chair, sat her uncle Rey. He seemed stoic, resigned.

Vanessa thumbed through a few more pictures so I could get a sense of his apartment. It was a familiar one to me, the standard bottom-floor layout of the Brooklyn brownstones many of my own relatives lived in. One of the key features was an entry to a backyard, a prized treasure for anyone who lived in Brooklyn. The picture Vanessa presented told me that the yard hadn't been tended to in years, maybe even decades.

"It took some doing, but my cousins and I, my mom and dad, and my aunt Maria spent a few weekends fixing up Uncle Rey's place."

Vanessa told me they painted the entire apartment and removed all the heavy drapes, replacing them with white miniblinds and simple curtain valences.

"Wow, this is great. You can really see the woodwork and moldings in the place. It's beautiful," I said eyeing the "after" photos.

"We cleaned the windows. And, god, the screens. They were caked with soot and who knows what else. It was disgusting," she said, laughing through a pinched smile.

Vanessa shared that a tag sale helped clear a lot of the clutter and how the family divvied up some of the vintage clothing and items Uncle Rey didn't want anymore. With a "less is more" eye for design, the apartment became a study in colors and function. The bedroom was simple but dressed in new navy blue sheets and a checked comforter. The bathroom had grab bars placed in the stall shower with towels that kept the navy theme going. The living room was completely uncluttered and the plaid wing chair and the nearby sofa were slipcovered in a navy print. The kitchen was reorganized, with the family suggesting paper plates and cups for Uncle Rey to use so the sink didn't get overloaded with dishes. Her cousins cleaned up and organized a stack of old records and fixed his stereo so Uncle Rey could play his favorite music. Finally, Vanessa showed me a picture of the take-out menus she clipped to the telephone for easy access.

"You laminated all the menus?" I said. "That's brilliant."

Vanessa brimmed. "We still have some work to do in the backyard, but at least all the junk and weeds are gone."

"So, how's your uncle doing with all this?"

"At first, he wasn't really into it. But I think he's really happy with things."

"How do you know?"

"He's going out more. He's smiling, telling his stories."

"That does sound good. How will you know if Uncle Rey isn't doing well with things again?"

"I guess time will tell. If he starts to do the same kinds of things, maybe he'll need to see the doctor again."

I arched my eyebrows and nodded my head in agreement.

"For now, he seems like he's back to his old self." Vanessa swiped to a photo of him. "Look."

I took the phone and saw a picture of Uncle Rey, standing in the middle of his newly vamped living room, his arms outstretched with a big smile on his face, and then another one of him wearing his hat, sitting on the stoop of the brownstone flashing a gangsta pose peace sign.

"Oh my god, he's so funny."

"Yeah, he's great." Vanessa stopped a second before continuing. "He totally needs a cane, but that intervention's for another day."

6

HOW TO MAINTAIN SUCCESS IN TREATMENT

If you only learned about the symptoms and treatments of depression in later life, you'd just be seeing half the picture. This chapter highlights the often unwritten and unaddressed aspects of depression so you can keep your treatment successful.

THE GOALS OF THERAPY

Simply stated, the goal of therapy is, of course, to get you to feel better—but there is much more that goes on in treatment of geriatric depression. Sometimes it helps to break the process down into manageable chunks. There are three goals involved in the treatment of depression: response, remission, and recovery. Understanding what each is and the importance of monitoring them is the key to your successful treatment.

The first goal in the treatment of your late-onset depression is to get you to a **response** level. "Response" is clinically defined as "an improvement from the initial onset of your illness."[1] Think of the last time you needed an antibiotic for an infection—let's say, a sinus infection. You begin taking your medicine as prescribed and slowly start to feel less pain. Your body is in a response mode. Treatment for depression follows a similar course. You involve yourself in psychotherapy and/or pharmacotherapy and soon find yourself feeling better. The example of staying on your antibiotic for the full, recommended course is the same as remaining on task with your depression treatment—both require a pledge to see it through to completion. If you stop taking your antibiotic or miss doses because you feel better, your sinus infection is likely to return. The same goes for the treatment of your depression. You need to participate fully in your treatments so you can get to this response level.

The second goal in treating your late-life depression is to bring you to a full state of **remission**. "Remission" is clinically defined as "the experience of being symptom-free from illness."[2] This differs from response in that you not only report an improvement from when you started treatment but also describe the presence of well-being, optimism, self-confidence, and a return to a healthy state of functioning. Diagnostically speaking, remission is achieved when fewer than three of the *Diagnostic and Statistical Manual of Mental Disorders* criteria are noted, and your feelings of well-being continue for three consecutive weeks. Continuing treatment toward a full remission requires you to consistently follow your treatment plan. If not, you may fall into what's called a **partial remission**—an experience of significant improvement but where mild symptoms still exist. These mild depressive symptoms, called "**residual symptoms**," are often overlooked in the maintenance of depression and can lead you into a false sense of feeling truly better.[3] Studies show that seniors who are depressed report that "feeling better" is their decisive factor for gauging remission, while practitioners look at clinical data from symptom checklists and diagnostic criteria. Given this discrepancy, it's vital for you and your healthcare professional to have a clear working definition of remission.[4] Using symptom checklists at the beginning of treatment, during treatment, and at remission stages can solidify the diagnostic and emotional features of your late-life depression. Remember, if you're still experiencing depressive symptoms, you have not reached a full remission. Partial remission with residual symptoms signals the need to continue with treatment regimes. Depression has a trajectory that is unique. If you're in psychotherapy and/or taking medication longer than most seniors you know, remind yourself that "one size fits all" doesn't apply to depression.

As covered in previous chapters, treatment-resistant depression (TRD) poses another hurdle in attaining full remission. Treatment-resistant depression is *not* diagnosed if you or your loved one is refusing to go to treatment, if treatment is discontinued prematurely, or if co-morbid mental or physical diagnoses are operating but are currently undetected.[5] Generally speaking, treatment-resistant depression for seniors is defined as an inability to achieve a response with two or more trials of different antidepressant medications, including **augmentation**, which is the use of an additional medicinal agent to boost the effect of a currently prescribed antidepressant.[6] Treatment-resistant depression is more common in the elderly than in younger individuals and is estimated to occur in upward of 40 percent of seniors.[7] Even though some of the reasons your depression may be resistant may be due to genetic, structural, or biological issues that occur as we age, it's important to evaluate if nonadherence to treatment is happening when TRD is suspected. Studies suggest seniors who fail to adhere to their medication regime range from 40 to 70 percent.[8] Sometimes seniors forget to take their medication or misunderstand the dosing instructions for antidepressants. Fixing this oversight may improve your symptoms—thus eliminating the notion of treatment-resistant depression. If, however, it's deemed that your late-onset depression is treatment resistant, it's vital for you to immediately seek alternative treatments to address your needs.

By now, you've learned that depression has its own unique trajectory. But did you know that the goal of recovery has a course all its own? Well, it does—and the experience of your recovery will be as personal and distinctive as was your depression. "**Recovery**" is clinically defined as "the absence of symptoms for at least four months following the onset of remission."[9] Recovery presents with periods of improvement and growth as well as with setbacks and stumbling blocks. Your personal biography and biology will have a bearing on the ebb and flow of your recovery, so refrain from measuring the arc of your progress with anyone else. Just know that, at times, recovery may be like a smooth-paved superhighway, moving quickly, easily, and effortlessly, and at other times it may be like a simple, single-lane country road, progressing slowly and gently. Recovery could also hit a rough and potholed street, leaving you broken down on the side of the road. The important issue here is to use your newly learned skills from psychotherapy to solve problems, reframe reality, and create detours if necessary so you get yourself back on the road to recovery.

RELAPSE AND RECURRENCE

Traditional treatments for geriatric depression aim to get you from response, to remission, and then to full recovery. For many of you, this process may readily occur. However, there will be some of you who may experience depression again. "Relapse" and "recurrence" are terms commonly used to describe a return of depressive symptoms. "**Relapse**" is defined as a "full return of depressive symptoms once remission has occurred—but before recovery has taken hold."[10] "**Recurrence**" refers to another depressive episode after recovery has been attained.[11] Depression, be it late onset or early onset, is often a chronic condition, where upward of 80 percent of treated individuals experience subsequent episodes. Additional statistics report that 60 percent of adults who've had one depressive episode are prone to relapse. Individuals with two depressive episodes are 70 percent more likely to have a third recurrence, and 90 percent of seniors with three depressive episodes will have a fourth episode.[12] Significantly important is research showing that relapse rates are radically lower in adults who've reached full remission—further emphasizing the importance of treatment commitment.

Just as there are risk factors for developing depression, so, too, are there risk factors for relapse and recurrence. Variables that increase risk begin with your family history. Your likelihood of relapse and/or recurrence will be higher if you have a relative with a depressive disorder. Another cause of relapse and recurrence involves your own unique neurobiology. "**Antidepressant tachyphylaxis**" (AT) occurs when your body no longer functions to counteract or control serotonin, norepinephrine, or other neurotransmitters.[13] Sometimes called "poop-out syndrome" or "drug tolerance," antidepressant tachyphylaxis can be monitored by your prescribing doctor and regulated by increasing the dosage of your current medication or by adding a supplementary medication to augment therapy.

Another reason relapse or recurrence might happen is if you stop your medication prematurely. Often, professionals prescribing medication will take you through a very detailed list of how to take your medications. This is a very important process and one that you should follow with regularity (which is why I recommend getting such instructions in written form from your doctor). Medication success has a great deal to do with timing of your doses and consistency in taking them as prescribed. Usually, you'll begin your antidepressant medication at a low dose, with a possible increase over time to reduce symptoms. At this stage, your neurochemistry is gently shifting, working slowly to bring you closer to well-being. It generally takes approximately three to six weeks for medication to reach its full effect. Hopefully, at this point, you're experiencing a reduction in your depressive symptoms. If so, you'll remain at this dosage. If not, another increase may be recommended to find your optimal dosage.

Sometimes taking medication comes with side effects, sometimes they're not noticeable. For some seniors, side effects are so terrible that they decide on their own to stop the medicine—but a serious issue can arise if you do this without the instruction and support of your prescribing doctor. Not many people are aware—even including some health professionals—that there is a need to come off medications in a specific way. If not, a variety of physical experiences may leave you feeling ill. This is known as **antidepressant discontinuation syndrome**. Sometimes shortened to "**discontinuation syndrome**," abrupt halting of medication will set into motion experiences that can include dizziness, nausea, headache, numb or shock-like sensations, diarrhea, and sweating, just to name a few.[14] Unlike withdrawal effects from addictive drugs or alcohol, there is no drug craving. Antidepressants are not addictive, but they do affect your body. If you come off your prescription(s) carefully, your neurochemistry will slowly return back to its original functioning. However, hastily stopping medication jars your system—and your body takes the hit. Most seniors who experience discontinuation syndrome think they have the flu or a very bad cold—and don't attribute these symptoms to the stopping of antidepressant medication. Coming off medication in a controlled way, overseen by your health professional, avoids this uncomfortable experience. In addition to experiencing antidepressant discontinuation syndrome from hastily stopping your medication, you'll likely find your depressive symptoms returning again. Now, I don't want the idea of taking medication to be a scary one for you or, if you're a caregiver to a depressed senior, worry that medicine may be more harmful than helpful. The truth is, with careful and appropriate usage, antidepressants are an enormously helpful treatment for geriatric depression.

Another reason relapse and recurrence happen is due to **gaps in treatment**, defined as treatment-avoidant behaviors like skipping your scheduled therapy sessions, missing doses of your medication, canceling your rTMS or ECT to a later date, or not following up on your health-care claims. Sometimes these gap behaviors happen because you begin to feel better and don't think treatments are needed anymore. You start to get casual with attending your treatment sessions, thinking it's no big deal. But it really is a big deal! Studies show that *the* biggest cause of relapse of geriatric depression is a gap in treatment.[15] What can also stall your healing is **treatment lag**, the time of onset of your depressive symptoms and the delayed time it took to finally get care.[16] The longer you wait to get treatment, the worse your recovery. This is why it's vital to seek treatment as soon as symptoms present. Other times, the reasons behind your decision that cause gaps in treatment aren't as easy to understand. If this is the case, you and your therapist can explore the causes for these behaviors and take steps to address them.

STIGMA AND DIAGNOSTIC TRAUMA

Fear of aging is an especially predominant inclination here in the Western world. **Ageism**, the stereotypical and misinformed attitudes toward the elderly, frequently shoehorns itself into pop culture, media, politics, and your community.[17] The myths that circulate from one generation to another insinuate that getting older means mental decline, physical rot, nonexistent sensuality, impending loneliness, being a burden to others, and feeling useless. Though this myopic view of later life is filled with misrepresentations and untruths, many adults buy into it and feel significant loss of self-esteem with every gray hair.[18] If we stack the deck with being diagnosed with a later-life mental illness, self-worth virtually all but evaporates. Studies show the consequences of late-onset depression deepen a senior's sense of failure, helplessness, and hope for the future.[19] Mental illness **stigma** can be defined as shaming from others that labels, stereotypes, separates, discriminates, and results in a loss of status for someone living with mental illness. Studies show that depressed seniors feel shunned not only by family and friends[20] but also by many in the healthcare profession[21] because they possess the stigma one-two punch of being old and having a mental illness.[22] These issues can make it harder for seniors to get the psychological care they need. There are ways to kick stigma to the curb. Figure 6.1 illustrates four proven approaches that help reduce ageism and mental illness stigma in older adults.

- *Language*: The power and importance of sensitive language is a central theme in research studies. Limiting words like *crazy*, *wacko*, and *psycho*, and phrases like *frequent flier* or *hard-to-serve* in families, healthcare organizations, media and journalism, workplace, and schools needs to be emphasized. Teaching words like *neurobiology*, *genetic predispositions*, and *compassionate care* are more appropriate and less stigmatizing.
- *Awareness of Stigma*: Educating others about stigma increases awareness. Debunking myths of aging and mental illness will create more mindfulness in the general public and healthcare sectors. Furthermore, reduction of stigma emerges most successfully when others are shown living well in spite of having a chronic

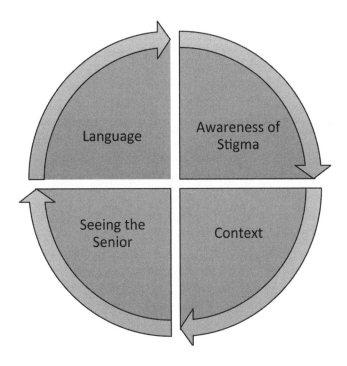

Figure 6.1. Reducing Stigma in Depressed Seniors

mental illness. Media campaigns need to encourage positive stories of seniors living with depression instead of sensationalizing
tragic or headline-grabbing narratives.

- *Context*: Take into consideration the relationships the depressed
  senior has with family, friends, caregivers, and healthcare professionals. Doing so shifts the context away from viewing him or her
  as seemingly frail or feeble.
- *Seeing the Senior*: Make sure you see the senior as a unique individual. Challenge your preconceived notions about mental illness
  and the elderly. Pledge to treat the senior with depression with
  dignity and respect while tending to whatever needs or circumstances present.

In addition to ageism and stigma, diagnostic trauma (the experience of
receiving life-changing news about your health) can leave you unsettled
and upset. Social psychologist Dr. Jessie Gruman poignantly writes
about her own personal experiences with diagnostic trauma: "Each of
the four times I have received a life-altering diagnosis, I have felt like a
healthy person who has been accidentally drop-kicked into a foreign
country: I don't know the language, the culture is unfamiliar, I have no
idea what is expected of me, I have no map, and I desperately want to
find my way home."[23] I have worked with many seniors where putting a
name to their symptoms—panic, anxiety, phobias—was an empowering
moment. It was as if delivering the diagnosis helped confirm their own
suspicions of what was going on. "Yeah, I thought that's what it could
be." But more often than not, seniors who learn they're living with a
form of geriatric depression don't find it so empowering. Many are
surprised. Others fall silent, overcome with grief. More than a few cry,
while some argue that I'm surely wrong. Absorbing this news and making decisions about tending to your health becomes an odyssey of epic
proportions. Getting support while you navigate these new waters can
help you gain access to treatment more swiftly. Otherwise, research
warns that diagnostic trauma and the recognition that stigma is waiting
in the wings lowers rates of treatment success.[24]

CONTINUITY OF CARE

One of the best ways to ensure treatment success is to insist on communication between and among the members of your health team. A collaborative approach involving your every need limits gaps in treatment and builds what's commonly called *continuity of care*. In fact, studies show that depressed seniors who have a health team that works collaboratively improves recovery and remission rates compared with those seniors who work independently with healthcare professionals.[25]

Care coordination—a planned integration of patient care between two or more healthcare providers, caregivers, or organizations involved in a patient's care to deliver treatment—is a gold-standard approach for any individual living with chronic illness.[26] However, seniors with depression can experience care that is poorly coordinated. They may see many different healthcare providers working in multiple clinical locations. As such, poor communication between providers and seniors is common.[27] These factors interrupt treatment success.

When I work with a senior with late-life depression who lives independently, the collaborative care model looks like figure 6.2. In this model, I get a release of consent signed from my senior patient so I can talk to his or her primary care physician, psychiatrist, spouse, or caregiver about relevant treatment information. My senior patient and I go over what kinds of issues will be addressed ahead of time and what the goals are for this collaborative approach so continuity of care occurs. I find that I'm often the liaison, making more phone calls to providers or taking more initiative about treatment follow-ups. This is because my patient caseload is significantly smaller than that of a physician, nurse practitioner, neurologist, or psychiatrist. It takes less time for me to monitor the 10 senior patients I treat each month than the hundred senior patients the other healthcare professionals treat each month.

Continuity of care gets more difficult when a depressed senior is in assisted living, a nursing home, or being cared for by a loved one or private nurse/aide. As figure 6.3 shows, the collaborative team is larger and requires more active communication. Think of the game of telephone we all played when we were young children: You'd start a phrase and then the message would pass from one friend to another via a whisper. The longer the chain of friends, the more likely the original message would be unintentionally changed. Collaborative care with a

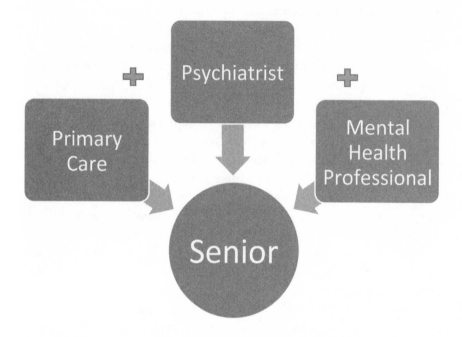

Figure 6.2. **Collaborative Care Model with Independent Senior**

large health team can present in a similar way. To minimize this risk, a case manager may be assigned to take on the exclusive role of coordinating care.[28] If you're a spouse or caregiver to a loved one with depression, I recommend that you shadow the case manager. I encourage you to call the other health team professionals too. Keep a file and ask for copies of relevant reports. I often tell caregivers and spouses that if we all get the same information from the others on the health team, that means we're all on the same page. It makes me feel that everyone is working toward the same goal. Research supports that seniors with better continuity of care were less likely to be hospitalized, less likely to visit hospital emergency departments, had lower rates of complications, and had lower overall costs for their episodes of care.[29]

WHY VS. WHAT

Another way to help your treatment success is to not dwell too long or too much on why you're experiencing depression in late life. I don't

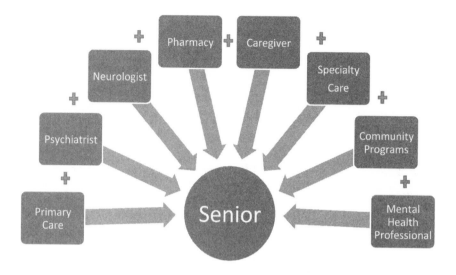

Figure 6.3. Collaborative Care with Many Agencies

mean that you shouldn't try to figure out why this has happened! It is very important to learn what **triggers** you have, what kind of genetics you possess, and other such things. What I'm trying to emphasize here is that getting stuck in the *whys* is neither helpful nor conducive to getting better results.

Why is this happening to me right now?
Why do I have to be dealing with this in my life at this age?
Why can't things be easier?
Why don't I have it easier like other people?
Why am I not feeling better right away?

"Why" can derail you from getting to "what." As in: What can I do right now to get help? What do I need to change to reduce my negative thinking? What things and people in my life now get prioritized? What treatments are needed for my depression? When you're in a crisis, lingering in the question of "Why?" can be a tactical error. Asking "what" will get more done.

Positive: *What* has directionality.
Negative: *Why* keeps you stuck in circular thinking.
Positive: *What* offers solutions.
Negative: *Why* offers no game plan.

So, when late-life depression hits, give yourself permission to ask why this has happened, but don't stay on the sidelines too long with this line of questioning. Instead, use the power of *what* to help you move into a successful route toward treatment success.

SUMMARY

Understanding how late-life depression is diagnosed and treated is only part of treating depression. The other aspect of managing depression is learning how to spot gaps in treatment so you can successfully move from recovery to remission. Here are some tips to help you streamline your treatment.

1. *Don't skip scheduled sessions with your therapist.* If you feel great or aren't in the mood to go to sessions, make it your business to be there and talk about your reluctance. If adjustments in the frequency of sessions are warranted, you and your therapist can make changes. Missing sessions on a whim can arouse feelings of guilt, which can set into motion self-defeating thoughts. Personally, the times I skipped sessions with my own therapist showed me that I was avoiding profound subjects or that I was reacting defensively to something in my life. *Talking* instead of *walking* showed me how self-defeating patterns were operating and that I needed to address these tendencies.

2. *Be consistent with your medication.* If you're taking prescription medication for your depression, be diligent about taking doses in a timely manner. Set an alarm for your medication. Some of my seniors use their reminder settings in their iPhones or computer tablets. Set up weekly pill boxes with all your medications so you can keep track of their management. Carry a portable pill box so if you've forgotten your dose, you can remedy the situation easily by popping in your medication.

3. *Never stop taking your medication(s) without talking with your nurse practitioner or prescribing doctor.* If side effects are intolerable or you just wish to not be on medication anymore, an open and honest forum can ensure that you come off your dosage in a safe manner.

4. *If you've been instructed to lower your dosage, follow the instructions given by your prescribing healthcare professional to the letter.* If you begin experiencing symptoms of discontinuation syndrome, immediately contact her or him. You may need to take a higher dosage for a longer period of time and step down more slowly in dosages before weaning your body completely off of the medicine.

5. *If not being on medication causes a relapse or recurrence of your late-life depression, consider returning back to another medication as a treatment.* There is no shame in having neurobiology that requires pharmacological help. I've come off my antidepressant medication twice, gradually discontinuing dosages with the help of my doctor, only to discover that my depression recurred. I have been taking antidepressant medication for my unipolar depression for over 20 years. And I know I'll continue to need it.

6. *Create a healthcare team.* Make sure you put together a team of professionals to help manage your geriatric depression. Collaborative care ensures that professionals are aware of how treatments are going and if any difficulties are presenting, and keeps other organizations, family members, or caregivers in the communication loop. Remember, together the team will help you move from a state of response to remission to the goal of recovery.

7. *Create a relapse-recurrent prevention plan for yourself.* Design a way to monitor and track your symptoms to understand the state of your well-being. You can do this on your own or with your therapist. The goal is to learn how to pay attention to subtle changes of thinking, feeling, and behaving that mark either a return or a repeat of your depression. If you're a caregiver, talk to your loved one about the steps to take if relapse occurs (calling therapists, asking for an increase in medication, using holistic treatments, considering alternative forms of treatment). Being proactive will help keep geriatric depression at bay.

CASE STUDY: YVONNE

Yvonne, age 68, was brought to the emergency room by her husband, Frank, after he couldn't "seem to control her anymore." Frank reported that over the past few weeks Yvonne had been agitated and confused. She was also emotionally unstable, moving along a range of tearfulness, anxiety, and recklessness (throwing items, pulling at her skin). The reason Frank finally brought Yvonne to the ER was that after several days of not sleeping, she insisted on going food shopping in the evening, without changing from her nightgown.

The emergency room hospitalist initially believed Yvonne was experiencing a form of dementia, so full physical and neurological evaluations were done. She was admitted from the ER to a hospital room. After several days of testing, lab work and brain scans were negative for stroke, metabolic, or vascular issues. A seasoned staff psychiatrist stepped in when Yvonne's symptoms worsened. A full psychiatric profile indicated that Yvonne appeared to be in the midst of a manic episode, which can often be misdiagnosed in later life.

Paul had never seen Yvonne like this, nor did he say that she ever displayed any other manic behaviors in the past.

"She never spent money like crazy or was careless," Frank reported. "She was sad on occasion, but never in the dumps too long," he continued.

Yvonne indicated that she had never been in therapy or even formally diagnosed with bipolar disorder at any time in her life. "This is such a sudden thing to happen," she said.

After Yvonne was stabilized enough with medications to be released from the hospital, she was discharged and continued seeing the psychiatrist who diagnosed her. She began working with me days after her discharge to help her transition to these new sets of issues that appeared to be interfering in her life.

From the outset, Yvonne was reluctant to accept her diagnosis. I suggested that she seek a second opinion with another psychiatrist, but she refused. The contact I made with Yvonne's psychiatrist and primary care physician showed that Yvonne wasn't complying with treatment recommendations. The health team shared these issues with Frank, who appeared overwhelmed, saying "he could never get his wife to change her mind once it was made up."

In sessions, Yvonne was more concerned about why this was happening to her and why no one had ever diagnosed her before. I spent some time teaching Yvonne and Frank about the different subtypes of bipolar disorders, especially helping them understand how bipolar II (a less intense form of bipolar disorder) can be present but sometimes undetectable to many. I suggested that once we got Yvonne from a state of response to a level of remission, we could review her past history for possible hypomanic or depressive episodes that weren't significantly disruptive—and as such, weren't picked up as a concern by her, Frank, or others. But for now, it was all about stabilizing her. But Yvonne couldn't shift forward. She kept ruminating about why this was happening to her now.

"I was in a car accident a few months back. Could that have done it?" Yvonne asked.

Another moment later, "Menopause was really hard for me. I still have issues with estrogen. Maybe that's why?"

Onset of bipolar disorders can occur after a trauma like a car accident, illness, or stressor. Research also links a worsening of bipolar symptoms with estrogen. Yvonne wasn't wrong to consider such things.

"It could be any one of those, Yvonne. But let's focus on consistency with your treatments before we start looking at the origin of things," I said.

The early sessions were like putting out a wildfire that moved from one place to another—never fully getting one out before the next one started and needing to tend to them all because they'd sputter and spark, threatening to ignite again. Increasing sessions to twice a week helped, but the focus of work was not doing much to help Yvonne adhere to her treatment plans. She wasn't taking her medicine regularly, stopping and starting them at will. She wasn't keeping a good sleep schedule either. As a result she was becoming agitated again. When she began missing or arriving very late to her scheduled appointments, I shoehorned my concerns via a phone call.

"Yvonne, we had an appointment scheduled today," I said, concerned.

"I know. I know. But I was feeling okay and didn't need to come," she explained.

Two weeks later, Yvonne missed another appointment.

"Hi, Yvonne. It's Deb. You need to keep your scheduled appointments with me. I'm so worried that you're not here today. Please call me so we can reschedule."

Yvonne returned my call within the same day and we rescheduled it to later in the week. However, Yvonne arrived 15 minutes late to it. Though she paid her fee, the check would later bounce.

"Yvonne, I don't think you're committing yourself to treatment, and I have to tell you that I won't work this way," I finally said at the next appointment.

"What! Why?" she said, clearly annoyed. "I'm doing fine. I don't see what the issue is."

"Psychotherapy requires you to be consistent with sessions. You've missed a few, been late to many, and I can't work like this with you. We've spoken about this many times." I took a long breath. "You need to ask yourself if you really want to be here."

"So, you're dumping me?"

I shook my head. "No. I'm saying that if you can't commit yourself psychotherapy, being here consistently, you and I can't work together anymore."

Yvonne grew quiet. "No. I want to be here."

Yvonne never showed for her next appointment and didn't return my phone call when I reached out to talk to her. Contact with her psychiatrist revealed she'd missed two appointments in a row. I reached out to tell Yvonne's general practitioner that treatment was unsuccessful on my end and that I'd no longer be part of the collaborative team.

Finally, I spoke to Frank who was bewildered at his wife's decision to not continue treatment. I told him I was here as a resource if Yvonne had a change of heart. And I also encouraged Frank to seek counsel on his end to help him deal with the chaos and upheaval with Yvonne. Before we ended the phone call, Frank shared something important.

"I've been reading about bipolar II and I think Yvonne's been living with it for a long time now."

"What makes you think that?" I asked.

"Her lack of needing to sleep, her talkative ways, and then her being irritable or withdrawn after. This has been something I've seen for years. I just thought she was moody."

"Could have been a mild case . . . or subclinical," I replied.

"Maybe the car accident. The wreck totaled the car even though neither of us was hurt beyond a few scrapes." Frank stopped a beat. "Could be the menopause too, like Yvonne says. Or it could be—"

I interrupted Frank and gently reminded him, "Don't let the *whys* keep you stuck. Focus on getting Yvonne to be consistent with treatment. It's the only way she'll ever get better."

Frank agreed.

"Good luck," I said before hanging up.

I knew Frank was going to need it.

7

SUICIDE IN LATER LIFE

Suicide is a significant risk for anyone with a mental illness but is exponentially higher for seniors with depression.[1] Though suicide is the most preventable kind of death, over 3,000 people die by suicide each day.[2] Mathematically measured another way, one million people a year die by suicide. Worldwide, more people die from suicide than all the deaths caused by accidents, natural disasters, wars, and homicides around the world—*combined*.[3] Another way to understand the enormity of depression and its unyielding grip is that every 40 seconds someone dies by suicide.[4] And every 41 seconds, loved ones are left behind trying to make sense of it all.

When it comes to suicide in later life, research reports that seniors have the highest death by suicide rate.[5] What I've come to know from my own depressive episodes and also as a trained psychologist is how the illness of depression distorts thinking. Of all that depression does, this is the worst of the worst. The danger arrives when the neurobiology of the illness slows the executive functioning of the brain's frontal lobes, areas responsible for problem solving and judgment. This causes reasoning and possibility to fade. This is when all hope is lost, where a momentary impulse sets into motion life-ending actions. The corrosive effect of depression is what makes it one of the most lethal of psychological disorders.

Studies tell us that many seniors find deeper meaning in life and experience more stable well-being than at younger ages, but research also reminds us that later-life suicide is a serious concern. These ex-

tremes make the argument that the golden years should be characterized *both* as a time of greater well-being and a time of greater risk of
suicide.[6]

STATISTICS FOR SUICIDE IN LATER LIFE

According to a 2010 report from the Centers for Disease Control and
Prevention,[7] the overall rate for late-life suicide is 14.3 per 100,000
people—or described another way, a senior dies by suicide every 97
minutes. By gender, nearly 85 percent of late-life suicides are completed by men, 15 percent by women. Within the senior age category,
death by suicide was highest for Caucasian males aged 75 years and
older, with 36 deaths per 100,000. Breaking this into more specific
demographics, here are suicide rates for other categories:

Asian and Pacific Islanders: 10.6 per 100,000
Hispanics: 7.9 per 100,000
Non-Hispanic Blacks: 5.0 per 100,000
Non-Hispanic Whites: 15.8 per 100,000

What is perhaps the most difficult sentence to read about this subject
are the following words: Studies report that one out of two suicide
attempts among the elderly succeeds, as compared to one out of 200 for
those under age 25 (the group with the second-highest suicide rate).
This staggering statistics tell us that for seniors struggling with depression, suicide is not a cry for help but the means to an end.

Though suicide rates for seniors vary across countries and cultures,
data show that 85–90 percent of persons aged 65 years and over who
took their own lives had a diagnosable major psychological disorder at
the time of death.[8] Other issues learned from studying late-life depression and suicide show that older adults tend to plan their suicides more
than younger peers.[9] Seniors are also less likely to survive a suicide
attempt because, unlike their younger counterparts, they're physically
frail.[10] Older adults who die by suicide generally live alone, are socially
isolated, and receive mental health treatment at strikingly low rates.[11]
Nearly two thirds of seniors who die by suicide had been seen by primary care physicians within the month prior to their deaths, and up to

half had been treated within one week.[12] This makes the need for identifying at-risk seniors all the more urgent.

Losing a loved one to suicide in later life is also an enormous financial burden. Studies put the economic toll on caregivers, family, and friends from lost wages, absenteeism to deal with the loved one's suicide, and slowed work productivity after returning back to work upward of $44 billion annually in the United States and $51 billion in Canada.[13] In addition to the measurable economic costs of suicide, there are emotional costs: the loss of love, the loss of hope, the loss of potential, the loss of a future.

RECOGNIZING SUICIDE RISK IN SENIORS

The goal of understanding why seniors are at such a high risk for depression begins with piecing together the emotional and environmental histories of those who've died by suicide, a process that's clinically called the *psychological autopsy*.[14] Data is also meticulously collected from interviewing seniors who attempted but did not die by suicide. We owe a great deal of gratitude and respect to the families who invite researchers into their heartbroken homes for this purpose and to suicide survivors who've come forward to share their own personal narratives and reasons behind their suicide attempts. It's from these inquiries that researchers have been able to target five domains that raise the risk of suicide in later life: 1) psychiatric illness, 2) personality traits and coping styles, 3) physical illness and pain, 4) social disconnectedness, and 5) functional impairment.[15]

- *Major Psychiatric Illness*: As mentioned previously, psychological autopsy studies report that seniors who died by suicide had psychiatric illness. But a notable statistic is that approximately 80 percent who died by suicide also suffered from depression.[16] This means that elderly adults who are depressed are either not getting proper treatment for their depressive symptoms or not being identified early enough to prevent suicide.
- *Personality Traits and Coping Style*: Another factor noted in studies is the inability to cope well with difficulties and life stressors. Data shows that rigid coping, poor problem solving, anxiety, and

obsessive traits are strongly linked to late-life suicide. In contrast, research noted that emotion-focused coping skills (expressing and exploring your emotions as you problem solve) were protective against suicide.[17]

- *Physical Illness and Pain*: Risk of late-life suicide increases with chronic illness, with seniors being nearly four times higher to die by suicide than age peers who did not have an illness.[18] Furthermore, research has shown that risk of suicide increases with the number of diagnosed illnesses. Seniors recently discharged from a hospital or nursing home demonstrated an elevated risk for suicide, suggesting that the experience of transition is an exceedingly vulnerable time for seniors.[19] The presence of pain, be it mental or physical, also raises completed suicide in the elderly. Pain has a set of singular characteristics. It's intrusive, demands attention, interrupts a sense of peace, slams to a stop any activity you're doing, is physically unbearable, and is mentally inescapable.[20] Pain leaves a senior feeling defeated, helpless, and overwhelmed by seeking relief, which can often lead to the decision to die by suicide.

- *Social Disconnectedness*: Being alone, lonely, unmarried, single, or disconnected from a source of social support are tremendous risk factors for late-life suicide. Although social disconnection is a factor for children, teens, and adults contemplating suicide, studies have shown that depressed seniors who had lower levels of perceived social support (that is, they felt no one was there for them in spite of others being there) and experienced bumpy interpersonal relationships with others were more inclined to be suicidal than depressed seniors who perceived good social support.[21] This suggests that social disconnection may be real or perceived and that geriatric assessments must formally inquire about both possibilities.

- *Functional Impairments*: When you cannot physically take care of yourself the way you used to or have to rely on others to perform simple tasks for everyday living, withering self-esteem and feelings of inadequacy emerge. Studies show that older adults who contemplate suicide not only experience these kinds of functional impairments, they additionally feel a loss of personal control, independence, and a rockslide of depressive symptoms.[22] Functional impairments are not just physical. When you begin to lose your abilities to think, remember, and process information, an unspeakable anguish takes over. Studies suggest there's a distinct association between dementia and suicidal behavior in later life.[23] Specifically, evidence suggests that suicide risk may be increased soon after receiving a dementia diagnosis. The 2014 death by suicide of Oscar-winner and comedic treasure Robin Williams highlights this finding when his family shared that a diagnosis of Lewy body dementia shattered his world. When someone like Robin Williams, a beloved icon, dies by suicide, it stuns and confounds. The collective experience is "How could this happen?" The truth is that many people, even healthcare professionals, are uninformed about depression and functional impairments. But those of us who struggle with depression, chronic illness, and the loss of autonomy understand. We know that being funny isn't the same thing as being happy. And studies warn if you're a senior who is struggling with depression and are losing physical and cognitive abilities, you're significantly at risk for suicide.

INTERPERSONAL THEORY OF SUICIDE

When Dr. Thomas Joiner, psychologist and distinguished research professor at Florida State University, was in graduate school, his father died by suicide. This tragedy changed him personally and shifted the trajectory of his professional life. Dr. Joiner is a leader of suicide research and media go-to expert focused on reducing stigma about suicide. Though the interplay of genetics, life experience, and environment influence suicidal thinking, imminent risk for suicide happens, Joiner argues, when a person simultaneously experiences two specific psychological states: the perception that one is a *burden* and the sense that *one does not belong*. The last feature in this model is having access to lethal means to die by suicide. Dr. Joiner's interpersonal theory of suicide offers much in helping us understand late-life suicide, as shown in figure 7.1.[24]

To begin, let's define **thwarted belongingness** as a lack of meaningful connections to others. For the senior, this means being a widow or widower, separated, divorced, living alone, experiencing a strain

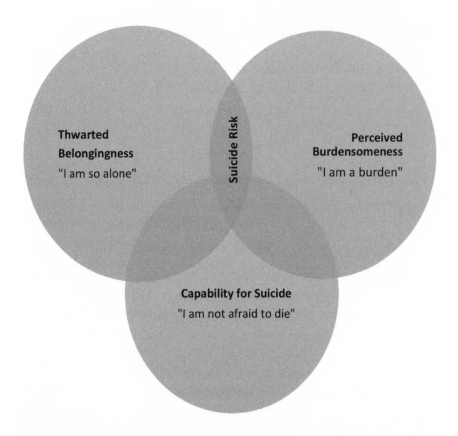

Figure 7.1.   Interpersonal Model of Late-Life Suicide

from previously solid relationships, or feeling isolated from belonging to a family or community, just to name a few. The sense of belonging is a fundamental need, deeply moving us to feel connected to others.[25] When a lasting, positive, and meaningful sense of connection is lost, the senior's sense of safety, security, and love is set adrift. No longer does the senior feel a part of something . . . or someone. When this occurs, the senior says, "I am so alone."

The next feature in this model is *perceived burdensomeness*, which is when a senior believes he or she is a burden to others, is no longer a valued contributing human being to society, and is a liability to others. Studies have shown that perceived burdensomeness was a significant predictor of suicidality indicators, even more so than the most robust predictors of suicidality, hopelessness.[26] The feelings of being a burden that a senior may feel include being a physical drain on her or his caretaker or loved ones, a financial weight to the bank account of others, and an emotional strain that taxes the minds and hearts of family or friends. Here, suicidal seniors say, "I am a burden" and believe that subtracting themselves from life's equation is an answer.

Acquired capability for suicide is the third factor, and considers the degree to which a senior has access to items or materials to put a suicidal thought into action. Once belongingness is thwarted and burdensomeness is realized, the suicidal senior takes thought and places it into action. Decisions are made, access is sought, and then the plan to die by suicide—be it a firearm, medication, hanging, or other lethal means—is carried out. Here, the senior affirms, "I am not afraid to die."

RISK FACTORS FOR SUICIDE

As mentioned earlier in this chapter, there are categories of risk that heighten late-life suicide. Risk factors are often confused with warning signs of suicide, but the two are very different. **Warning signs** indicate an immediate risk of suicide, whereas risk factors indicate someone is at heightened risk for suicide but not at a level of immediate risk.[27] We'll be talking about warning signs regarding suicidality in just a little bit. Right now, I want to highlight a list of evidence-based factors for late-life depression. Take time to familiarize yourself with them. The knowledge you gain can help monitor your own late-life depression or assist in the detection of suicide risk in someone you know or love.

Access to Lethal Means	Alcohol Abuse
Atheism	Borderline Personality
Celebrity Suicide	Chronic Pain
Cigarette Smoking	Clusters of Suicide in the News
Comorbid Mental Illness	Culture Beliefs Supporting Suicide
Dementia	Diminished Problem-Solving Skills
Divorce	Failing Health
Family History of Suicide	Financial Hardship

Functional Impairments	Gaps in Treatment
Helplessness	Hopelessness
Impulsivity	Isolation
Lack of Healthcare	Loss, Death, or Separation
Mood Disorder	Negative Life Events
Perceived Burdensomeness	Recent Hospitalizations
Sleep Disturbances	Social Disconnectedness
Substance Abuse	Transitions and Major Changes

PROTECTIVE FACTORS THAT MINIMIZE SUICIDE RISK

Protective factors are features that help inoculate a person from engaging in suicidal behavior. Protective factors include personal, cultural, and religious attitudes; cohesive support from family, friends, and community; and access to treatment for mental illness. Just as you did in the risk-factor section above, familiarize yourself with the kinds of positive influences that can protect against suicide. It is important, however, to understand that protective factors don't necessarily balance or cancel out risk factors; keep in mind that evaluating risk for suicide is not like setting up a list of pros and cons. There is no specific formula for detecting and preventing suicide. What I recommend is to look at your own biology, life history, environment, risk, and protective factors as well as your current level of depression to determine if a suicide attempt is a real possibility. Here are examples of suicide protective factors:

Access to Healthcare	Adherence to Medication Treatment
Belief in Future	Belongingness
Cigarette, Drug, and Alcohol Avoidance	Cohesive Family Structure
Community Prevention Programs	Continuity of Treatment
Cultural Discouragement of Suicide	Good Physical Health

Healthy Avoidance of Risky
Behaviors

Hopefulness

Resilience

Restricted Access to Lethal Means

Spiritual or Faith-Based Beliefs

Stable Retirement/Work/Social
Environment

Strong Self-Esteem

Trust in Others

WARNING SIGNS OF SUICIDE

Research has noted that 75 percent of individuals who die by suicide often give clues or warning signs.[28] Warning signs may be observed in a person's behavior or by the words he or she speaks. When warning signs are observable, suicide can be a preventable death. But studies suggest a suicidal senior's clues can go unnoticed because loved ones, friends, and even health professionals miss the warning signs or fail to know what to do with them.[29] In fact, research says four kinds of responses arise from the warning signs of elderly suicidal adults. Let's note them here to heighten your awareness.

1. *Not taken seriously*: Many caregivers, loved ones, or health professionals don't take a senior's warning signs seriously. They minimize the signs or totally misunderstand the gravity of the disclosures.
2. *Exhaustion*: Sometimes a senior may talk about a wish to die or a plan of action so much that loved ones find it exhausting. The longer the period of time a senior expresses suicidal thoughts, the more others may view them as empty threats, wearying, or even irritating.
3. *Helplessness*: Many family relatives and caregivers can feel powerless when faced with warning signs of suicide in a senior. They become helpless and don't know who to turn to, how to get help, or that a warning sign signals an emergency.
4. *Acceptance*: Sometimes family members respond silently to a senior's warning signs because they understand their loved one's desire to die. In chapter 9, I am going to write about compassionate care, also known as physician-assisted suicide. This is quite

different from the suicidal thoughts of untreated geriatric depression. When it comes to late-life depression and suicide, any warning sign needs to be regarded as an emergency. Furthermore, all members of your care team need to share information once a warning sign is noted. This can help piece together if other warning signs were observed.

One way to narrow the margin of missing these lifesaving clues is to become familiar with warning signs for late-life suicide, listed in table 7.1.

Another way to help identify if you or a loved one is at risk for suicide is to use the American Association of Suicidology's mnemonic device: IS PATH WARM.[30] Ask yourself if you've been experiencing any of the following or, if you're a caregiver, see if your loved one is demonstrating these risk factors and warning signs.

Table 7.1.   Warning Signs for Late-Life Suicide

Warning Signs for Late-Life Suicide

- **Avoidant, secretive**
- **Breaking medical regimens or halting treatments**
- **Buying items that if used are lethal: rope, poison, gasoline, plastic bags, aspirin**
- **Distancing oneself from religious or faith-based activities**
- **Giving things away: money, possessions**
- **Increasing the use of alcohol or drugs**
- **Making arrangements for issues to be taken care of by others**
- **Making changes in wills**
- **No longer engaging in self-care and grooming**
- **Purchasing a firearm**
- **Preoccupation with death**
- **Remarks or statements that reflect a lack of concern about personal safety:** *It's no big deal if I don't wear a seatbelt. I think people live too long these days.*
- **Remarks or statements that reflect a time limit on being alive:** *I don't think I'll be around this Christmas. This is the last time you'll see me.*
- **Researching ways to die by searching online**
- **Showing rage or talking about seeking revenge**
- **Stock-piling medication**
- **Suddenly happier, calmer**
- **Suddenly wanting to visit or call people**
- **Talking about being a burden to others**
- **Talking about feeling hopeless or having no reason to live**
- **Talking about feeling trapped or in unbearable pain**
- **Talking about where to find paperwork, wills, bank statements, etc.**
- **Talking about wanting to die**

I	**I**deation	(thinking or talking of death)
S	**S**ubstance Abuse	(alcohol, drugs, over the counter, prescription medicines)
P	**P**urposelessness	(feeling useless, no sense in living anymore)
A	**A**nxiety	(excessive worries, nervousness, restlessness)
T	**T**rapped	(feeling there's no way out, wish to get away from it all)
H	**H**opelessness	(having no hope for the future)
W	**W**ithdrawal	(isolating from others)
A	**A**nger	(irritability, angry outbursts)
R	**R**ecklessness	(impulsivity, risky behaviors, not tending to self-care)
M	**M**ood Changes	(variability in moods)

UNDERSTANDING SUICIDALITY

Suicidality is defined as a series of ideas and behaviors, ranging from mild to severe. Detailing these distinct categories teaches that suicidality begins at subconscious levels that, if ignored, grow more menacing . . . and if left unaddressed at the more serious levels, become fatal. There are seven levels of suicidality. Learn them. Understand them. Make them part of your self-assessment if you live with late-life depression. Use them as a benchmark for your loved ones if you're a caregiver.

1. *Self-harm behavior with subconscious suicidal intent* is the category that describes the actions of seniors who hurt, wound, or harm themselves without understanding the intention of their behavior. Often, the self-harm act has a careless or ambiguous origin that may stem from a subconscious wish to die. "I don't know how I cut my arm." "The car came out of nowhere and hit

me as I crossed the street." "I didn't realize I took too many pills." Inquiring further about "unintended" wounds, self-destructive behaviors, or "accidental" overdosing may reveal feelings of unworthiness, guilt, despair, and pessimistic attitudes—symptoms that suicidal thinking is percolating just under the surface of awareness. *Intervention*: Check in immediately with your physician, psychiatrist, or therapist to talk about this very concerning occurrence.

2. *Suicidal ideation*, sometimes called "suicidal thinking," is the stage in which a person consciously thinks about suicide. The thoughts of sleeping forever, not wanting to wake up, or being dead are sometimes uttered aloud by seniors. So if you're a caregiver, listen for such statements. If you're a senior with depression, examine your thoughts, fantasies, or wishes to see if they take on these qualities. *Intervention*: Immediate intervention is needed here to explore suicidal ideation. When a senior or a caregiver tells me that these kinds of thoughts are being expressed, I schedule an appointment *that day* to further explore suicidality.

3. *Suicidal intent* is the category in which thought is now dangerously accompanied by an intention of carrying a plan out. Sometimes intent is mild, where a senior may say, "I've thought about taking a handful of pills, but I'd never go through with it." Others, though, express intent in a specific manner. "I'm gonna wait till everyone's asleep and then take all the pills." *Intervention*: This is an extremely serious concern and immediate contact with a health professional is recommended. If you cannot get a prompt appointment, an emergency room visit to the hospital is advised.

4. *Preparatory acts toward imminent suicide* is the category in which suicidal ideation and intent move into full-on action. A number of seniors will start taking care of personal issues, like giving things away or asking for others to oversee matters. I've worked with seniors who made sure the house was clean and the bills were paid. This is also the stage where you may hear remarks like "I won't be here next summer" or "I don't need any more appointments scheduled." Suicidality at this level is where the suicide plan becomes actualized and the items or methods for suicide are needed—like drugs, firearms, rope, a knife. *Interven-*

tion: Immediate contact with health professionals and admission to the emergency room at the nearest hospital.

5. *Interrupted suicide attempt* is the category where a senior has started a plan to die by suicide but was interrupted by either another person, an outside circumstance, or by their own self-reflection. No physical harm or injury occurs in this category. An interrupted suicide generally does one of two things. Some seniors may recognize the critical event and call 911 or reach out to a loved one or health professional to get help on their own. There are others who may stop in the moment but will reorganize to complete suicide at another time. *Intervention*: If you're witness to a loved one in the middle of a suicide attempt, take him to the nearest hospital emergency room. If you cannot get him there or are fearful to leave him alone, even for a second, call 911 and ask for help.

6. *Nonfatal suicide attempt* is the category that describes a suicide attempt that was carried out by an elderly adult but was not fatal. Perhaps the overdose wasn't toxic enough, the rope frayed and broke apart, the cut wasn't lethal, or the gun misfired. Results of nonfatal suicide attempts can range from no physical injury to mild, moderate, and serious injury. *Intervention*: Call 911 and get an immediate transfer to the nearest hospital emergency room.

7. *Completed suicide* is the category describing a death by suicide. *Intervention*: Sadly, there is no way to prevent the suicide at this level. The intervention herein is for family, friends, and loved ones to get immediate support to deal with the completed suicide. Research has long shown that suicide survivors move through very distinctive bereavement issues. Family and friends are prone to feeling significant bewilderment about the suicide: "Why did this happen?" "How did I not see this coming?" Overwhelming guilt about what they should have done more of or less of becomes daily, haunting, and inescapable thoughts. Survivors of suicide loss struggle for years trying to make sense of their loved one's death—and even longer, making peace, if at all, with the unanswerable questions that linger.

SUMMARY

I know this has been a difficult chapter. But understanding how late-life depression can blur into the margins of suicide is mandatory reading. As discussed in previous chapters, self-monitoring and prevention plans can help you keep track of your depressive states. Before we leave this topic, I want you to put together a *suicide prevention plan* to ensure your safety, or if you're a caregiver, the safety of your loved one. Here are some suggestions.

- *Make a "life plan."* Keep a list of suicide-intervention names, doctors, professionals, agencies, and hotlines, and their respective contact numbers near all landline telephones. These should also be programmed into cell and cordless phones and bookmarked in personal computers and laptops. Please refer to appendix C for resources.
- *Ask others to keep you informed.* Don't be shy to invite trusted people to let you know if they detect any changes in how you're thinking or behaving. Suicidal intentions can be observed in how you think, communicate, and behave—so others may see these high-risk symptoms before you do. If you're a caregiver, gently express to your loved one that you are noticing changes or concerns.
- *Choose life-affirming experiences.* Resist reading and viewing tragic or trauma-filled books, news stories, and films. These negative experiences can worsen feelings of hopelessness and despair. Instead, embrace nature, feed your senses, and surround yourself with children and adults who brim with purpose and pulse with life. Remember to dodge isolation as much as possible. Seclusion heightens the likelihood of death by suicide. If you're a caregiver, use these tips in your caretaking.
- *Sequester lethal means.* Consider having your spouse, family, or friend hold your prescription and over-the-counter medications. Keep trigger items like razors, knives, firearms, rope, and other items out of reach by throwing them out or having someone safeguard them. Sequestering such items subdues the impulse for their use. If you're a caretaker, make sure all lethal means are out

of the home, and monitor prescribed and over-the-counter medications.

- *Keep away from drugs and alcohol.* Substance use increases impulsivity and dulls cognition. Refrain from this fatal combination by keeping all alcohol and drugs out of reach. Avoid socializing with people who don't adhere to this policy or who push the agenda that alcohol and drugs will mellow you out. They won't. In fact, using drugs and alcohol significantly increases your odds of dying by suicide. If you're a caretaker, be a role model and don't use drugs or alcohol.

- *Pay attention to signs of suicidality.* Exercise your self-awareness by frequently analyzing your inner thoughts and feelings. Are they positive, hopeful, and realistic? Are they becoming negative and morbid? If you're a caretaker, observe your loved one in a similar way. Remember that subtle changes in thinking, feeling, and behaving can not only signal a relapse or recurrence of depression but can also set the stage for suicidal behavior. Become familiar with the seven categories of suicidality. Knowing their textures and subtleties before you actually experience them can hasten intervention.

- *Have an "action plan."* You already know that suicidal thinking hijacks reasoning and common sense. If you detect your judgment worsening, immediately contact a healthcare professional, take yourself or your loved one to the nearest hospital emergency room, or call a friend or family member. *Do not wait.*

CASE STUDY: MY FATHER

"Dad was sitting on the edge of the bed with his gun," my mother said.

"What?!" I yelled back into the phone.

"It was a few days ago. We took away the guns," she continued.

My mom was never good about telling me important things in the moment—partially out of misguided sense of protection and, to another degree, denial.

"I think he's better now, but I thought you should know," she continued.

"Dammit, Mom," I snapped, doubting my father was better. "I'm coming over."

My dad had always been a strong and active man. A first son born to Italian immigrants who ran a successful restaurant in New York City, he excelled as a kid in sports and music. He became an accomplished accordionist and played professionally in his teen years until he was drafted. After serving in the Korean War, my dad became a New York City firefighter and during his off-duty time trained to be a chiropractor. He was health conscious, working out at the firehouse, keeping things holistic in our home as well as in his small practice. My formative years with him were spent sailing and camping in good weather, learning how to rebuild a car engine or cooking a meal from one his family's restaurant recipes in bad weather. My father was also a skilled sportsman. He was a 7-handicap golfer, bowled three 300 perfect games, and won ribbons in marksmanship. And though he was flawed, as we all are, I admired him greatly. In my eyes, there wasn't anything he couldn't do. He was my superhero.

His superman status lasted until his middle 50s, when a heart attack hit. From there, my dad slowly deteriorated. Though he looked fit on the outside, thirty years of breathing in smoke, soot, asbestos, and toxins were wreaking havoc on the inside. The FDNY didn't have masks or oxygen tanks in my dad's days, and many of his friends were sidelined from related illnesses like lung cancer and cardiac issues. It was scary for me to see how just one of my father's illnesses taxed the functioning of additional organs, which burdened other metabolic functions—and so on and so on. The next 30 years of his life were filled with challenging illnesses—the most serious being kidney failure. I watched as my strong dad withered into a frail shell of a man.

"Where are the guns?" I asked, grabbing my things to leave. I needed to know who had them. I wanted to be sure they were sequestered away.

"He wouldn't let us take them out of the house, but we managed to get him to agree to take them apart." My mom sighed one of her legendary heavy sighs. "He has pieces of them in the closet. The others we have."

I shook my head, nonplussed. "I'll be there in half an hour," I huffed, frustrated with this fact. I drove quickly and arrived 20 minutes later.

As a family, we had watched my dad's love of life dim with every new medical diagnosis that was delivered. He tried psychotherapy a few times and didn't like it. He wasn't much of a talker and so I agreed to stop pushing him to do that. Instead, my sisters and I, along with my mom's help, were successful in getting him to take antidepressant medication in his late 60s, which helped enormously. But in his late 70s, my dad was given devastating news that his kidneys were failing, and he began dialysis. It was a grueling routine, requiring him to sit for a five-hour treatment every other day to keep him alive. He endured it as well as could be expected, but after three years, his spirit seemed irreparably broken. Bump-ups in his antidepressant medication helped, but after months, suicidal thinking began.

First it was the wish spoken aloud that he "didn't want to go to dialysis anymore," that he thought it would be better if he "didn't celebrate another birthday," that dying gave him comfort.

An immediate conference with his health team suggested another increase in his medication and for psychological services at the dialysis center. It helped for a short time.

Soon after, he started to behave in self-destructive ways like not taking his medications, drinking too much liquid (a hazard if you're a dialysis patient), and eating foods that would dangerously increase his creatinine levels (another danger if you're a dialysis patient). As a result, he had to be hospitalized to stabilize his physical and mental health.

Now, he was holding a gun.

"Dad, I'm so worried about you," I said, seeing him in his bed, resting with his beloved dog, Abbey, beside him.

"Was just a bad moment," he said.

"It would be terrible if you killed yourself."

He nodded.

"It'd be so hard for us to lose you like that," I said, emphasizing the point.

He nodded again, tearful.

I stopped for a moment to recall my own suicide attempt some 30 years earlier, with the very same gun. The access to lethal means was too easy for me then and so very easy for my dad now too. *Goddamn guns*, I thought to myself.

We remained quiet for a long time. In the silence, I considered how my sisters and I had to get rid of any bullets or ammunition in the house, as well as any other lethal means that might tempt my father in his fragile state. My eyes brimmed at the thought of having to do that, but I knew it had to be done.

"Things have been hard on you for so long now, Dad. And there's a part of you that wants to let go." I was trying to stay strong, but the tears spilled downward.

I took in a breath and tried to steady myself. "We can talk to the health team and figure out a way to create a compassionate care plan. Where you can stop dialysis, be at home here, and get medical care to . . . make you comfortable," I finally said.

"We can do that?"

I nodded. "Of course."

"I don't think your mother or sisters will like it."

"Well, it's better than sitting on the edge of the bed with a gun."

My dad and I talked for a long time that day—about life, about death, about regrets and losses, how so much of his later life was controlled by illness, and how he missed feeling free. We agreed to look into this further with his health team, and we gathered the family to talk about this arrangement. Although it wasn't wholeheartedly welcomed by all, it shifted my dad in a profound way. It seemed to lift his suicidal thinking. I think it gave him a sense of freedom—to choose this option should he want it. And it gave him a sense of dignity, where he could leave this world in a way that wouldn't haunt those who loved him, the way a suicide would.

My dad decided not to go further with a compassionate plan and continued going to dialysis every other day. In the last year of his life, he was admitted to the emergency room 22 times for kidney-related issues. And during the blizzard of that year, he had the local fire department take him to and from dialysis, appreciating the irony of that arrangement. My dad wasn't a superhero, but he was, as my sister rightly declared, a warrior—a real-life man of flesh and blood who fought and battled physical and mental illness, and showed me what courage truly was. He taught me how to appreciate the small things, the ordinary, the laugh amid the tears.

He died early one December morning getting ready "for work"—the phrase he used for his dialysis treatments. I like to think that despite his years of physical illness, of depression and suicidal despair, he died in his own home, preparing his favorite morning cereal.

And knowing more than anything else that he was deeply, deeply loved.

8

WHAT TO EXPECT SHOULD YOU NEED HOSPITALIZATION

If you are a senior with a late-life depression, you may require acute, short-term hospitalization if your symptoms are serious or if traditional treatments haven't brought significant results. You may also require hospitalization if your late-onset depression leads to suicidal thinking. In my experience, educating a person about what to expect at the hospital can make for a better experience and smoother transition.

THE HOSPITAL SETTING

For starters, the inpatient psychiatric unit is not straight-jackets, rubber rooms, and metal beds. Those are the images the general public gets from Hollywood, where drama trumps realism. Those inaccurate descriptions breed ignorance and stigma, so don't let those images be your guide. Adult inpatient psychiatry units treat individuals ages 18 and older experiencing a mental health crisis. When possible, I recommend seniors to seek **psychogeriatric units**, which are specifically designed inpatient programs for older adults. Your location will dictate where you can access inpatient care, but if a geriatric unit is within driving distance, it is often the better choice. Generally speaking, geriatric inpatient programs offer single beds and dressers; common areas for socializing; a garden, greenery, or sanctuary area for finding peace; large meeting rooms for group sessions; and smaller rooms for individual treatment. On site is a café area for meals and snacks, and a family room so loved ones can share a visit with you. It is, however, a locked and secured environment. This is to keep you and others safe, and enables the geriatric team staff, who are present throughout the day and night, to manage everyone on the floor with continuity. The team of professionals will likely include a psychiatrist, psychologist, neurologist, social workers, nurses, nutritionists, physical therapists, art therapists, and pharmacists. Other seniors experiencing an acute mental health crisis will be there as well, some having more complicated issues or less pressing matters than you.

The average length of stay for a senior at a regular acute care psychiatry unit for adults—that is, a hospital unit for individuals aged 18 and older—is approximately 10 days.[1] Studies show the average length of stay for seniors hospitalized in specialized psychogeriatric units is shorter, approximating six days.[2] Furthermore, psychogeriatric units have been found to be more effective than regular psychiatric units in reducing depressive symptoms for late-life depression and lowering readmission rates to hospitals.[3] I recommend finding a psychogeriatric unit, even if it means traveling further than where you live, rather than going to a regular inpatient psychiatric unit for these reasons. But if you don't live near a geriatric inpatient facility, a regular adult inpatient unit will offer supportive treatment and stabilization.

ADMISSION

There are two ways to be admitted to an inpatient psychiatric unit. The first way is called a voluntary hospitalization, where you agree to go to the hospital. This can be done either by going through the emergency room, where your give your consent to be admitted into the psychiatric unit, or you and your and your health team coordinate a scheduled intake for admission with the unit directly. The other form of admission is called an *involuntary hospitalization*, where an admission is being sought in spite of the fact that you won't give your consent. A majority of older adults suffering with severe depression may show limited insight into their illness and therefore resist going to the hospital, thus necessitating an involuntary admission. Although the laws differ for involuntary hospitalization from state to state, most require what's called a "Two Physician Certificate" (where two physicians certify that the order for inpatient hospitalization is medically necessary). A decision for hospitalization can also be court ordered. Forcing treatment, though it might be lifesaving, can make seniors noncompliant and irritable. It fills caregivers or loved ones (like spouses and children) with enormous guilt, especially if they oversaw the involuntary placement. The most troubling statistic is that involuntary hospitalizations lead to higher rates of death by suicide.[4] Therefore, involuntary hospitalization is a decision of last resort.

In all my years in practice, 25 years and counting, I've never had to seek an involuntary hospitalization. Although it may be different for other therapists, I like to extend the session with a depressed or suicidal patient and work until there is a cooperative theme in play. The same follows if a person has called in crisis on the telephone. I work and talk and process the issue, with the goal being that my patient will agree to go with a friend or family member to the hospital, or go with the police if I've called them to my patient's home. When you agree voluntarily to enter the hospital, you significantly increase your rate of recovery.

Once you're admitted to the inpatient unit, an intake will be done with staff members to determine your treatment plan and goals for discharge. If you're an independent senior, you'll directly participate in the intake. If you are a senior in assisted living, a nursing home, or require a caregiver, your intake will involve others *including* you. A clinical case worker will be assigned to you and will be your go-to liaison for all in-hospital care.

For safety purposes, there will be rules regarding acceptable clothing. I educate those heading to the hospital to pack a bag with clothing that doesn't have ties or belts, favoring elastic waist sweatpants, jeans, or trousers; slip-on shoes or Velcro sneakers; sweatshirts; and crew-neck tees with long and short sleeves (in case you need to layer your clothing for temperature comfort)—and don't forget your pajamas. There may be limits on what kinds of accessories you may bring in, but seniors are generally given permission to have certain toiletries, an extra pair of glasses, slippers, and a book or two to read, just to name a few. All your nutritional requirements will be assessed prior to admission, and meals are geared to your unique needs. Coffee, tea, and snacks will be readily available throughout the day on the unit floor, so there's no need to pack any extra food. Just make sure you bring a list of your medications, a list of your health team's contact numbers, and any other relevant reports or information.

One of the first things you may feel is afraid or unsettled once you're alone on the floor. Studies report that many seniors feel this way upon admission, but once they've had some time to settle into their room and get used to the surroundings, such feelings faded.[5] Another issue that improves with time is getting used to the daily routine on the floor. As previously mentioned, you'll likely meet other adults who have similar, less-intense or more-involved, issues. Research has shown that while some seniors found interactions with those who had severe cognitive or psychiatric needs objectionable, others expressed tolerance—even gaining new insights and coping strategies from the diagnostically mixed population on the floor.[6]

INPATIENT HOSPITAL TREATMENTS

The inpatient hospital setting provides a safe space for treatments to be delivered in a sensitive and caring manner. The goal of your stay is to return you to a higher level of functioning mentally and physically. You'll be seen daily by specialists from a variety of treatment fields. Another objective is for your family members and caregivers to participate in your treatment plan so they can learn about your depression, discover better ways to help you manage your geriatric depression, and gain insight into ways they can be more attentive to their own well-being as well. Treatments will involve different kinds of individual, group, and family therapy, as well as support services that are meant to offer self-reflection, respite, and peace. Here are but a few of the many treatments you may receive:

Art Therapy	Caregiver Support
Crisis Intervention	Discharge Planning
Exercise Therapy	Family Therapy
Individual Therapy	Group Therapy
Medical Management	Mindfulness Training
Movement Therapy	Music Therapy
Occupational Therapy	Pet Therapy

Psychoeducation	Neuropsychological Assessment
Pharmacotherapy	Physical Therapy
Recreational Therapy	Sand Therapy
Safety and Fall Prevention	Spirituality Services
Stress Management Support	Tai Chi

It's important to understand that while you're receiving inpatient treatments, all of your outside therapies are on hold. It's during this time that someone like me will have contact with your inpatient team, as will your psychiatrist, neurologist, or other members of your care team—and we will await your discharge so our work can resume again.

I like to keep in touch with any patient who's hospitalized in a psychiatric unit, be it a child, teen, or an adult. With seniors, I coordinate a phone call during their scheduled free time so I can check in and chat with them. I also make sure to know who the case manager is and how treatment is going. Of course, releases for shared consent are obtained, and sometimes I even talk to a senior's spouse, child, or caregiver to prepare for when my patient returns back home. If a senior happens to be at a psychiatric facility that's new, I arrange for a visit so I can experience the setting. I like knowing where my patients are going, what the environment is like, how the staff works, and other such things. I want to be able to say that I could feel comfortable being in such a setting so I can endorse it wholeheartedly.

TIPS FOR FAMILY MEMBERS OR CAREGIVERS DURING INPATIENT CARE

Just as the inpatient hospitalization will be a time of adjustment for your loved one, you too will likely move through some difficult moments. One of the most challenging issues is that inpatient hospitalization may upset or frighten you, or make you worry that you'll be judged or criticized because you've failed in some way to care for your loved one. These feelings are not uncommon. Remember, depression isn't a result of poor caretaking, and suicidal thinking doesn't happen because you weren't able to fix things or do a better job at caring for your loved one. Geriatric depression is a serious illness that has numerous causes. Professionals at the inpatient program know this, and they know how hard it was for seniors and their caregivers to make such a decision. Another moment that may hit you hard is if your loved one doesn't want to see you or have any visitors at first. This often happens and it's recommended that you respect this wish for privacy. You will be included in the treatment plan in time, so be patient and sensitive.

Here are some other tips for you to consider:

- There may be privacy regulations on the unit that prevent you from finding out about your loved one's treatment. To avoid this, ask your loved one to sign a consent form allowing you to be part of the communication exchange.
- Learn about the kind of geriatric depression (unipolar, bipolar, vascular, etc.) your loved one is experiencing.
- Keep a running list of questions to ask hospital staff and their answers. Having paper and pen when you're on the unit to keep track of things is essential.
- When bringing items during visiting hours, check with hospital staff regarding which objects and foods are acceptable, and which are not.
- If your feel your loved one is not receiving adequate care, speak up. If you don't see a change or you're still concerned about the quality of care, get in touch with the hospital administration department. Be assertive but calm and clear about your concerns.
- Make a file and keep a record of all your communications with hospital staff, including e-mails, phone calls, reports, etc.
- Before your loved one is released, make sure to get written instructions for transitional care. You want to know medication dosages, follow-up appointments, what health professionals are to be seen, any dietary changes, and other outside care-related issues.
- Remember that depressed seniors who have been recently hospitalized are at a greater risk for suicide upon their return home. Make sure you know the warning signs and promise to keep a consistent treatment schedule for your loved one so there are no gaps in treatment.
- Remember that inpatient care is to stabilize, not cure, your loved one's depression.

- Finally, believe in your loved one's ability to recover. Research shows that family support is vital for recovery from any mental illness.[7]

DISCHARGE PLAN

Once your depressive or suicidal symptoms have stabilized, a treatment plan beyond your hospital stay will be developed. This is called a discharge plan. In actuality, your discharge plan begins the day you are admitted and remains an important aspect of your hospital stay. Your discharge plan will be unique and tailored just for you, and it'll be updated daily until the actual moment you leave the hospital. Your discharge plan is like an architect's blueprint: an overview of what needs to be assembled in order for you to keep a solid sense of well-being.

Elements of this plan involve your active participation as well as that of family members, caregivers, and outside health professionals. The plan itself has two aims: 1) to create short- and long-term goals to maintain your stabilized level of health, and 2) to devise a prevention plan to reduce the risk of relapse.[8] These aims are essentially a form of **transitional care**, a plan of action that facilitates your safety and treatment from hospital to home.

Although a length of stay was estimated upon your admission, an exact date of discharge will be created by your inpatient care team using the following criteria:

- Your severe depressive symptoms have reduced.
- You are no longer a danger to yourself or to others.
- Your functional abilities have improved.
- Goals in your hospital treatment plan have been met.
- Continued treatment can be accomplished outside the hospital setting.

TRANSITIONING BACK HOME

Most seniors who are discharged from an inpatient unit are not free from depressive symptoms. The goal of inpatient hospitalization is to stabilize, not cure. The rest of the recuperation process takes place outside the hospital, at home, with continued care from your health professional team, family, caregivers, and friends. This period from hospital to home is a very critical time. Remember, statistics show that risk for suicide is enormously high once a senior returns home. So, too, is relapse of depressive symptoms. To help strengthen your recovery, the discharge plan will include an order for immediate scheduled appointments with your outside healthcare professionals. Doing so creates what's called seamless care, the smooth and safe transition of a patient from the hospital to the home.[9] So make sure you get to your therapist and/or psychiatrist right away. Other things to be mindful of include not pushing yourself too much once you arrive back home. Give yourself more time to rest. If possible, ask others to help you with food shopping, household chores, banking, bills, and so forth. If you've returned to assisted living or a nursing home, allow yourself time to readjust. Let caregivers and nursing staff understand your need to slowly settle back into a routine. Whether you're at home or in a care facility, expect the helicoptering effect of friends and family hovering over you—watching your every movement—to make sure you're safe and sound. This is common and should diminish as you grow stronger.

I like creating a style of communication that helps you convey what you need and to balance it with the safety and concern loved ones have. A good starting point begins with:

- Deciding what ways you want others to check in on you (looking in on you with an unscheduled or a scheduled visit, actually finding you in whatever room you're in at any given time, phoning you, e-mailing you, etc.).
- Talking about how often you'd like others to check in on you (hourly, daily, weekly).
- Creating a number scale from 1 to 5 to measure distress. 1 = no stress; 2 = mild stress; 3 = moderate stress, 4 = extreme stress; 5 = I need to go to the hospital again. Using this scale as shorthand code helps you and others communicate without a long, drawn-out conversational exchange on your state of health.
- Talking about how often you'd like others to use this scale with you (hourly, daily, weekly).

- When it comes to talking about your hospitalization to others, find a way to disclose information that makes you feel comfortable. Remember, it's up to you to choose what to share about the situation because this is your personal narrative. Try not to deny your experience or avoid talking about it. Instead, understand that talking about your inpatient hospitalization is part of your recovery process.
- Finally, create an "action plan" for you and your loved ones to put into play should your depression worsen or self-destructive urges increase. Practice the sequence of who'd be called, where the contact information will be listed, where the location and address of the nearest hospital is, what to do if you become reluctant or resistant to going back to the hospital, etc.

I also want you to know that it's normal to feel worried about yourself and your ability to continue healing once you arrive home from your hospitalization. This is an expected reaction. In fact, I tend to worry if seniors aren't overwhelmed in some regard or don't display any levels of stress. Risk for suicide is heightened when a person demonstrates what's called a **flight into health**, where a sudden improvement appears. A senior's attitude that everything is good and easy may underlie an impending suicide plan. Another risk factor is that inpatient hospitalization can revitalize your physical energy and motivation before your depressed mood and hopefulness improve—so you may still be feeling despair and suicidal upon your return home, but now you've got the energy to carry out your plan. Talking about these issues helps you understand where you are along the range of these emotional reactions. And talking about how you're feeling and what you're thinking is encouraged—even if the content is unpleasant. One of the myths about suicide is the belief that talking openly about such things increases the likelihood of suicide. Research debunks this myth and states that talking about suicide actually reduces suicidality.[10]

Once you've settled back home, research says that getting back into a routine, especially one with a main focus on well-being, can reduce depression.[11] Here are some ideas for you to consider:

- *Daily routine*: Make sure to design what I like to call a "Goldilocks daily routine"—that is, not doing too much or too little. Give yourself enough things like self-care, chores, and socializing so the day feels "just right."

- *Look after yourself*: Make sure you choose healthy habits like eating well, keeping a set sleep schedule, and most of all, being kind and practicing self-compassion.
- *Set boundaries*: Setting limits for yourself and for others will stop you from becoming overwhelmed. Tension in your life raises levels of the stress hormones cortisol and adrenaline—and this leads to irritability, a weaker immune system, and other negative outcomes. Learning how to say "no," to ask for help, to delegate things, or to just give yourself some time out will increase the feel-good hormones dopamine and serotonin.
- *Identify your triggers*: Put a name to the things, people, thoughts, and experiences that make you feel vulnerable. By doing so, you'll learn to recognize the *whos*, *whats*, *whys*, and *whens* of your emotional and physical life—and will be ready to deal with them before they trigger you.
- *Label your support systems*: Identify your resources for support and encouragement by having friends, family, and therapist contact numbers readily available, soothing music ready to go, and calming activities on hand to bolster your well-being.
- *Get to your all your appointments*: In the weeks immediately following inpatient discharge, severely depressed seniors are at risk of "falling through the cracks"—so make sure you get to all your follow-up appointments and scheduled therapy sessions.[12] Research shows that not getting to appointments increases the likelihood of readmission.[13]
- *Believe in your recovery*: Studies show that when you believe in yourself and in your recovery, your healing occurs more swiftly.[14]

SUMMARY

Inpatient hospitalization is still a stigmatized and fearful proposal to many. While there are many aspects that can make you feel afraid and alone, the treatment provided can be lifesaving. Studies suggest that many seniors, and their loved ones, appreciate the hospital experience in retrospect.[15] I have found this to be quite true with patients and families who've received inpatient treatment for their depressive disorders. Though many felt abandoned, angry, or resistant to going to the hospital, hindsight offered a different perspective. Seniors I've worked with were able to reframe their inpatient experience, accepting the need for hospitalization because a deeper understanding of their illness was now known. Others used their inpatient experience as a stepping stone toward more formal care, as the following case study shows.

CASE STUDY: RUBY

I met Ruby for consultation when her self-described "cozy chaos" became too overwhelming for her to manage. She was part of the **sandwich generation**, working full-time while raising her four children in their late teens with her husband of 25 years, and caring for her elderly 87-year-old mother, Gloria. All of them lived together in a split ranch home, her mother living in the small downstairs area, while Ruby, her husband, and children occupied the upstairs section.

Ruby reported being a worrier and anxious as a child but learned to deal with things by keeping lists, being scheduled, and running a lot. Literally. She ran about ten miles a week to calm her nerves. When she married and began raising children, the fast-paced life kept her physically active, but the balancing act required to parent, run a house, maintain a marriage, and work continued to tax her anxiety levels. Ruby felt stressed but always managed. She moderated her agitated state by adding yoga to her workout regime when knee injuries began sidelining her running. In her 50s, Ruby had her mother move in after Gloria became a widow. At first, things went well, but over time, they became more difficult. Though discussions of assisted living were considered, they were never acted on because Gloria balked at the arrangement. Shortly after one such discussion, Ruby began having terrible panic attacks at work and at home.

Psychotherapy focused on helping Ruby learn how to balance her needs and the needs of her family in more healthy ways. We did this by setting boundaries—delegating, minimizing her people-pleasing ways. Her husband and children took to the changes well, but her demanding mother didn't. Gloria had medical issues and insisted that Ruby, and *only* Ruby, drive her to her appointments. Part of our work in sessions revolved around getting physical therapy and visiting nurse services in the home to reduce the stress on Ruby. Gloria, though, was uncooperative. She didn't like anyone coming into her part of the home. Using the senior bus to get her to outside physical therapy and to her internist was out of the question because she wasn't independently mobile, so that option was tossed. When it came to mental health, we also tried arranging home services, but again, Gloria refused to work with the arrangements. She did, however, agree to take antidepressant medication to alleviate some of her irritability and sadness—and did so regularly along with her other cardiac and blood pressure medications.

Ruby reported that her mother didn't do much outside of the home but kept a routine that included making her own breakfast, showering, watching television, making lunch, then reading a book until the family dinner was ready. Gloria had no social life because many of her friends and family had died. Even though the grandchildren were in close proximity, they led busy lives, often out at school or sporting events, or socializing with their own friends. As a result, Gloria relied heavily on her daughter, sometimes calling her at work several times a day to talk. After several weeks of working together, Ruby came into one particular session quite upset. Her face and cheeks were puffy and red, her eyes a watery mess.

"I have to get my mother into assisted living." She dabbed her tears with a tissue and continued. "I came home from work last night, found her in her chair still in her nightgown. And she was staring into space."

"Did she recognize you?" I asked.

"Yes, right away. But she looked terrible."

"What do you mean, *terrible*?"

"She hadn't showered or dressed for the day. I don't think she ate either . . . there weren't any dishes in the rack." Ruby patted her nose. "I don't know . . . she didn't look good."

"Has this ever happened before?"

"No, never." Ruby blinked hard.

"Did she have a fall? Was she sick? Anything like that?"

"No, nothing."

"Anything happen this past week?"

Ruby thought for a moment. "Her oldest friend died."

We both remained quiet, taking that news in.

"She didn't seem too bothered by it," Ruby said. "She hasn't seen Darlene . . . or talked to her in years."

"Well, maybe it really did."

Ruby lowered her head and pursed her lips. "Hmmm," she said thoughtfully.

"Talk to your mom about this and schedule an immediate appointment with her GP," I suggested.

And with that, we moved onto other issues in the session.

Ruby called later in the day to tell me she had taken her mother to the doctor, who thought Gloria was having a grief reaction to the news. He upped her Cymbalta and took blood and urine tests to make sure nothing else was going on. I praised Ruby for her attentiveness to her mother's health and told her I'd see her next week.

But just three days later, I got a frantic phone call from Ruby.

"My mother's staring off into space!" Ruby huffed heavily into the phone. "Debbie, she won't respond to me."

"Where is she, Ruby?"

"In her chair." Ruby began crying. "And, oh my god, she soiled herself too."

"Okay, Ruby," I said aloud. "Stay on the phone with me but call 911 on your cell. Is it nearby?"

"Yes."

I heard Ruby rummage for the phone and then dial the numbers.

"Get an ambulance there," I instructed. "Don't hang up on me though, okay?"

I waited as Ruby talked to the dispatcher.

"Anyone else in the house with you?" I piped in once I heard her hang up with the dispatcher.

"Ronnie and the girls."

"Okay, get your husband to put together a bag of clothes for your mom. Tell him to find her medical cards and her prescriptions."

"Okay," Ruby said in between short breaths.

"Listen. Your mom may be having a depressive episode. A really serious one, a psychotic depression. It's very possible with what you've told me that she could also be having some serious medical issue."

"Yeah, okay. Okay," Ruby said, panic stricken.

I heard Ruby find her husband and her daughters. The chaos began to increase as they all moved into action.

"Ruby. The ambulance is gonna take your mom to the nearest hospital. That will be St. Martin's. I'm gonna call ahead and see if I can get one of the psychiatrists on staff to be ready in the ER. Do I have your permission to do this? "

"Yes," Ruby said just before the ambulance arrived.

"Okay, I'm gonna hang up and do that now," I said to Ruby. "Remember, I'm just a phone call away."

Within minutes, I was on the phone with the emergency room triage nurse to let her know Ruby would be coming in with her mother and for the hospital to alert the on-call psychiatrist.

Ruby called me later that night and told me that her mother was being treated in the emergency room and that the psychiatrist had arrived about an hour after her admission. The medical team ordered tests to rule out a stroke, dementia, and other medical issues. Based on the history Ruby shared about her mother, the psychiatrist believed a psychotic depression was operating. Ruby said she'd call back after the tests came back.

Over the next few days, Ruby let me know that Gloria was, indeed, experiencing a psychotic depression and had been admitted to the adult inpatient unit at St. Martin's. It wasn't a psychogeriatric unit but a regular adult inpatient unit. Ruby reported the staff and healthcare professionals were very attentive and spot-on with their approaches. They helped Ruby and her family understand what Gloria was going through and had created a treatment plan, adding antipsychotic medication and a recommendation for ECT.

"How's your anxiety level?" I asked at our next session.

"Not that bad." Ruby sat back in her chair and dropped her shoulders. "It's kind of a relief to have my mom there. She needs more care than I can give her."

Ruby told me she had learned from the inpatient support program that older seniors slip into psychotic depressions more than younger adults. And it can happen from many kinds of trauma—an accident, a fall, an illness, even grief. We talked about how her mother's depression will need great care and how Ruby will need to structure herself emotionally and physically to deal with this. We also spoke about the trauma of getting Gloria to the hospital and what a great job Ruby did through it all.

"How long do they think she'll be inpatient?" I asked.

"They want her to have a series of ECTs. She's been there a week already. Maybe another week. Then she'll come home, I think."

"You and Ronnie were talking about assisted living for your mom before you started working with me. With her illness, that may not be an option anymore."

"Well, if she bounces back from inpatient, we'll see."

"It's more likely she'll need a skilled nursing home, unless you want to think about getting private home care . . . but I don't want to jump too far ahead. I'm sure her caseworker will look into things."

"Yeah, they already mentioned that to us."

"How are feeling about your mom being on the unit, Ruby?"

"Okay. It's scary sometimes. You know, there's people yelling or crying. And the families—how hard it is for us all." Ruby stopped a beat before she spoke again. "It's a temporary thing. But if it wasn't, I don't think I'd be so okay with it."

"How is your mom doing? Does she look more like herself?"

"She's got a long way to go. She keeps asking if Darlene—you know, her friend who just died—is coming to visit."

I tightened my lips. "Aw, that's rough."

Ruby agreed. She blinked back tears and said, "Getting old sucks."

"Yes. Sometimes it really does," I replied.

9

CONSCIOUS AGING WITH DEPRESSION IN LATER LIFE

If you think having depression in later life means the last chapter of your life will be limited, think again. Although there will be many seniors whose level of unipolar, bipolar, or vascular depression will impair their quality of life, there will many more who can recover. Any chronic illness comes with challenges, but what science says about living well in spite of having one is this simple word: *perspective*.

This is where the theory of **conscious aging** comes in. Yes, I know it sounds an awful lot like Gwyneth Paltrow's "conscious uncoupling"—but she's not just throwing trendy phrases around. She's actually highlighting the practice of self-transcendence that has been spiritually practiced for centuries and cultivated clinically by psychology for decades. Many psychosocial approaches have emerged over the years in addition to conscious uncoupling, like conscious childbirthing, conscious coupling, conscious dying, and this chapter's focus: conscious aging.

Conscious aging, also known as conscious eldering, conceptualizes the notion that the golden years should be a time for appreciating your earned wisdom as well as becoming more self-aware in a deeper, more profound way than was possible in earlier life.[1] Conscious aging grounds itself in the importance of awareness, acceptance, and personal evolution. While as seniors we can't control many circumstances that come our way (frailty, illness, cognitive decline, loss, etc.), we can control what we bring to the situation.[2] Before we start working on strengthening your consciousness muscle, let's get to the topic of aging and what it truly means.

WHAT IS AGING?

Aging is defined as a gradual, natural, continuous process of change that occurs in all living things, including plants, animals, and people. Aging is a process. It is *not* a disease. Aging does not need to be treated or to be fixed—despite all the commercials, print ads, and social messages that suggest otherwise. Aging is part of our genetic design and needs to be valued and understood as such.[3]

Perspective about aging differs in countries and cultures. For example, Asian countries like China, Korea, Japan, and Vietnam revere the elderly. The populations in these cultures follow the Confucian philosophy called **filial piety**, which is the expression of devotion and respect to elders. Mediterranean countries like Greece, Spain, and Italy care for their elders, living as multigenerational families under one roof. Hispanic and Latino cultures hold their elders in high esteem as well, and consider old age as a most positive and prolific time of life. Traditionally, Native American and Inuit people revere community and family, placing elders in significant roles and caring for them when they become aged. But many media-savvy countries like the United States, Canada, Australia, and the United Kingdom aren't very good about honoring age and accepting it in a positive light. As a result, depression in seniors tends to be higher in these countries and less so in parts of the world that revere their elders.

Also prominent in countries that don't embrace aging are negative beliefs about being old. This is called **ageism** and is a form of discrimination and prejudice. Most seniors live well into old age and have much to offer society. However, the general population that uses ageism marginalizes seniors, making them feel unwelcome and obsolete. The by-product of this skewed way of thinking is that many seniors believe this narrow view, deeming themselves as undesirable too. Another misinterpretation that comes with ageism is that being elderly reminds us that youth and beauty will fade, that illness and disability await us, that loneliness casts a long shadow, and that death is a certainty for everyone. But consider framing these observations in anti-ageism ways: Being elderly reminds us that there is beauty in a time-worn face, that grace can be found in frailty, that the spell of loneliness can be easily broken by human kindness, and that death makes life worth living.

You see, it's all about perspective.

DIFFERENT MEASURES OF AGING

So now you know that aging is valued differently around the world. But did you know you can be different ages at the same time? Well it's true. Comedian George Burns, who lived to be 100 years old, said, "You can't help getting older, but you don't have to get old"—and he is right. Age is measured in many different ways. One manner of measuring aging involves genetics, another uses the calendar, while others consider your state of mind or your abilities. So being "old" takes on an entirely different view using the following categories.

- *Biological age* refers to the arc and trajectory of the aging process in your body. Sometimes called *physiological age*, this measurement considers the interplay of your genetics and your chosen lifestyle as a means of preserving, worsening, or enhancing your body age.[4] So, if you're a man in your 70s who eats and sleeps well, exercises, socializes regularly, and has genetics that shield you from illness and disease, you may really have a biological age of 60. On the other hand, if you're a 65-year-old woman who smokes, is sedentary, lives alone, and has a genetic predisposition for high blood pressure and stroke, your biological age may be 75. Biological age is all about the interplay between your lifestyle and your genetics—what I like to call the "Two B Approach": your biology and biography.

    Biological age testing has been a fad in the past decade, with Dr. Michael Roizen and Dr. Keith Roach leading the pack with *Real-Age*, a scientifically based test that yields your body's true age.[5] Although these kinds of quizzes can be found in magazines, online, and on television shows, advances in aging research offer more precise ways to detect biological age. Specifically, a blood test that measures the length of *telomeres* (a genetic protein structure found on the tip of chromosomes) can indicate one's true lifespan. Studies have shown that size matters when it comes to telomeres—the longer the better.[6] For example, an 80-year-old woman with long telomeres indicates that she's aging slowly and is considered to have a young biological age—and therefore she has better health and longer to live than an 80-year-old woman with shorter telomeres.[7] Though testing for telomeres as a means of measuring age and health risks is in its early stages, it's expected to be a common lab practice by 2030, so our lexicon will have to make room for "How long are your telomeres?" as another way of asking "How old are you?"

- *Chronologic age* is the most popular way we measure age. All over the world, people mark the day of their birth—their birthday—as a way of recording their age. This is done by calendar time, using the earth's revolution around the sun to measure one full year. Chronological age is more clinically defined as the number of years lived[8] or as the distance marked in years and months or days from birth.[9] Measuring your age in this way is easy. You take the year of your birth, the month, and the day and subtract it from the current year, month, and day. Chronological age, however, is limited because it simply measures age solely on the passage of time.[10] It doesn't take into consideration anything else like the biological, physical, or behavioral aspects of a person. We know that aging is a universal phenomenon, but the truth is that we don't all age at the same rate. So while chronological age may similarly group, for example, 90-year-olds in the same classification, some of these **nonagenarians** (that's 90 year olds in Latin) may experience rapid declines while others do not. The bottom line here is that chronological age is static, meaning it's fixed. It's a singular statistic, a numerical value that holds little else than marking a moment in time. For example, at this exact moment as I sit and write this sentence, my chronological age is 54 years, 7 months, and 0 days. Nothing more. Nothing less.

- *Functional age* was first coined by Robert McFarland in 1943 as a substitute for chronological age assessment in the workforce.[11] Arguing that the proficiency of aged workers was more valuable than looking at their actual calendar age, McFarland devised a way to calculate a worker's true functional abilities with standardized checklists that rated age-related skills. In recent years, functional age has looked at the ability of seniors to perform everyday tasks that are clinically called "activities of daily living." Functional age is often measured for the elderly to evaluate if independent living can occur successfully. Testing looks to see how proficient a senior is at dressing, grooming, cooking, making the bed, getting the mail, shopping for food, and other self-care skills. Functional age can be obtained with self-report scales administered directly to seniors or from caregivers who can detail the skill level of their loved one. There are many who feel that functional age is a more meaningful way to gear the process of aging. It's all about what you can do and are still able to do, no matter what the timetable says about your age.

- *Psychological age* is a way of calculating age based on how you feel, think, and act.[12] Sometimes called *mental age* or *personal age*, this kind of aging has long been studied in the fields of longevity, psychology, and well-being.[13] Generally, psychological age looks at several dimensions, including self-esteem, perception, and memory, as well as how old a person feels, how old a person looks, how involved a person is when doing age-related activities, and how similar a person's interests are to members of an age group. What researchers have learned is that how old you feel is equally as important as how old you are. Tests that measure psychological age ask you to describe your self-experiences about life, love, thoughts, and feelings without factoring in chronological or biological age. The results scored by this way of measuring age resonate with the famous saying "young at heart" or "age ain't nothing but a number." Psychological age explains why a senior woman in her 60s, who has a mental age of 40, can pal around with younger people and feel great. Or why a man of 70, with a psychological age of 80, prefers hanging out at the senior table than with the younger hipsters at the bar. Psychological age also helps describe why large age difference in marriages work. It's likely that the chronologically older partner has a much younger mental age . . . and the chronologically younger spouse has an older psychological age. Simply said, the way this couple feels, thinks, and acts is more similar than their chronological age.

Take a moment now and think about your chronological age. Now consider calibrating it by using these different measures. Perhaps you'll find that you have many different age levels, and that this newfound appreciation will broaden your view of age—and just how old you really are.

LIFE STAGES

Another way of looking at aging is to understand Erik Erickson's **life cycle**,[14] which is illustrated for you in table 9.1. From birth on, we age and move through a series of psychological and social experiences that help us develop. Each of these "stages" embodies a fundamental need that, if left unresolved, leads to an unhealthy outcome—but if resolved, leads to life satisfaction.[15]

When we head into our senior years, we start to realize—more than ever—how finite life is. Our *golden years* are described in that way partly because we're in the sunset of our lives, where the golden hue of the sun begins to slowly fade into the horizon. Later life brims with the recognition that there isn't enough time remaining to right all of the wrongs in life, to get a do-over for your lost moments, or realize all your unfulfilled dreams.[16] Erickson's life cycle stage of Ego Integrity versus Despair reminds us that we all will face this issue. As with the other stages in life, if you successfully work through this stage, you'll find acceptance and fulfillment. If you fail to make peace with your life, you'll feel despair and regret.

How can a person with late-life depression navigate this stage of life? Facing old age and death are massive issues. Having a depressive disorder on top of that can make moving through this stage feel impossible, but there are ways to move through this. The key is to find meaning by using your inner knowledge and deepening your insight. Let's get into that now.

ATTAINING WELL-BEING

Many people misunderstand the word *well-being*. Typically, they believe that it means *to be well*. It's true that those actual words are right

Table 9.1. Erickson's Eight Stages of Psychosocial Development

Age	Stage	Healthy vs. Unhealthy Outcome
Infancy (Birth to 1 ½ years)	Trust vs. Mistrust	A baby will develop a sense of trust from caregivers who are nurturing, constant, and reliable. Unhealthy caregiving will lead to mistrust.
Early Childhood (2 to 3 years)	Autonomy vs. Shame/Doubt	This stage requires toddlers to develop a sense of independence. Success will lead to confidence and autonomy, failure will have the outcome of shame and doubt.
Preschool (3 to 5 years)	Initiative vs. Guilt	Preschoolers will learn to take control of their environment, with success leading to initiative—a sense of having purpose. Those who control too little or too much will feel a sense of guilt.
School Age (6 to 11 years)	Industry vs. Inferiority	Children at this stage must learn to cope with academic, peer, and cultural demands. Success leads to industry—a sense of competency—while failure will lead to feelings of inferiority.
Adolescence (12 to 18 years)	Identity vs. Role Confusion	The goal of this age is for teens to discover their personal likes and dislikes, which will lead to a strong sense of self and identity, while failure will lead to insecurity and role confusion.
Young Adulthood (19 to 40 years)	Intimacy vs. Isolation	Young adults will seek out others to bond and form intimate relationships. Success leads to intimacy, while failure results in isolation.

Age	Stage	Healthy vs. Unhealthy Outcome
Middle Adulthood (40 to 64 years)	Generativity vs. Stagnation	This stage is where adults consider leaving a legacy—be it family, social change, etc. Success leads to feelings of accomplishment and purpose, while failure results in feeling stuck or stagnant.
Maturity (65 years & older)	Ego Integrity vs. Despair	The goal of this stage is to review one's life. Success will lead to sense of fulfillment, while failure fills one with despair and regret.

in there . . . *well being*. The phrase, however, is actually an umbrella term for acceptance, happiness, and reaching one's optimal functioning.[17] Well-being is the experience of learning how to live as well as you can with all the good in your life but also by accepting all the bad and everything in-between too. Well-being is not an either-or experience but rather a way of learning how to live with things that are unchangeable, and finding ways to bring meaning to your life in spite of them. Being happy when you're happy is easy for us all. But learning how to accept and adjust to adversity—or make lemonade from the lemons— this is where **resilience** rewards you with well-being.

For some seniors, cognitive and physical decline are probabilities. For others, dementia or mental illness may present. Even for seniors who don't experience significant illness, they know that death is a certainty. So how do you find a sense of well-being with all of that, you ask? Well, the answer is . . . by facing it all. You see, the anxiety that surrounds the prospect of decline and death, clinically called *death anxiety*, can actually motivate you to search for meaning in your life. Research tells us that elderly adults who experience connection to others and a sense of belonging to something bigger than themselves have greater satisfaction with life.[18] Studies also report that seniors who hold more realistic views about aging live more meaningful lives.[19] The realization that the last chapter of life comes with significant endings can actually become a source for new personal discoveries and self-realization.[20] As psychologist Victor Frankl so wisely wrote, "Death is not the end but rather the beginning of the birth of meaning in human living."[21]

But living with late-life depression can make finding this well-being hard. This is where conscious aging can help.

CONSCIOUS AGING

Conscious aging is an offshoot of the 1987 model of *successful aging*, which was defined as an elderly person moving through the last chapter of life without disease and disability.[22] Given that we're living longer, the notion of successful aging is now obsolete because older age yields a greater risk of illness. Aging is a challenge, especially when one lives with depression, but it's also a time of great opportunity. The approach of conscious aging invites such possibility by encouraging you to find answers, significance, and enlightenment from within.

Consciousness is defined as a process that involves your acute awareness of the world around you and of yourself, including your inner thoughts, feelings, sensations, and identity. Consciousness essentially shapes your understanding of who you are, what the world is, and even influences how you feel about your late-life depression and well-being.[23] Making mindful changes to allow yourself to live with self-compassion because of your depression and be skilled at learning how to cope with the changes and impermanence of old age releases you from those very confinements. When you shift away from beliefs of self-limitation, fear, or anger about life, you can gently accept and, perhaps, find comfort in the process of aging.

What I've discovered living with depression and working with individuals with late-life depression is that the key to well-being is all about *adaptation*—the ability to adjust to challenging new experiences. Deepening your consciousness can lead to that, so let's go into detail about how to strengthen your consciousness. Figure 9.1 takes us through eight steps to get you there.[24]

1. *Attention*: The first and perhaps most essential ingredient to heightening consciousness is acute attention. This is done by turning your focus toward your senses, your thoughts, and your bodily feelings. This concentrated effort increases self-awareness and, by doing so, gives you the necessary pause to turn inward.[25] Conscious aging is all about taking this time of your life and using

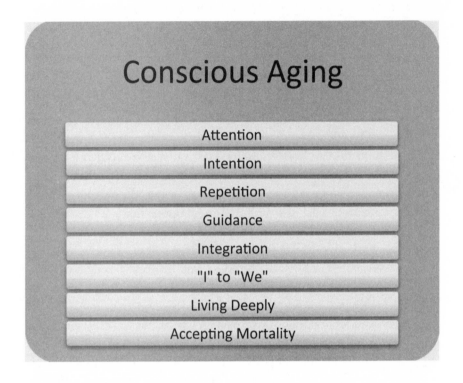

Figure 9.1. Conscious Aging. *Source:* **Marilyn Mandala Schlitz et al., "Conscious Aging and Worldview Transformation,"** *Journal of Transpersonal Psychology* **43 (2011).**

it to deepen its meaning. Let yourself get in the moment and then be in the moment. Listen to your breath. Sense your heartbeat. Feel the sun. See the beauty of nature. Feel the textures of this mind, body, and soul moment.

2. *Intention:* A second element of conscious aging involves your worldview and your perception of what's possible.[26] This is called intention. Understanding your intention will help you see what you're valuing. Is it healthy? Is it toxic? Do your beliefs lead to possibility or are they self-limiting? Ask yourself: What matters most in my life? What brings me meaning? What people, places, and things make me feel safe and loved? What purpose can I have now? What values are essential to my life? What can I live without? Where does my heart go when I let myself think freely? What can I let go of?

3. *Repetition*: The next step in developing deeper consciousness involves practicing your new insights so they become habit. This is certainly more challenging than it sounds, but you can do it. Learning to live with awareness, intention, compassion, and forgiveness leads to new ways of being—and even creates adaptive neural pathways in brain functioning.[27] Just like efforts to build up a new muscle groups require repeated exercise, so too does the process of conscious aging.[28] You'll practice by reminding yourself: This is a normal part of aging. It's okay that I'm not as strong as I used to be. There's grace in every one of my wrinkles. I have much to offer to others. It's good to let go of unfinished business.

4. *Guidance*: Finding sources of inspiration can help you maintain the approach of conscious aging.[29] Look for books, workshops, study groups, social networks, exercise classes, and other such activities that emphasize consciousness or mindfulness. Consider spiritual guidance, religion, or faith-based practices to help you deepen your insight. Even agnostic or atheist-based beliefs can offer guidance, comfort, and support that ground you in being in the moment.

5. *Integration*: Conscious aging is not a trendy fad to be sampled. It's a transformative way of living that requires you to integrate it into your everyday lifestyle. Once you've heightened your awareness and deepened your insight, it becomes easy to keep it going if you use its practices every day. Give yourself some quiet time each morning and ask yourself: How am I feeling today? When I become quiet, what do I truly hear? How can I make today great?

6. *Moving from "I" to "We"*: Conscious aging is not just a personal process of creating a sense of acceptance about life in your golden years. It's also about a shift beyond your own journey to one that goes beyond your own self. The process of moving from "I" to "we" invites you to find meaning not from within but from without—from your loved ones, your community, the world.[30] This is where you'll create your legacy. Here's where you'll ask: What can I be remembered for? How can I leave my mark? Who can I inspire? What can I offer others?

7. *Living Deeply*: All of the steps you've done to this point will bring you to a level of **self-actualization**, which is a peak experience

gained finding fulfillment and accepting oneself. Conscious aging techniques free you to heal, to forgive, to let go. Conscious aging also encompasses finding a balance of safety, security, love, belongingness, and self-esteem so you can live deeply, with meaning and wisdom.[31] This is the stage where you learn to be fully in experiences. Lingering in the entire moment, drinking it in so to speak, and accepting limitations so you can make the most of an experience, such as: It's hard for me to shake this depression, but I can appreciate how beautiful it is to be with my grandchildren today. I'm feeling so very tired, but I'm going to nap so I can be ready for the concert tonight. It's okay that my partner doesn't get my depression, what matters most is that I get it—and that I do what I need to live well with it.

8. *Accepting Mortality*: Contemplating death is a vital aspect of conscious aging. This doesn't mean that you have no fear of it. But by lifting the veil of denial of death and accepting your own mortality, you allow yourself to invest your focus, energy, and time to live as well as you can in spite of the inevitable.[32] Conscious aging reminds you that death means different things. Biologically, it is the permanent ending of all vital functions. But it can mean other spiritual, cultural, or psychological things to you personally. Remind yourself that everyone dies but not everyone lives, and that "life is not measured by the number of breaths we take but by the moments that take our breath away."

LATE-LIFE DEPRESSION AND ACCEPTANCE

Throughout the aging process, depression is not an expected outcome.

Let me write that again: Depression is *not* a part of getting older. This is yet another myth that surrounds old age. In truth, it is not normal for a person of any age to experience depression.

I learned long ago that my depression was a chronic illness and that for the rest of my life, I'd be working without a wand. There'd be no magic to relieve its scorching sadness, no enchantment to sway its corrosive power over my thinking, no tricks to erase its existence from my life.

I had to acknowledge it.

Accept it.

And learn to live with it by using evidence-based techniques.

Living with depression has left me suicidal, despondent, and woefully lost. But it has also taught me many other things. It has shown me that I'm strong and resilient, that I'm a survivor. Living with depression has made me more aware of what's truly difficult in life, like summoning every bit of your physical strength against the colossal weight of gravity just to merely get out of bed, or knowing how to sidestep the mines that set off self-destructive urges. But getting stuck in traffic—yeah, that's not a big deal. Listening to the latest gossip or scandal du jour? No thanks, I ain't interested. Wishing for some material luxury or pining for a lavish experience? Meh, give me simple comforts. Living with depression has also made me aware of what's truly wonderful in life: a child's laugh, the amazing colors I see in every twilight sky, hearing a well-crafted joke, how awesome it feels to drive through a series of green lights. Simple things. My perspective about life is very different because I almost lost mine to depression.

When you add the acceptance and insight that comes with conscious aging, you learn to view your depression as offering gains, in spite of the losses.[33] You learn to identify your regrets, sufferings, longings, and self-limiting beliefs so you can face old age with a deeper appreciation. The new reality of living with late-life depression and letting go of what you can and can't control becomes a form of transcendence—a life you define, not a life that depression defines.[34]

One of my favorite passages about aging is by Pulitzer Prize–winning writer Leland Stowe.[35] I share it with you and hope you'll find significance in his words whether you're someone who is living with depression or caring for a senior who lives with this disorder.

> If it doesn't take courage to grow old.
> What does it take?
> Faith in living,
> I believe, faith that its compensations will multiply with time. . . .
> It all adds up to this equation:
> Attitudes + Habits = Motivations;
> Motivations + Goals + Dreams = Character
> All cindered into solid bricks for the passageway into growing old.

SUMMARY

Outcome research over the past 50 years has shown the single largest contributor to finding life satisfaction as a senior is *you*.[36] This fact illustrates how important it is for you to find well-being in spite of having depression in later life. Although getting older is unavoidable, it can offer new ways of defining yourself. And when we talk about consciousness and transcendence, these phrases aren't some hippy-dippy, zany psychobabble trend. Deepening your awareness and acceptance is *the* definitive way to design a life in your golden years that's superlatively meaningful. Science says so. I say so. And so does the following case study.

CASE STUDY: DAWN

I began working with Dawn to address her late-life depression when she was almost 70 years old. Though she was formally diagnosed with depression in her senior years, both she and I agreed that she had most likely experienced a mild form of depression throughout her life. Dawn reported having many of the symptoms of dysthymic disorder (a chronic depression) as a young adult but never sought treatment. Only now, as she began to acknowledge how fast life had gone by, did she begin having trouble coping day to day.

Dawn was still happily married to her husband, Ben, and lived in the small harbor town cape house where they had raised two boys. Now that her boys were married with kids of their own, Dawn and Ben enjoyed visiting with their grandkids, watching them grow, even teaching them how to fish and kayak just as they had done with their sons. Dawn started having trouble sleeping, was tearful, and found herself thinking about death way too much around the time her last grandchild graduated high school. From there, she began having aches and pains in addition to her other depressive symptoms and was at the doctor for every little thing to make sure she wasn't dying. After falling into a puddle of tears during one appointment for severe stomach pains, her doctor referred Dawn to me. Dawn cried easily at our first session, saying how hard turning 70 was going to be. She knew it was a number she hoped she'd reach but was surprised at the breakneck speed it seemed to arrive. "It all went by too fast," she said, her eyes wide in disbelief.

"I know. It can feel like the blink of an eye," I said supporting her. "Was there ever a time you felt time was passing more slowly?"

"Not really. I was always busy. Got married right out of high school. Had kids. Worked." Again through a cascade of tears, she said, "Too fast. It's all done too fast."

Through psychotherapy, Dawn and I learned that she approached life with passion and enthusiasm, trying to make everything count. She'd put her heart into her relationships, her work, and her family, but keeping that momentum would often burn her out. The effort she put into others wasn't often returned, so she also felt unappreciated. Dawn would then immerse herself in new moments trying to recapture that lost recognition. Our sessions helped Dawn see that there was a wash-rinse-repeat cycle to this way of living for her that intensified her depressive symptoms. Furthermore, Dawn learned that she was in the throes of death anxiety, overwhelmed by the notion of her life's end. Our work uncovered a series of losses that had happened in a short amount of time when she was small that intensified this subject: the death of her beloved dog by a car accident, her grandmother's death, and her brother heading off to college.

"My head was spinning," she said, recalling that time. "So much was going on then."

"Yes, a lot to lose. Too much, too fast, and too soon," I replied, hoping she'd bridge this piece of her history to her current experience of life going by so fast.

Dawn's eyes brightened. "Oh my god, just like now."

Great, she grabbed it, I said to myself. Then I said aloud, "Tell me what you mean by that."

"Everything felt so big then. I didn't have time to deal with it because . . . because the next loss came. I just couldn't deal with it."

"It went by all too fast," I said again.

As psychotherapy often does, we were able to weave all these story strands together to help her make sense of things. I believed that while Dawn was emotionally invested in life, she wasn't always really experiencing it. I suggested the idea of using conscious aging techniques and more mindful kinds of practices. Dawn ran with it. First, I taught Dawn about focused breathing and guided imagery, and we practiced it in sessions.

"I want you to close your eyes and relax. Take a slow, deep, long breath though your nose and hold it down in the bottom of your belly. Focus on the sound of the air going in and how your body lifts ever so slightly as you take it in. Hold it for five seconds and then slowly release it through your mouth, pursing your lips. Feel the air flow out, how soft it feels. The sound it makes. Do this again, but you're going to think of something beautiful. Imagine the sparkling blue ocean rising up to the shore as you breathe in. And the waves of water flowing back out as you exhale."

"This is so great," she said. "I feel such peace."

"Wonderful!" I replied. "Let's do it again, but for a longer period of time."

I suggested that Dawn learn to do this and other mindful techniques on her own, outside of sessions, and also recommended a senior yoga class that a friend of mine was teaching. She signed up and even managed to get Ben to go with her to a few classes. Dawn poured herself into her consciousness training, buying books, watching videos, and seeking workshops, dragging her not-so-sold-on-this-idea husband when she could. I reminded Dawn to be careful not to be in "doing" mode and to remain in a "being" mode.

Dawn worked long and hard to deepen her awareness and calm herself into a mindful stillness. Our session work expanded too, coming to terms with the regrets she had in life, like not having more children, not taking more time from work to vacation as a family, arguments that ended in falling-outs that seemed trivial now. Dawn also talked about death and what it meant to her. We profoundly explored the religious, cultural, and spiritual aspects about death, afterlife, reincarnation, and other cosmic issues. Dawn also considered the possibility that death was an ending of everything for her, and how much that frightened her to think of that. Raising her awareness about this subject brought forth a serious contradiction that Dawn hadn't shared with anyone. She revealed that her sadness and grief revolved around her Catholic upbringing and the rejection of its religious tenets: the pull of science (there is no God) versus religion (there is a God) making it hard for her to accept death. She couldn't find balance with her belief system. It left her living in an either-or state.

Death is nothing.

Or.

Death is life everlasting.

"I just can't imagine never seeing the ones I love again." Dawn shook her head, fighting the thought. "Time just goes by so fast. I want to slow everything down."

"Mmhmm. I get that. But . . . we can't slow time. We can linger more fully in it though."

"I know," Dawn huffed. "I'm trying." She lowered her head. "Then I think, I really shouldn't worry because, you know, I've been taught to believe in the afterlife. That I'll be there with my parents, my grandparents. And my children and grandchildren—and their children—will be there one day with me and Ben too."

"I can see the comfort you get from that. Is there any comfort from your belief that death is a final ending?"

Dawn's eyes widened almost twice their normal size. "What comfort comes from *that*?"

"Well, I'm trying to help you define some way to accept the scientific thoughts you believe about death. Some people believe death is an ending as we know it, but that it's part of a bigger circle. We become part of the earth, part of the universe. Others believe that death isn't a vast nothingness, it just *is what it is*. A ceasing. Some find comfort in those ideas."

"Let's not even go there today, Deb."

We both laugh. The subject begins to feel too big for the session.

"You know, it's okay not to know what happens when we die. You don't have to pick a team or have your flag planted." I leaned forward a bit in my chair. "You don't have to have a definitive belief."

Dawn bobbed her head in agreement.

"Making memories, living life—that's what our work's about. Extraordinary things happen when we become fully present with others and at peace with life, even if the peace comes from not knowing," I said.

My work with Dawn continues as I write this book. She celebrated her 70th birthday with a long getaway weekend with her family, booking a guest house at a retreat that overlooked the Hudson River. She cried many times during that time, though she said "for *good* reasons."

"I just loved every minute of it," she said, showing me photos.

"Was it easy or hard to slow time down?"

"Actually, I tried not to think about that," Dawn replied. "Just wanted to hike the trails with my grandkids, listen to their stories, spend time connecting."

"Sounds super."

"It really was." Dawn thumbed through some photos and handed me one. "I thought you'd get a kick out of this," she said. It was a picture of Ben in a tai chi class.

I smiled, "He's got good form!"

"He tells me he doesn't really like doing this, but he went by himself that morning before breakfast. Asked a passerby to take the shot. Isn't that a riot?"

I agreed it was funny. And so were the stories Dawn would come to share in our work together. She was definitely learning to live deeply and live well.

10

LONG-TERM CARE AND LATE-LIFE DEPRESSION

For those of you struggling with late-life depression and other medical issues, the conversation of long-term care may have to be discussed. I know this is a tough subject to consider, but waiting until you need long-term care is a recipe for disaster. Emergency caretaking without being informed leads to impulsive choices and poor financial decisions. It is better to educate yourself about the different kinds of long-term care and how they may best suit your needs.

When it comes to long-term care, there are several kinds. There's home health care, assisted living, skilled nursing homes, and community care retirement communities. I'm going to detail the structure of each one along with tips on how to create well-being in each environment.

HOME HEALTH CARE

Many seniors with depression consider living at home with supportive services the most desirable. If your late-life depression is well managed, this can be a terrific option. In this form of long-term care, you reside in your own home or apartment with care from private-pay aides or insurance-funded licensed therapists and nurses. The costs for home health care that involves medically necessary treatments like physical therapy, occupational therapy, speech therapy, psychotherapy, or skilled nursing is generally picked up by your health insurance, Medicare, and Medicaid. Other kinds of assistance—like cleaning, cooking, or shopping—are provided by private companies. You can arrange for care every day, several times a week, or weekly depending on your needs. According to a 2013 Centers for Disease Control (CDC) report, there over 12,000 home health care agencies listed as active.[1]

A great place to find home health care services begins with contacting your local county or town senior agencies or local hospital. Word-of-mouth referrals are also a good reference and can help you narrow your search. Medicare offers medical, social, and long-term care services for seniors with depression who want to remain in their homes and to maintain their quality of life under the Program of All-Inclusive Care for the Elderly (PACE), so check out their website for more information.

Also, if you're lucky enough to live in a county that has free senior services, you may be able to get transportation to and from medical offices and shopping centers, Meals on Wheels, adult day care, visitor programs, and other such helpful resources.

Once you've selected a few sources to interview, the Administration on Aging[2] recommends asking the following questions:

- How long has the agency been serving this community?
- Does the agency have any printed brochures describing the services it offers and how much they cost? If so, get one.
- Is the agency an approved Medicare provider?
- Is the quality of care certified by a national accrediting body such as the Joint Commission for the Accreditation of Healthcare Organizations?
- Does the agency have a current license to practice in the state you live?
- Does the agency offer seniors a "Patients' Bill of Rights" that describes the rights and responsibilities of both the agency and the senior being cared for?
- Does the agency write a plan of care for the patient (with input from the patient, his or her doctor, and family) and update the plan as necessary?
- How closely do supervisors oversee care to ensure quality?

- Are agency staff members available around the clock, seven days a week, if necessary?
- Does the agency have a nursing supervisor on call 24/7 for emergencies?
- How does the agency ensure patient confidentiality?
- How are agency caregivers hired and trained?
- What is the procedure for resolving problems when they occur, and who can I call with questions or complaints?
- Is there a sliding fee schedule based on ability to pay? Is financial assistance available to pay for services?
- Will the agency provide a list of references for its caregivers?
- Who does the agency call if the home health care worker cannot come when scheduled?
- What type of employee screening is done?

When securing home care services, chemistry is going to be as important as skill level. You'll want to feel comfortable with the providers in your home, so arrange for a meet-and-greet before signing any contracts. Make a list of questions and detail your own special needs to go over during your trial visit. And don't be shy to request another service provider if you don't feel confident. You'll also want to look into your private healthcare insurance to see if there are any allowances for medically necessary care. If so, you'll want to use certified aides or nurses as opposed to noncertified ones—otherwise, you won't be able to seek reimbursement for your private-pay treatments.

Case in point, when my 84-year-old mother went into a state of depression after a serious operation, our family contacted a local agency for a certified aide to come in nightly at her home. Medicare covered her daytime visiting nurse, but at night she needed more assistance. We went that route, instead of choosing a noncertified aide, because her secondary insurance allowed for "medically necessary" treatment in the home. Though we paid out of pocket for the services, we kept receipts in the hope that once the crisis ended, we'd look into reimbursement from the insurance company. After several months, my mother improved and became more independent. We stopped the home care services at night and were able to gain a moderate percentage back from the insurance company.

ASSISTED LIVING

If you can't live independently with caregiver assistance or more medically provided services, assisted living is an option. It's important to know that this type of long-term care is not supported by Medicare, Medicaid, or health insurance. It is a private-pay arrangement. Costs vary yearly, ranging from $25,000 on up depending on your service contract. Many seniors use their Social Security to help offset costs, sell their home and use the proceeds, or use long-term care policies to pay for coverage. Family members can also pay for assisted living with payment plans. If medically necessary services are needed, Medicare/private insurance will take care of such treatments, but you need to inquire further in your state about this. According to a 2013 CDC survey, over 22,000 assisted living facilities are listed as active.

Residents of assisted living communities have their own room or apartment on the grounds of the facility. Staff members are generally not licensed nurses or certified aides. Furthermore, assisted living centers are not regulated like skilled nursing homes, so there can be some leeway regarding standards of care.[3] Services provided include assistance with daily living skills like showering, dressing, grooming, and eating, as well as light cleaning, laundry, and medication monitoring. Consider asking the following questions recommended by the Administration on Aging[4] if you're thinking about assisted living:

- How long has this assisted living facility been operating?
- What will your future needs be if your health changes, and how will the facility meet those needs?
- How close is the assisted living facility to family and friends?
- How close are shopping centers or other businesses nearby? Are they within walking distance?
- Does the facility provide a written statement of their philosophy of care?
- What kinds of social, recreational, and spiritual activities are offered?
- What kind of training does the staff receive and how frequently are they updated with new practices?
- What kind of security is there in the facility?
- What kind of transportation services are offered for residents?

- What kind of emergency services are available?
- Where can you review the state's licensing report on this facility?
- Have there been complaints with the Better Business Bureau or Health Department?

I frequently advise seniors with a mild or moderate depression who have no other serious health issues to consider assisted living if they can afford it. It provides a great sense of autonomy and independence. However, if you have more serious health issues along with depression, assisted living may not be an appropriate setting. A more inclusive long-care facility may be more fitting.

SKILLED NURSING HOMES

Higher levels of care may be necessary for seniors who have severe late-life depression and/or other health issues. This is where a skilled nursing home, sometimes called a **skilled nursing facility**, is needed. Skilled nursing homes are different than nursing homes, and it's vital to understand the difference. A skilled nursing home is a licensed facility, regulated by the state and federal government, and participates regularly in unannounced visits from the local health departments. On the other hand, nursing homes may have certified professional healthcare workers on staff like nurses and doctors, but they are not covered by Medicare or Medicaid because they are not certified and not regulated by state or federal agencies. Nursing homes are more often run by charitable or religious organizations, and don't provide the full spectrum of care that a skilled nursing facility does. The bottom line here is to learn which type of nursing home is available in your area for you or your loved one—and understand how funding and payment occur. According to a 2013 CDC report, more than 15,700 skilled nursing homes were listed as active.[5]

Skilled nursing homes have changed in appearance over the past 20 years. Gone are the hospital-like dreary settings and smells. Long-term care facilities that have skilled nursing are more like a community, with green spaces, aquariums, and warm décor. Bedrooms for residents are semiprivate, having two queen-size beds, armoires and dressers, a telephone, and a television, as well as a private bathroom. Private rooms are also available but for a higher cost. Each bedroom has a window and easy access to the common areas throughout the facility. Residents are encouraged to make their room their home by decorating it, bringing in blankets or duvets (sheets are changed by the staff daily), and other personal items. There are many services offered in skilled nursing homes in addition to medical care—like social, recreational, holistic, and faith-based activities. Most skilled nursing homes have a salon in house as well. The goal in living in this facility is to provide residents with the comforts of home as well as the needed medical care and supervision required for well-being.

While some seniors with late-life depression may find comfort entering long-term care in a nursing home because they're no longer a burden to loved ones, most will likely feel a variety of negative feelings: loss, grief, anger, abandonment, and resentfulness, just to name a few.[6] This is understandable given the loss of privacy, limits on independence, and decreased autonomy that come with these new living arrangements. Remember from previous chapters in this book, transitions are hard on depressed seniors, and significant care needs to be taken when you or a loved one takes up residence.[7] Some skilled nursing homes have transitional programs that allow for extra support if you require hospitalization, rehabilitation, or a return to your own home. Long-term care living in this kind of setting also presses heavily on family members, who often feel sorrow about their loved one living there. Studies show that caregivers who are offered support when their loved one enters a skilled nursing home experience less grief than family members who were not offered such intervention.[8]

There are some negatives about skilled nursing homes that I'd like to highlight. A 2011 report by the Department of Health and Human Services' inspector general found that one third of the residents in skilled nursing facilities suffered an adverse event or other harm. These events were deemed preventable, resulting from staff training errors.[9] Another disconcerting statistic is that these facilities are not always "elderly" based. Figures show that over 125,000 nonelderly adults with serious mental illness were living in skilled nursing homes in 2008.[10] Research has cited another concern when it comes to depression in later life and living in skilled nursing homes. It shows that not only is depression common in the elderly population living there but also that it's not always treated successfully.[11] Studies point to four different kinds of depression that occur most often—major depressive disorder, dysthymic disorder, minor depression, and depression—as a result of the medical condition Alzheimer's.[12] Residents are not often screened for depression—or, for that matter, rescreened after an intervention has begun—so if you choose to live in this structured setting, you're going to need to be proactive about having such assessments done.

I know that reading about all these negatives is upsetting, but the truth also gives you the power to be preemptive about the care and treatment you or a loved one with late-life depression receives. When you have to consider skilled nursing homes as way of managing depression in later life, these are the questions to ask.

- Is this long-term care facility a skilled or general nursing home?
- How long has this facility been operating?
- Is this facility Medicare and Medicaid certified?
- How many beds are in this facility?
- How many residents live here now?
- What is the age population of the residents here? How many are elderly?
- What is the nursing staff per resident ratio?
- What are the nursing staff hours per day?
- What is the staff ratio per resident at night?
- How many full-time doctors or nurse practitioners are on staff each day and night?
- How are prescriptions monitored and prescribed?
- Is there a full-time psychologist or social worker on staff each day?
- How do I request further medical assessments for myself or my loved one?
- Who will be the case manager for me or for my loved one?
- What is the ratio of residents per case manager?
- What other healthcare professionals are available (dentists, ophthalmologists, speech language therapists, physical or occupational therapy, podiatrists, neurologists, etc.)?
- What staff training and continuing education is mandatory in this facility?
- What kinds of background checks are done for healthcare workers and staff?
- What is the procedure if I need to report elder abuse?

- What kinds of social, recreational, holistic, grooming, and spiritual services are offered?
- Does this facility have private and/or semiprivate rooms?
- Does every bedroom have a window?
- Does every bed have a private bathroom, private television, and private phone?
- What nutritional programs are offered? Are snacks available throughout the day?
- Can family and/or friends visit any time of day?
- What kind of security is there in the facility?
- What kind of emergency services are available?
- Where can I review the state's report on this facility?
- Has this facility garnered any awards, distinctions, or honors?

Of all the long-term care settings, skilled nursing home recommendations are accompanied by sadness, guilt, and regret for all involved. It is never a choice that one wants but rather is a choice that one needs. If you or a loved one living with depression is crossing this bridge, make sure to visit as many facilities as possible. Educate yourself, talk to other families and residents, and map out a guide to include the best quality of life possible given your physical, mental, and emotional needs.

CONTINUING CARE RETIREMENT COMMUNITIES

Continuing care retirement communities (CCRCs) are self-contained communities that offer various kinds of long-term care for seniors. There are over 22,000 continuing care retirement communities in the United States, some operating for profit, other nonprofit.[13] The grounds are all inclusive, including an area of single-family homes or apartments for seniors (called independent living units) who can live independently, assisted living units for those who require more support, a skilled nursing home facility, and respite and hospice care.[14] This long-term care guarantees housing for the rest of your life, calling the approach "aging in place"—making the promise of offering seniors a continuum of care by tailoring their living arrangements as their needs change. Roughly half of continuing care retirement communities are faith based, with the others working under a university, private health system, or military umbrella. According to the American Association of Retired Persons, a CCRC is an expensive long-term option, with entry fees ranging from $10,000 up and include a monthly fee in the thousands. Fees will depend on the kind of contracted care you seek. Another important issue is that seniors must move into the CCRC when they can live independently. Not all continued care retirement communities are accredited or regulated. However, medically necessary treatments will be covered by your health insurance, Medicare, or Medicaid policies.

According to the U.S. Government Accountability Office, movement to the higher levels of care in a continued care retirement community may only be temporary to restore the health of the senior.[15] This means if you're in the skilled nursing home because you're in a hypomanic bipolar state, you'll return to your assisted living unit once you're stabilized. If you're having a serious major depressive episode and need more medical monitoring, you may be moved to assisted living until you recover, and then you'll move back to your independent living unit.

If, however, a change in care level is meant to be permanent, decisions by case managers will be made. Some CCRCs have specific standards they use to assess this treatment change, while others have very ambiguous policies. Some research has shown the tiered approach to living in a CCRC with vague rules for status changes leaves seniors feeling disempowered, socially disengaged, and fatalistic about their life.[16] We've learned from research that successful transition for a senior to a retirement community happens when development of attachment to their space and the formation of strong social ties occurs.[17] So, if you're considering a CCRC to manage your late-life depression, make sure the facility has specific standards for such decision making.

Other questions to ask include the following:

- How long has this CCRC been in business?
- Are you a profit or nonprofit facility?
- Is this facility accredited?
- Is this facility regulated by the state?
- Are independent units rented or owned?
- How many assisted living units are there?
- How many beds are available in the skilled nursing home?

- What happens if the assisted living units or nursing home beds are full when I need them?
- What is the staff-to-resident ratio in *each* living setting?
- How are living arrangement transfers determined?
- How close is the nearest hospital?
- Is there security 24/7 on the grounds?
- Are independent living units pet friendly?
- What kind of emergency care is available in *each* living setting?
- What amenities do you offer (gym, pool, theater, salon)?
- Is there transportation to and from each of the communities on the grounds?
- What other health professionals are available on the grounds (dentists, ophthalmologists, speech language therapists, physical or occupational therapy, podiatrists, etc.)?
- What kinds of background checks are done for healthcare workers and staff?
- What refund policies do you have?

Continued care retirement communities offer a broad range of services. When you're thinking about how to live with late-life depression in your elderly years, you need to consider your own physical, mental, and spiritual needs, calculate your finances, and explore living accommodations. Perhaps most important is the fact that treatment of your unipolar, bipolar, or vascular depression needs to be at the forefront of your life plan. Long-term care facilities are notoriously bad at identifying, treating, and maintaining recovery for seniors with mood disorders. Be proactive yourself, or if you're a family member of a senior with depression know that this will require a full-on commitment.

ADVANCED DIRECTIVES

Even though you're done reading the difficult portion of this chapter on long-term care, I'm sorry to write that I have another complex issue to address with you. It's about making sure you create—in advance—a plan of your healthcare wishes should you fall into a serious or terminal medical crisis. Legally speaking, these are called **advanced directives**.

Advanced care directives began in 1967 when human rights activist lawyer Luis Kutner created the first living will to help secure the rights of seriously ill people who wanted to control decisions about their own medical care.[18] It took a very long time for advanced directives to become part of the state and federal legislature, but in 1992, all 50 states, as well as the District of Columbia, passed legislation to legalize advance directives.

Advanced directives come in three forms: *psychiatric directives* (how you wish your psychiatric treatment to occur if you're in a mental health crisis), *medical directives* (which detail the kinds of medical interventions you choose or refuse in a crisis), and *legal directives* (which detail how you assign power of attorney or wish your possessions to be distributed).

When it comes to taking care of these important health directives, few think about it. And even fewer actually complete the paperwork. Studies show that only 20 percent of the aging population with chronic illnesses complete advanced directives.[19] The good news, though, is that studies show that making advance directives promotes autonomy, dignity, reassurance, and empowerment for seniors.[20]

I recommend seniors with late-life depression to consider these arrangements as soon as they reach a state of recovery or remission. There are several reasons why. First, you want to be in a good state of mind so these directives can remain sound and legally binding.[21] In legalese, this is called testamentary capacity . Second, by planning ahead and talking about your healthcare wishes, you ensure that your loved one won't be left with feelings of doubt or guilt because you've created these instructions with care and thought. They won't second guess or think you want or don't want a specific action. They'll know because you've detailed this information. Finally, you, yourself, will feel empowerment and peace of mind because you've taken action to outline what you choose and refuse.

Psychiatric Advanced Directives

Psychiatric advance directives (PADs) are legal documents signed by you to indicate your specific instructions or preferences regarding future mental health treatment.[22] Psychiatric advance directives can be used to plan for the possibility that a senior with late-life depression may lose capacity to give or withhold informed consent to treatment during acute episodes of depression. Your PAD can be used for emergencies like hospitalization but also can be a resource in long-term care treatment. There are two kinds of psychiatric advanced directions, Instructive PADs and Proxy PADs.[23]

- *Instructive PADs* are documents in which you, the senior, write instructions about the kind of mental health treatment you want to experience in a psychiatric crisis. You can choose or refuse certain kinds of medications, hospitalization, use of restraints, use of seclusion, ECT, or other treatments.
- *Proxy PADs* are documents in which you, the senior, name a healthcare proxy to make treatment decisions if you're unable to do so. You need to communicate your thoughts and wishes to this trusted individual by making an Instructive PAD.

The National Resource Center of Psychiatric Directives offers step-by-step guides to create these psychiatric advance directives. Also, the National Alliance on Mental Health provides support and guidance on this subject. It's important to know that you don't need an attorney to set up these directives. What's required is your writing of instructions, assignment of a proxy, and an adult to authorize the document as a witness or via a notary public. When using a psychiatric PAD, let your loved ones know where it's located (make it an accessible place) and also share your psychiatric PAD with your mental health team too (so your wishes can be further supported). Currently, 46 states allow you to complete a legal advance document for your future mental health treatment.[24]

Medical Advanced Directives

Medical advanced directives (MADs) are instructions that outline how you want your medical treatment to occur should you be incapacitated in any way. No attorney is needed for these documents and you can find standardized forms online. For example, Care.org has downloadable PDF forms for each of the 50 states in the United States, with tips and instructions. Generally speaking, there are three steps to completing an

MAD. Step 1 is assigning a healthcare proxy, step 2 is creating a living will, and step 3 is having it witnessed or notarized.

- *Healthcare Proxy* is a document where you assign a loved one, partner, or friend to be your health "agent"—the person who will make decisions about life-sustaining treatment if you're incapacitated. Your health agent can provide not only medical decisions that are detailed in your living will but also ones that may not be covered in your advanced directives. Your healthcare agent will also have the right to enforce your healthcare wishes in court, if necessary, to hire and fire doctors or medical staff, have access to your medical records, and have visitation rights. Your healthcare agent will be able to make decisions both in a medical crisis *and* also in end-of-life decisions for you. Creating a healthcare proxy ensures that your wishes for medical treatment are honored and respected whether you are in a hospital, long-term care facility, hospice, or at home.
- *Living Will* is a detailed list or summary about your specific wishes about healthcare in the event you are incapacitated. In your living will, you write down whether you wish to receive CPR, intubation, hydration or artificial nutrition, dialysis, donate your organs, and other such issues.
- *Witnessing Provisions* is the last step in creating a medical advanced directive. Based on your state's requirements, you'll either need an adult 18 years or older to witness your documents or a notary public.

Your medical advanced directives go into effect when you sign them in the presence of appropriate witnesses. They remain in effect throughout your life unless you change or revoke them. The hope is that you'll never need to rely on them, but should a doctor determine you're unable to give informed consent because you're in a medical crisis, your healthcare proxy and living will offer dignity and a sense of control.

Legal Advanced Directives

I think it's just as vital to have all your ducks in a row when it comes to finances and personal possessions as it is to have your healthcare wishes structured. The last of these directives is for legal and financial issues. Again, you don't need a lawyer to create these legal advanced directives (LADs) but, of course, feel free to seek one should you want a more professional opinion. My husband is an attorney and says that while many people come in to ask him to draw up wills, powers of attorney, and other such matters, he's also had clients come in with standardized legal forms that were obtained online that were useful and legally binding. There are many different kinds of legal directives you can choose, but I think these two are the most important.

- *Durable Power of Attorney* is an advanced directive that legally allows you to assign an "agent" or what is sometimes called the "attorney-in-fact" to make financial and legal decisions for you should you become incapacitated. You don't need a lawyer to draw up this document but will need witnesses or a notary public, depending on your state. A durable power of attorney can be written so that the transfer of responsibilities occurs immediately—or you can instruct that the power of attorney goes into effect when you become incapacitated. Up until that point, you can continue to make decisions for yourself. The durable power of attorney is an important tool because if your depression worsens or you become incapacitated by a severe episode, the attorney-in-fact can maintain your financial affairs until you recover—without any need for court involvement. That way, your needs and your family's needs continue to be provided for, and the risk of financial loss is reduced. If a durable power of attorney is not set up, your partner or family friends cannot pay bills, access Medicaid or Medicare planning, or make legal or financial decisions without being appointed as a legal guardian by a court.
- *Last Will and Testament*, sometimes shortened to just *Last Will*, is a set of instructions that details how your personal possessions (known as *property* or *estate*) will be distributed upon your death. You appoint a person who will execute your wishes for your beneficiaries. As a senior, you'll likely have a legacy to leave your family and friends, be it personal items, money, or more. Having a last will eases the pain and confusion that comes with dealing with your property after you're gone. If you die without a valid last will, your personal property will be distributed by a court-appointed

administrator according to a predetermined state law formula. Furthermore, without a last will, you can't give your estate to nonrelatives, so if you don't have next of kin, your property will go to the state.

There are other kinds of legal advanced directives that you can look into, such as trusts or estate and financial planning, but it's best to seek out professional advice from an attorney who specializes in elder law.

SUMMARY

Living with late-life depression requires seniors to think about—and act on—a variety of difficult issues. When you're in good health (meaning that your depression is in recovery or remission), talk with your loved ones and healthcare team about how you'd like to be cared for should the need for long-term placement occur. Investigating home care, assisted living, skilled nursing homes, or continued care retirement communities before you need them allows for thoughtful decision making. Along similar lines, planning ahead by completing advanced directives for psychiatric healthcare, medical healthcare, and legal support gives your family and friends a way to manage your personal issues without needing the court system to get involved. The advanced directives I've outlined in this chapter offer you empowerment and peace of mind, and can be simply done by downloading forms, talking with your family and health team, and setting them up for future use. Remember, studies show that taking care of these kinds of matters fosters a sense of confidence for your loved ones, health practitioners, and yourself.[25]

CASE NOTES: REUBEN AND MARTA

Reuben and Marta, both in their mid-70s, were referred by their elder lawyer, Barbara Smith, for consultation. During one of their legal meetings together, Marta became overwhelmed, breaking down in tears. Reuben, too, was emotional. Given that they were creating legal documents, the attorney felt it was best for Marta and Reuben to address these psychological issues before continuing forward with estate planning.

Our initial session was spent getting to know Reuben, a retired surgeon, and Marta, a retired nurse, and their life together. Both talked openly about their early life and how their careers were, at first, a big priority in the marriage. When they wanted to have children, it didn't happen so easily. Several miscarriages and stillbirths left them heartbroken.

"We considered adopting but never went further with things," Reuben said, looking at Marta.

"We have many nieces and nephews, and adored taking care of them when we could." Marta offered a thin smile. "We just became very busy working at the hospital—and never really looked back."

Marta began to cry. Reuben laced his fingers within hers as he did too.

"The loss of not having a child is enormous, I see."

"A big emptiness, yes." Marta's tears spilled over.

"And meeting to draw up wills really opened the wound," Reuben offered, plucking a few tissues from the box. He gave one to Marta and dried his eyes with the other.

Marta and Reuben wanted to come to terms this, as well as with dealing with getting older. Because they had no children, they wanted to set up long-term care so other family members and friends wouldn't have to be burdened with the responsibility. They spoke about feeling afraid of losing one another, the fear of being alone, and what that would mean for each of them. More so than anything else was the loss of not having children or creating a legacy in that regard.

"I can sense your heartache," I said.

"We didn't realize how hard it'd be until we were in the office with Barbara," Reuben said.

"Truth is, I think we've both been functionally depressed for years," Marta said. "Just sad enough to feel the pain but not strong enough to move beyond it."

I agreed. So many people live with symptoms of depression not knowing that it's there. It shadows their life in imperceptible ways, so much that they become unaware of its existence. But when depression finally bursts through the surface, it becomes unimaginable that it ever *didn't* exist—because the intimate edges are so suddenly recognizable.

Together, we decided that psychotherapy would help them deal with the feelings of loss, as well as the anxiety about making these arrangements. Once things stabilized, they'd resume working with Barbara and their estate planning.

In the weeks that passed, Reuben and Marta poured out their feelings of despair and loneliness of not having been parents not only to me but to one another as well. For years on end, they had never broached this subject, each wanting to protect the other from feelings of inadequacy, pain, and loss. We also discussed the topics of illness and disability and how they'd move through needing short- and long-term care. We addressed many other difficult subjects like funeral services, burial wishes, and even discussions about marrying someone else if either one of them was ever single again. What started out as a goal of healing pain from long ago flourished into a journey of self-discovery and self-awareness for Marta and Reuben, and it fortified their bond as a couple too.

"I know it's more expensive, but I'd feel better if you're in a retirement care community. If I'm not in the picture, that is," Reuben said to Marta.

"Same here," Marta replied.

"I want you to have everything you need not to feel alone," Reuben said. "And it'd be a good way to make sure we don't have to ask family to get too involved."

Marta nodded her head in agreement.

"How about advanced directives? I'm sure you have medical ones, right?" I asked.

"Oh yes," Marta said. "Both being in a hospital made us very aware of what's needed. We have a living will and health proxies. Set that up a long time ago."

"When it comes to a last will or estate planning, what are you guys thinking?" I asked.

"We were talking with Barbara about the risks and benefits of certain kinds of trusts, of gifting our nieces and nephews each year now as opposed to making them beneficiaries later, and other estate planning issues," Reuben said.

"I got very upset thinking about all that," Marta said. "It was important to give these things to the kids, but it brought such feelings of loss. Such sadness about what is and what never was."

I leaned forward in my chair. "How does it feel today to think about these things?"

"Still such a loss, but it seems easier to talk about it," Marta said tearfully.

Out of the corner of my eye, I saw Reuben quietly moving his head up and down.

"Well, let's outline things in more detail here and explore the feelings you have about them. Then you can head back to Barbara and take care of your arrangements. How does that sound?"

Marta and Reuben agreed. We continued working for a few more weeks. I thought it was important for them to create a legacy more personal than the one of leaving behind money to family members. I introduced the idea of creating a scholarship or charity that would help their parental feelings of loss. Marta and Reuben found meaning in this idea and explored many different avenues. Shortly thereafter, they met with Barbara and created an estate plan that satisfied their legal, financial, and most importantly, their emotional needs. We met one last time as a check-in to see how things had been going.

"So, how are you guys feeling?" I asked.

Marta and Reuben looked at each other. "I think we're good," Reuben said, tapping her hand.

I looked more directly at Marta, raising my eyebrows, inviting a response.

"Yes, we're good," she smiled.

"You're satisfied with what you and Barbara set up?"

"Very much," Reuben stated.

"Gives us great peace of mind now," Marta said.

"That's terrific to hear," I replied. "What did you end up doing with the charity idea?"

"We arranged for a donation to the Compassionate Friends in our will," Marta said.

"Who are they?" I asked, unsure of the name.

"A national organization that offers support to parents who've lost a child," she continued.

"Hmm . . . sounds like a great plan," I replied, sensing the choice was a meaningful fit for them. "So, what's next for you guys?"

Marta and Reuben turned toward each other, locked in a gaze of connection but comfortable uncertainty.

"I don't know . . . travel a little?" Marta offered.

Reuben curled his lips. "I'd like that. But none of those tours again. I want to go somewhere and be able to go where we want, when we want."

Sometimes sessions create a kind of poetry that seamlessly floats like ether in the air. Much of Marta and Reuben's work was about accepting limits and taking control in the name of finding freedom. I grabbed Reuben's phrase and wove it into a sentence I knew they'd instinctually appreciate.

"I wish you that now and always," I said.

I like to think of Marta and Reuben living their golden years with a better sense of their life's accomplishments and losses since our work together. I like to imagine their plans for healthcare, be it together or apart, short term or long term, offering them peace of mind; that preparations for their estate and personal belongings has given them comfort; and that while they may not have had the chance to be parents to a child themselves, they can feel the meaningful impact of their caregiving to their family, friends, and cherished loved ones.

11

15 LATE-LIFE DEPRESSION MYTHS EVERYONE SHOULD KNOW

What are myths?

Why do they hold such power over public opinion?

And how do they get started in the first place?

Myths are fabricated stories that attempt to define the existence of things that frighten or confuse us. Myths have been around since the dawn of civilization and are most notably linked to the Ancient Greeks for describing issues like thunder, fire, dreams, or death. Since these couldn't be described or fully understood, the Ancient Greeks explained their existence as a result of the supernatural powers of specific gods and goddesses. These tales, of course, were never based in science but were instead rationalized stories that offered comfort to the masses.

Fast-forward several thousand years, and you'll find that myths still have a stronghold on humanity despite the fact that science debunks them. And if you thought myths only exist in cultures and societies that are primitive or underdeveloped, you'd be wrong. English professor and myth aficionado Dr. Jan Brunvand writes that myths aren't just found there but also gain traction in highly industrialized and well-educated cultures. [1]

SOCIAL CONTAGION

One of the reasons myths persist is the psychological phenomenon called **social contagion**. Just like you can catch a cold, you can also catch a myth—but instead of a pathogen seeping into your body system, it's a social message that penetrates. Social contagion follows a unique pattern. It begins with the expression of a piece of information, the power of its belief, the reach of its trajectory, its perpetual flow, and its staying power.[2] So, one day when someone said "Twinkies have an infinite shelf life," that got passed along from person to person like a child's game of telephone. Slowly yet intensely, the message of the Twinkie's glorious status as an immortal snack spread here, there, and beyond. It became a socially contagious piece of information. And despite science telling us that Twinkies are edible for just about a month and then they go stale, the urban legend lives on. Why? Because the social message of the Twinkie's infinity status has Velcroed itself into our culture's psyche. And no amount of science seems to be able to debunk this myth. It lingers until someone comes along and bursts the Twinkie bubble.

Some myths carry little impact, like the myth that shaving your hair makes it grow in thicker. Science reveals that it doesn't, but because the razor slices the tip of the hair shaft in such a way that it *appears* thicker, many people shun the evidence.[3] How about the myth that cracking your knuckles will cause arthritis? It won't, so crack away if you must.[4] Or that Napoleon Bonaparte was really short. Well, he wasn't. He was almost five feet seven inches tall, which is very tall for a Frenchman at that time.[5] Then there are myths that become damaging and dangerous, particularly ones that are based on race, gender, sexual orientation, and even health. These social beliefs minimize people instead of acknowledging diversity, genetics, and human uniqueness. The hazard of these types of myths is how they evolve into rigid stereotypes that discriminate.

HOW MYTHS LEAD TO STIGMA

Derived from the Ancient Greeks, stigma was the primitive practice of burning or cutting a part of the body of an objectionable person as a means to identify them to the rest of the society. The bearer of this "mark" was to be avoided, rejected, and snubbed in public. Children and adults who were stigmatized were assigned to the most undesirable category in the community. Though modern use of the word *stigma* no longer involves physical markings, a person with mental illness carries an indelible mark of shame nonetheless.

To understand stigma, you have to learn about the history of mental illness and its treatments. Long ago, children and adults afflicted with depression, euphoria, or unusual behaviors were believed to be possessed or evil. As the primitive beliefs of mysticism, mythology, and demonology were prominent at that time, interventions for mental issues were cruel and barbaric. Remedies included blistering, bloodletting, and the drilling of holes in the skull to exorcise evil spirits. Some approaches were more direct in their deadliness, with hanging, burning, and drowning frequently being used to "treat" mental illness.[6] Although many of those ancient myths have faded away, others evolved into more contemporary ones, with people believing those with mental illness in the twenty-first century are violent, menacing, deviant, and unpredictable. Myths about mental illnesses are embedded in our culture by misrepresentations in news stories, movies, television, and other media outlets. The fallout from these stigmatizing beliefs causes many who live with depression to feel "tagged and labeled and set apart." According to the World Health Organization, people with mental illness are one of the most stigmatized populations in the world.

SENIORS AND STIGMA

According to Dr. Patrick Corrigan, professor of psychiatry at the Illinois Institute of Technology and expert on stigma research, there are three kinds of stigma that seniors need to be aware of.[7] They are:

- *Public stigma*—how the general public, healthcare providers, professionals, politicians, and others in the public eye exhibit negative stereotypes about seniors with late-life depression
- *Self-stigma*—how you, yourself, negatively use myths and stereotypes about depression in your own life

- *Institutional stigma*—how assumptions about seniors with depression are translated into public policy and funding decisions that discriminate against people with mental illness

When it comes to late-life depression, it's vital for you as a senior to measure if any or all of these stigma subtypes touch your life. For example, how do your loved ones treat you? And how do they treat your late-life depression? Is it with respect and dignity? What about friends and relatives? Are your healthcare professionals *professional*? Or are they dismissive?

Research shows that much of the public, even health professionals, don't readily understand depression in later lifer. Often medical professionals believe that a depressed senior's physical health problems are not real but a sign of depression.[8] This is clinically called **diagnostic overshadowing**, and it leads them to misattribute real health issues to an already preexisting mental disorder.[9] I actually call this *lazy medicine* and get very angry when it happens to me or to patients I'm working with. And when you live with late-life depression, this will happen a lot.

How you monitor your own thoughts and beliefs about living with depression in later life taps your self-identity. If you measure your value as a person beyond the limitations of your depression, that means you have a healthy self-regard. So, that's great! But if you judge your worth by some of the myths that surround mental illness, you're going to struggle with self-stigma—and clearly, that's bad. Some studies show that seniors who deny the neurobiological origins of their depression in later life and blame themselves for being weak, lazy, or not being strong enough to fight depressive symptoms experience a poor quality of life.[10] Other research reveals how older adults feel guilt, shame, inferiority, and a wish to keep their illness concealed when self-stigma occurs.[11] Probably the worst part about believing stigmatizing myths of mental illness is that science reports it's the greatest obstacle preventing seniors from getting treatment.[12] And if you don't get treatment, you don't get better. I hope you can see the paradox in that conundrum.

It won't be hard to miss when stigma presents itself in the agencies, institutions, or hospitals in your life. If you're living in a skilled nursing home, assisted living, or other long-term facility, ask yourself if the staff is tending to your needs appropriately. If you have to go to the emergency room, evaluate if the hospital staff is taking immediate care of you. Research shows that institutional stigma can leave seniors with late-life depression feeling neglected or lonely because they're avoided by staff.[13] Often, this comes from ignorant attitudes from employees toward people with mental illness, diagnostic overshadowing, or just plain discrimination.

The key to offsetting all of these stigmatizing issues is to be proactive. If you're a senior with late-life depression, demand that your family, friends, and healthcare professionals give you ample time to convey how you're feeling and what you're thinking. Stigma is a relational process, which means that you can debunk the myths that persist when you take charge and educate others.[14] Counter any negative self-beliefs about depression with positive, realistic ones. If can't do this on your own, consider working with a therapist to help you frame a more healthy outlook. If you're in a short- or long-term facility, or are a caregiver to a senior with depression, reach out to a supervisor to convey your concerns. The goal here is to not be passive if stigma finds its way into your life. Studies encourage patient empowerment, noting that it's both a process and an outcome.[15] The process begins when you use education as an intervention to those who have ill-formed views of mental illness. The empowerment then results in an outcome because change has happened.

LATE-LIFE DEPRESSION MYTHS

One of the best ways to help debunk stigma is to familiarize yourself with the myths of late-life depression. Once you understand the truths about depression and its treatment, you can challenge the stigma that comes your way, be it public stigma, self-stigma, or institutional stigma.

- *Myth*: Depression is a normal part of aging.
- *Fact*: Depression is not a normal part of aging. This is the biggest myth of aging and mental health. Depression at any age is not a normal part of the aging process.

- *Myth* : Being confused is a normal part of aging.

- *Fact* : This is another myth about aging, that it's common for seniors to be confused. Confusion in not a normal part of aging. Chronic disorientation, bewilderment, and mix-ups are hallmark signs of bipolar depression in later life or dementia.

- *Myth*: Falling is normal with advanced age.
- *Fact*: Falls should never be considered a normal part of aging. A change in functional status, including falls, can often be sign of depression in later life.

- *Myth*: Getting senile is a normal part of aging.
- *Fact*: The word *senile* actually means "to age or grow old," but it's a word that's often used to mean *dementia*. Dementia is not a normal part of aging. It is a neurobiological disease that affects the brain and nervous system. About 5 percent of seniors will experience dementia; depression often accompanies this illness.

- *Myth*: Depression isn't a real medical problem.
- *Fact*: Depression is a very real illness that affects the emotional, social, behavioral, and physical health of a person. There are genetic and biological factors that predispose a person for depression, but life experiences also influence its development. Rates of depression are higher than cancer, diabetes, heart disease, and AIDS combined.

- *Myth*: Depression in later life is not a major health concern.
- *Fact*: The World Health Organization has stated that depression is a global crisis. Late-life depression occurs in about 15 percent of seniors ages 65 and older. In the United States alone, approximately seven million older adults meet the criteria for a depressive disorder. However, over 90 percent of seniors who suffer from depression are not being diagnosed or treated for this illness, which places them at enormous risk. Depression in the most common mental health problem for the elderly.

- *Myth*: Depression will go away on its own.
- *Fact*: A serious mental illness cannot be willed away or brushed aside with a change in attitude. Ignoring the problem doesn't give it the slip either. Depression is a serious but treatable illness, with success rates of upward of 80 percent for those who seek intervention.

- *Myth*: Depression affects seniors in the same way it does younger people.
- *Fact*: Depression is not a one-size-fits-all illness. It actually presents differently in seniors than in younger individuals. Studies suggest seniors experience more structural changes in the brain and vascular issues, and aren't aware that they're feeling depressed. Seniors report more somatic complaints and irritability than sadness or despair as do younger people.

- *Myth*: My doctor says I'm not depressed and not to worry.
- *False*: Although upward of 80 percent of mental health treatment for elderly patients is delivered in the primary care setting, depression is frequently overlooked or misdiagnosed. If you're on the receiving end of a don't worry response from your physician and have any doubts at all, seek a second opinion from a mental health specialist.

- *Myth*: Major depression is more prevalent in seniors than subclinical depression.
- *Fact*: Statistics report that subclinical depression, sometimes called minor depression, is more common than major depression in seniors. Research also reports that seniors who have subclinical symptoms are not identified early and therefore not treated appropriately. Untreated subclinical depression leads to more serious late-life depressive disorders.

- *Myth*: Antidepressants don't work in the elderly.
- *Fact*: Antidepressants are useful in the treatment depression in later life. However, many seniors take more than one medication to treat other medical issues, so to minimize adverse reactions, it's wise to consider genetic testing. The clinical term for this is called *age interaction antidepressant response*.

- *Myth*: Talking about depression makes things worse.
- *Fact*: Research debunks this myth. Talking about depression reduces symptoms. This is the whole goal of talk therapy, to talk about your experiences, thoughts, feelings, and concerns. Although many seniors refrain from talking openly about things, encouragement with warm, supportive communication can be significantly meaningful.

- *Myth*: The risk of suicide in the elderly is greatly exaggerated.
- *Fact*: The population for the greatest risk of suicide is the elderly, with men age 85 and older having the highest death by suicide rate of all. Though suicide rates for seniors vary across countries and cultures, data shows that 85–90 percent of persons aged 65 years and over who died by suicide had a diagnosable depressive disorder. Also, two thirds of seniors who died by suicide were seen by primary care physicians *within a month* of their deaths, and up to half were treated by a primary care doctor *within one week* of their deaths. These statistics make the need for identifying at-risk seniors urgently crucial.

- *Myth*: When a senior I love is depressed and refuses treatment, there's nothing I can do.
- *Fact*: If you're a caregiver or family member of a senior who has late-onset depression and refuses to go to talk therapy or take medication, there are things you can do. You can seek therapy with a trained mental health specialist to learn how to help your loved one. You'll discover strategies to use to minimize depressive symptoms and also find ways to cope with frustrations and worries you have. In a crisis situation, you can drive your loved one to the nearest hospital emergency room, or contact family, friends, or the local police for assistance. In short, there is always something you can do.

- *Myth*: Seriously depressed people cannot lead productive lives.
- *Fact*: Seniors with depression can live full, productive lives. In fact, many high-profile people—even now in their golden years—are doing incredible things despite living with depression. Consider rocker Bruce Springsteen, actor Harrison Ford, talk show host and writer Dick Cavett, comedian Stephen Fry, entrepreneur Richard Branson, and tennis legend Cliff Richey. How about the greatness of President Abraham Lincoln, choreographer Alvin Ailey, Prime Minister Winston Churchill, film director Akira Kurosawa, and artist Michelangelo? It's considered that depression helped all of these significant icons achieve greatness. Appendix F lists over 400 names of famous people who've had depression and have led very productive lives. Let them help you feel less alone—and let this list inspire you.

CASE STUDY: BIG AND LITTLE JOE

"Look! It says here Buzz Aldrin walked on the moon," Joe shouted. "*On the moon*, Dr. Debbie."

"I know. Isn't that totally cool?"

Joe grabbed a crayon from the metal tin. "Uh huh," he said, scribbling with it on the fresh piece of paper.

I'd been working with Joe, seven and a half years old, since he began refusing to go to school in the mornings. The stressor that set his anxiety into motion was his grandmother's death, which was unexpected and quite sudden. Joe lived with his single mother, Bonnie, in the house she grew up in, living alongside Joe's grandmother, Dianne, and grandfather Joe in a sectioned-off part of the house.

"When was he depressed, Dr. Debbie?"

"Hmm. I'm not sure. Let's read more about it," I said to Joe, scrolling down the website.

Joe had been recovering moderately well from the loss of his grandmother, returning to school within a few weeks after treatment began with me. Our work involved helping him grieve, learning to discharge his anxiety in more productive ways, to fight the urges to hide or avoid when he became nervous, and to understand the sad feelings that seemed really big some days.

"Says here that after he came back from space, he started having trouble in his life. He was depressed, started drinking, and things kinda fell apart in his family," I looked at Joe for a moment. He snapped his head up because I stopped talking.

"C'mon, what else does it say?" he said, wagging the crayon.

"Aldrin was able to get well by going to psychotherapy and says facing adversity challenged but changed him for the better." I fanned my fingers toward Joe. "You know what *adversity* means, buddy?"

"Nope."

"It means difficult. To have a tough time."

"Hmmph. I know what *that's* like," Joe replied.

For the last several sessions, Joe had been very worried about his grandfather. Big Joe, as I called him, brought Little Joe, my patient, to our sessions, so I saw him every week. And though we had been working for several months now, Big Joe was looking worse for the wear. Grief is experienced differently from person to person, but instead of seeing Big Joe moving forward with the mourning process, I had seen him decline. He had lost weight. His grooming was negligible. His eyes were vacant and expressionless.

I told myself that maybe Big Joe was just beginning his grieving because until now he was holding things together for his daughter and grandson. Since Bonnie and Joe were doing better, it was okay for him to let go. So perhaps that was why he was in such bad shape. Concerned, I asked Big Joe to join Little Joe and me for sessions, but he bristled at the invite. I even asked if he might want to talk to someone on his own, but that wasn't going to fly either. Big Joe was not the kind of man who would go to talk therapy. It just wasn't his thing. So I reached out to Bonnie, who said her father believed things would get better on their own and not to bother him with talking further about issues. I winced that Big Joe believed such myths, but Bonnie said she'd be extra attentive and would let me know if anything further developed.

Over the last few sessions, Little Joe had shifted his focus in therapy from being worried about death, monsters, and not wanting to be alone to trying to cheer up his grandfather. It seemed that Joe was healing his own self, and his grandfather too, by showing him that it was okay to be sad and it was okay to talk about it—something Little Joe learned in his work with me.

First it started with asking if he could take some of the picture books on death and loss home with him, so he could read them to his grandfather.

Of course, I obliged.

Then, he wanted to make a memory lantern for his grandfather.

We made two of them, which Big Joe liked very much.

Now, Joe was drawing pictures of some of his grandfather's favorite heroes—to help Grandpa feel strong.

The first was Babe Ruth because "Grandpa wished he could be a baseball player as good as The Babe." Joe asked if we could go online and draw a picture of Babe Ruth. And so we did.

And it made his grandfather happy.

The next session Joe came in wanting to draw an astronaut, because "Grandpa always wished he could be one."

"Does he have a favorite astronaut?" I asked.

"Hmmm. I don't think so," Joe said, scratching his head. "Can we look some up?"

I talked about a few famous astronauts, and Joe liked the story of Buzz Aldrin best. I think what sold him on things was that his name was Buzz.

"Like Buzz Lightyear!" Joe giggled.

That Buzz Aldrin struggled with depression also sealed the deal. I made sure to share that little tidbit as we explored astronauts. I thought it would be a meaningful story for both Big and Little Joe. Sometimes therapists stack the deck, it's true, but I did it for a good reason: I wanted Little and Big Joe to learn that sadness crosses people's lives in big and small ways, and that even heroes can find themselves in the darkness of enormously sad feelings.

"Can you help me make a helmet?" Joe asked. "I want to draw one on Buzz."

"Sure thing," I said, and traced a light pencil line around for Joe to follow.

"Grandpa is gonna love this."

"Why do you say that?" I asked.

"Well, because I made it. And he loves everything I make."

I tried not to laugh at Joe's response, but it was too big to contain. I chuckled softly. "Why else might he love it?" I asked.

Joe stuck out his lower lip. "'Cuz . . . it's an astronaut," he finally said.

I thought Joe might run with the backstory of Buzz Aldrin moving through depression because Joe had asked about it earlier in the session, but he didn't go there. Instead, he colored his picture, adding details of rocket ships, stars, and of course the moon. All the while he did that, he talked about how irritated he's been with the longer bus ride to and from school since a new bus driver came into the mix. We worked on that issue until the session's end.

As I opened the office door, Joe bolted out of the room and delivered his masterpiece to Big Joe. I watched as his grandfather came to life, smiling broadly, ooh-ing and ah-ing over the picture.

"It's Buzz Aldrin, Grandpa. He walked on *the moon!*"

"This sure is a great. We'll put in on the fridge for Mommy to see," his grandfather replied.

"We had a great session, Big Joe," I said before closing my office door. "I'll see you guys next week, okay?"

"See you next week, Dr. Debbie," Joe said, taking his grandfather's hand.

And as they traveled down the stairs, I heard Joe tell his grandfather about Buzz Aldrin and "how he was a fighter pilot before he became an astronaut . . . and he has his footprint on the moon . . . on the moon, Grandpa! . . . and that he got depressed, but then he got better because he talked to someone like Dr. Debbie . . . and that it's okay to be sad, because you're not alone being sad because so many people get sad . . . and . . ."

I couldn't hear any more because Big and Little Joe were now out the door and walking down the driveway to their car.

But in case Joe needs some more heroes to inspire his grandfather, I have hundreds waiting.

Appendix A

DEPRESSION SCREENING QUESTIONNAIRE

Name: _____ Date: _____

Depression Screening Questionnaire	YES	NO
1. Have you felt irritable or easily agitated?		
2. Are you having trouble sleeping? Or sleeping too much?		
3. Do you feel unsatisfied with your life?		
4. Do you feel tired and zapped of energy?		
5. Do you have aches and pains that don't go away with rest?		
6. Have you lost interest in activities you once enjoyed?		
7. Do you have trouble concentrating or finishing tasks?		
8. Are you feeling hopeless for your future?		
9. Do you often feel helpless?		
10. Is this stage of life challenging for you?		

If you answered "Yes" to five or more questions, you need to be screened for late-life depression.

Appendix B

CURRENT MEDICATIONS AND SUPPLEMENTS

Name: _____ Date of Birth: _____ Age: _____

Current Medications and Supplements

Medication / Supplement Name	Dosage	Prescribing Doctor	Side Effects

Previous Medications and Supplements

Medication / Supplement Name	Dosage	Prescribing Doctor	Side Effects

Appendix C

HEALTHCARE TEAM CONTACT INFORMATION

Name: _____ Date of Birth: _____ Age: _____

Healthcare Team Contact Information

Professional's Name	Specialty	Address	Phone / Fax

Other Vital Information

Name	Address	Phone / Fax
Pharmacy:		
Emergency Contact:		

Appendix D

SIDE EFFECTS CHECKLISTS FOR SENIORS

Medication Side Effect Checklist for Seniors

Name: _____   Date: _____

Name of medication _____   Dosage _____

PHYSICAL SIDE EFFECTS

Please circle the level of each behavior you have experienced

Bites nails	none	mild	moderate	severe
Dizziness	none	mild	moderate	severe
Drowsiness	none	mild	moderate	severe
Fatigue	none	mild	moderate	severe
Frequent falls	none	mild	moderate	severe
Forgetfulness	none	mild	moderate	severe
Gastrointestinal distress	none	mild	moderate	severe
Headaches	none	mild	moderate	severe
Incontinence	none	mild	moderate	severe
Nightmares	none	mild	moderate	severe
No appetite	none	mild	moderate	severe
Pacing /restless	none	mild	moderate	severe
Physically aggressive	none	mild	moderate	severe
Radiating pain	none	mild	moderate	severe
Self-destructive	none	mild	moderate	severe
Sleeping long hours	none	mild	moderate	severe
Speech difficulties	none	mild	moderate	severe
Stupor	none	mild	moderate	severe
Tearful	none	mild	moderate	severe
Trouble sleeping	none	mild	moderate	severe
Unbalanced gait	none	mild	moderate	severe

Medication Side Effect Checklist for Seniors

Name: _____ Date: _____

Name of medication _____ Dosage _____

EMOTIONAL SIDE EFFECTS

Please circle the level of each behavior you have experienced

Anxiety	none	mild	moderate	severe
Apathy	none	mild	moderate	severe
Argumentative	none	mild	moderate	severe
Disconnected from friends/family	none	mild	moderate	severe
Depressed mood	none	mild	moderate	severe
Easily frustrated	none	mild	moderate	severe
Fearful	none	mild	moderate	severe
Feelings of helplessness	none	mild	moderate	severe
Highly emotional	none	mild	moderate	severe
Inability to cry	none	mild	moderate	severe
Insomnia	none	mild	moderate	severe
Loss of motivation	none	mild	moderate	severe
Loss of self-care	none	mild	moderate	severe
Mood swings	none	mild	moderate	severe
Not able to recognize familiar people, places	none	mild	moderate	severe
Tangential, incoherent speech	none	mild	moderate	severe
Thoughts of self-harm or death	none	mild	moderate	severe
Unable to sense reality	none	mild	moderate	severe
Worried, obsessive	none	mild	moderate	severe

Appendix E

RESOURCES

AGING RESOURCES

Administration on Aging
Website: www.aoa.gov

Aging Children of Aging Parents
Website:
www.acapcommunity.org

Aging in Place
Website: www.aginginplace.com

Aging with Dignity
Website:
www.agingwithdignity.org

Alzheimer's Association
Website: www.alz.org

American Association for Retired
People
Website: www.aarp.org

American Association of People
with Disabilities
Website: www.aapd.com

American Health Assistance
Foundation
Website: www.ahaf.org

Center for Positive Aging
Website:
www.centerforpositiveaging.org

National Resource Center on
LCBT Aging
Website: www.lgbtagingcenter.org

ASSISTED LIVING

Assisted Living Federation of
America
Website: www.alfa.org

LeadingAge
Website: www.leadingage.org

National Center for Assisted
Living
Website: www.ahcancal.org/ncal/
Pages/index.aspx

CAREGIVER RESOURCES

Eldercare Locator
Website: www.eldercare.gov

Family Caregiver Alliance
Website: www.caregiver.org

National Alliance for Caregiving
Website: www.caregiving.org

National Clearing House for
Longterm Care
Website: www.longtermcare.gov

National Family Caregivers
Association
Website: www.nfcacares.org

Veteran Affairs Caregiver Support
Website: www.caregiver.va.gov

Visiting Nurse Associations of
America
Website: www.vnaa.org

Well Spouse
Website: www.wellspouse.org

CONSCIOUS AGING RESOURCES

Center for Conscious Eldering
Website:
www.centerforconsciouseldering.
com

Conscious Aging
Website:
www.consciousageing.org

Conscious Aging Alliance
Website:
www.consciousagingalliance.org

Institute of NOETIC Sciences
Website: www.noetic.org

DEPRESSION AND BIPOLAR RESOURCES

Black Dog Institute
Website:
www.blackdoginstitute.org.au

Brain and Behavior Research
Foundation
Website: www.bbrfoundation.org

Depression Alliance
Website:
www.depressionalliance.org

Depression and Bipolar Support
Alliance
Website: www.dbsalliance.org

Families for Depression
Awareness

Website: www.familyaware.org

International Bipolar Foundation
Website: www.ibpf.org

Mood Disorder Association of
British Columbia

Website: www.mdac.net

Mood Disorders Society of
Canada

Website:
www.mooddisorderscanada.ca

National Alliance on Mental
Illness

Website: www.nami.org

National Network of Depression
Centers

Website: www.nndc.org

FINANCIAL & LEGAL RESOURCES

Social Security Administration

Website: www.ssa.gov

Equifax Credit Bureau

Website: http://www.equifax.com

Internal Revenue Service
Website: www.irs.gov

Low Income Home Energy
Assistance

Website: www.liheap.ncat.org/
referral.htm

National Senior Citizens Law
Center

Website: www.nsclc.org

Scam Awareness Alliance
Website: www.scamawareness.org

GERIATRIC ORGANIZATIONS

American Geriatrics Society
Website:
www.americangeriatrics.org

American Association for
Geriatric Psychiatry
Website: www.aagponline.org

Geriatric Mental Health
Foundation

Website: www.gmhfonline.org

International Psychogeriatric
Association

Website: www.ipa-online.org

HEALTHCARE RESOURCES

American Health Care Association
Website: www.ahcancal.org

Assisted Living Federation of
America

Website: www.alfa.org

Centers for Medicare & Medicaid
Services
Website: www.medicare.gov/
caregivers

HealthFinder.Gov
Website: www.healthfinder.gov/
findservices

Medicaid

www.medicaid.gov

Medicare

Website: www.medicare.gov

Medicare Rights Center
Website: www.medicarerights.org

National Council on the Aging Benefits
Website: www.benefitscheckup.org

National Hospice and Palliative Care
Website: www.nhpco.org

National Institute on Senior Health
Website: www.nihseniorhealth.gov

Veterans Administration Benefits
Website: www.va.gov

Visiting Nurse Centers of America
Website: www.vnaa.org

HOME CARE SERVICES

The National Association for Home Care
Website: www.nahc.org

Visiting Nurse Associations of America
Website: www.vnaa.org

MENTAL HEALTH ASSOCIATIONS

Mental Health America
Website: www.mentalhealthamerica.net

Mind
Website: www.mind.org.uk

National Alliance on Mental Illness
Website: www.nami.org

National Mental Health Association
Website: www.nmha.org

National Institute on Mental Health
Website: www.nimhinfo@nih.gov

R U Okay?
Website: www.ruok.org.au

SANE
Website: www.sane.org

SAMHSA
Website: www.samhsa.gov

PRESCRIPTION ASSISTANCE

Drug Card America
Website: www.drugcardamerica.com

Patient Assistance
Website: www.patientassistance.com

Partnership for Prescription Assistance
Website: www.pparx.org

Rx Assist
Website: www.rxassist.org

STIGMA RESOURCES

Active Minds
Website: www.activeminds.org

Bring Change 2 Mind
Website: www.bringchange2mind.org

The Carter Center
Website: www.cartercenter.org

Entertainment Industries Council
Website: www.eiconline.org

National Consortium on Stigma Empowerment
Website: www.stigmaandempowerment.org

National Stigma Clearinghouse
Website: www.stigma.net

No Kidding, Me Too

Website: www.nkm2.org

Shift

Website: www.shift.org.uk

StigmaBusters at NAMI

Website www.nami.org

Stamp Out Stigma

Website:
www.stampoutstigma.co.uk

SUICIDE HOTLINES

National Suicide Prevention
Hotline

T: 800-273-TALK (800-273-8255)

Website:
www.suicidepreventionlifeline.org

Samaritans

T: 877-870-HOPE (877-870-4673)

Website: www.samaritansusa.org

Appendix F

HIGH-PROFILE PEOPLE WITH MOOD DISORDERS

Name	Prominence	Diagnosis
Andre Agassi	American tennis player	Depression
John Quincy Adams	American president	Depression
Alvin Ailey	American choreographer	Bipolar
Alan Alda	American actor	Depression
Buzz Aldrin	American astronaut	Depression
Sophie Anderton	British model	Bipolar
Hans Christian Andersen	Danish writer	Depression
Louie Anderson	American comedian	Depression
Shawn Andrews	American football player	Depression
Adam Ant	British singer	Bipolar
Parveen Babi	Bollywood actress	Depression
Vin Baker	American basketball player	Depression
Alec Baldwin	American actor	Depression

Christian Bale	British actor	Depression
Azealia Banks	American rapper	Bipolar
Brigitte Bardot	French actor	Depression
James Barrie	Scottish writer	Depression
Drew Barrymore	American actor	Depression
Amanda Beard	American Olympian	Depression
Ingmar Bergman	Swedish film director	Depression
Irving Berlin	American composer	Depression
Hector Berloiz	French composer	Bipolar
Maurice Bernard	American actor	Bipolar
Leonard Bernstein	American composer	Depression
Halle Berry	American actor	Depression
Valerie Bertinelli	American actor	Depression
William Blake	British poet	Depression
David Bohm	British physicist	Depression
Kjell Magne Bondevik	Prime minister of Norway	Depression
Clara Bow	American actor	Depression
Lorraine Bracco	American actor	Depression
Terry Bradshaw	American football player	Depression
Wayne Brady	American actor	Depression
Zach Braff	American actor	Depression
Jo Brand	British comedian	Bipolar
Jon Bon Jovi	American musician	Depression
Helena Bonham Carter	British actress	Depression
Steven Bowditch	Australian golfer	Depression
David Bowie	British singer	Depression
Susan Boyle	British singer	Depression

Lord Melvyn Bragg	British writer	Depression
Russell Brand	British comedian	Bipolar
Marlon Brando	American actor	Depression
Sir Richard Branson	British entrepreneur	Depression
Charlotte Bronte	British author	Depression
Frank Bruno	British boxer	Depression
Art Buchwald	American humorist	Bipolar
Delta Burke	American actor	Depression
Carol Burnett	American comedian	Depression
Robert Burton	British academic	Depression
Tim Burton	British director	Bipolar
Barbara Bush	American first lady	Depression
Gabriel Byrne	Irish actor	Depression
Lord Byron	British poet	Depression
Beverley Callard	British actor	Depression
Anthony Callea	Australian singer	Depression
Alastair Campbell	British journalist	Depression
Robert Campeau	Canadian entrepreneur	Bipolar
Jose Canseco	American baseball player	Depression
Truman Capote	American writer	Depression
Drew Carey	American comedian	Depression
Jim Carrey	American actor	Depression
Johnny Carson	American talk show host	Depression
Dick Cavett	American talk show host	Depression
Raymond Chandler	American writer	Depression
Mary Chapin-Carpenter	American country singer	Depression

Ray Charles	American musician	Depression
David Chase	American writer	Depression
Kristin Chenoweth	American singer	Depression
Lawton Chiles	American governor	Depression
Agatha Christie	British writer	Depression
Winston Churchill	British prime minister	Depression
Louis C K	American comedian	Depression
Rosemary Clooney	American singer	Bipolar
Eric Clapton	British musician	Depression
Dick Clark	American entrepreneur	Depression
John Cleese	British actor	Depression
Jesse Close	Sister of actor Glenn Close	Depression
Leonard Cohen	Canadian musician	Depression
Natalie Cole	American singer	Depression
Judy Collins	American singer	Depression
Shawn Colvin	American singer	Depression
Pat Conroy	American writer	Depression
Calvin Coolidge	American president	Depression
Francis Ford Coppola	American film director	Bipolar
Patricia Cornwell	American writer	Bipolar
Noel Coward	British writer/ composer	Bipolar
Simon Cowell	British record producer	Depression
Courteney Cox	American actor	Postpartum
Michael Crichton	American writer	Depression
Sheryl Crow	American musician	Depression

Billy Crystal	American comedian/ actor	Depression
John Daly	American golfer	Bipolar
Rodney Dangerfield	American comedian	Depression
Larry David	American comedian	Depression
Ray Davies	British musician	Bipolar
Jack Dee	British comedian	Depression
Edgar Degas	French painter	Depression
Ellen DeGeneres	American comedian	Depression
Johnny Depp	American actor	Depression
Sandy Denton	American singer	Postpartum
John Denver	American musician	Depression
Charles Dickens	British writer	Depression
Emily Dickinson	American poet	Depression
Benjamin Disraeli	British prime minister	Depression
Scott Donie	American Olympic diver	Depression
Gaetano Donizetti	Italian composer	Bipolar
Mike Douglas	American TV host	Depression
Fyodor Dostoevsky	Russian writer	Depression
Richard Dreyfuss	American actor	Bipolar
Theodore Dreiser	American writer	Depression
Kitty Dukakis	First lady of Massachusetts	Bipolar
Patty Duke	American actor	Bipolar
Paula Duncan	Australian TV host	Depression
Kirsten Dunst	American actor	Depression
Adam Duritz	American singer	Depression
Bob Dylan	American musician	Depression
Thomas Eakins	American painter	Depression

Thomas Eagleton	American senator	Depression
George Eliot	British writer	Depression
T.S. Eliot	American writer	Depression
James Ellroy	American writer	Depression
Ralph Waldo Emerson	American writer	Depression
Eminem	American rapper	Depression
James Farmer	American civil rights leader	Depression
William Faulkner	American writer	Depression
Jules Feiffer	American cartoonist	Depression
Craig Ferguson	Scottish comedian	Bipolar
Sarah Ferguson	British duchess of York	Depression
Carrie Fisher	American actor	Bipolar
Eddie Fisher	American actor	Depression
F. Scott Fitzgerald	American writer	Depression
Larry Flynt	American publisher	Bipolar
Kevin Foley	South Australia deputy premier	Depression
Harrison Ford	American actor	Depression
Tom Ford	American fashion designer	Depression
Stephen Foster	American composer	Depression
Connie Francis	American singer	Bipolar
Stephen Fry	British actor	Bipolar
Lady Gaga	American musician	Depression
Peter Gabriel	British musician	Depression
Paul Gauguin	French painter	Depression
Francisco de Goya	Spanish painter	Depression

John Kenneth Gailbraith	Canadian economist	Depression
James Garner	American actor	Depression
John Gibson	Irish pianist	Bipolar
Mel Gibson	American actor	Bipolar
Sir John Gielgud	British actor	Depression
Kendall Gill	American basketballer	Depression
Paul Gascoigne	British footballer	Bipolar
Amy Grant	American singer	Postpartum
John Paul Getty	American philanthropist	Depression
Matthew Good	Canadian musician	Bipolar
Joseph Gordon Levitt	American actor	Depression
Tipper Gore	First lady	Depression
Cary Grant	American actor	Depression
Macy Gray	American singer	Bipolar
Graham Greene	British writer	Bipolar
Ken Griffey Jr.	American baseball star	Depression
Tim Gunn	Fashion icon	Depression
Dorothy Hamill	American Olympic skater	Depression
Linda Hamilton	American actor	Bipolar
Susie Favor Hamilton	American Olympic runner	Depression
Tyler Hamilton	American Olympic bicyclist	Depression
John Hamm	American actor	Depression
George F. Handel	German composer	Bipolar
Angie Harmon	American actor	Postpartum
Pete Harnish	American baseball player	Depression

Mariette Hartley	American actor	Bipolar
Juliana Hatfield	American singer	Depression
Stephen Hawking	American physicist	Depression
Lena Headey	British actor	Depression
Paige Hemmis	Television host	Depression
Robert Herjavac	Canadian entrepreneur	Depression
Hermann Hesse	Swiss writer	Depression
Audrey Hepburn	American actor	Depression
Abbie Hoffman	American activist	Bipolar
Hulk Hogan	American wrestler	Depression
Dame Kelly Holmes	British Olympic runner	Depression
Sir Anthony Hopkins	British actor	Depression
Victor Hugo	French writer	Depression
Janice Ian	American singer	Depression
Henrik Ibsen	Norwegian playwright	Depression
Natalie Imbruglia	Australian singer/ actress	Depression
La India	Latin salsa star	Depression
Jack Irons	American musician	Bipolar
Janet Jackson	American singer	Depression
Jesse Jackson	Civil rights pioneer	Bipolar
Henry James	British writer	Depression
William James	American psychologist	Depression
Kay Redfield Jamison	American psychologist	Bipolar
Thomas Jefferson	American president	Depression
Billy Joel	American musician	Depression
Andrew Johns	British rugby player	Bipolar
Dwayne Johnson	American wrestler	Depression

Russ Johnson	American baseball player	Depression
Elton John	British singer	Bipolar
Daniel Johns	Australian musician	Depression
Brad "Scarface" Jordan	American rapper	Bipolar
Ashley Judd	American actor	Depression
Franz Kafka	German writer	Depression
Kerry Katona	British singer	Bipolar
Karen Kain	Canadian ballerina	Depression
Danny Kaye	American actor	Depression
John Keats	British poet	Depression
Patrick Kennedy	American congressman	Bipolar
Ted Kennedy	American senator	Depression
Jack Kerouac	American writer	Depression
Alicia Keys	American musician	Depression
Margot Kidder	American actor	Bipolar
Anthony Kiedis	American singer	Depression
Soren Kierkegaard	Danish philosopher	Depression
Stephen King	American writer	Depression
Gelsey Kirkland	American ballerina	Depression
John Kirwan	New Zealand rugby player	Depression
Otto Klemperer	German conductor	Bipolar
Beyoncé Knowles	American singer	Depression
Joey Kramer	American musician	Depression
Kris Kristopherson	American musician	Depression
Julie Krone	American jockey	Depression
Akira Kurosawa	Japanese film director	Depression

Denise L'Estrange-Corbet	New Zealand fashion designer	Depression
Pat LaFontaine	American hockey star	Depression
Kendrick Lamar	American rapper	Depression
Queen Latifah	American singer	Depression
Peter Nolan Lawrence	British writer	Bipolar
Jenny Lawson	American writer	Depression
Hugh Laurie	British actor	Depression
Frances Lear	American TV producer	Bipolar
Yoon Han Lee	Korean writer	Bipolar
Vivien Leigh	British actor	Bipolar
Meriwether Lewis	American explorer	Depression
John Lennon	British musician	Depression
Neil Lennon	British footballer	Bipolar
David Letterman	American comedian	Depression
Jennifer Lewis	American actor	Bipolar
Abraham Lincoln	American president	Depression
Joshua Logan	Playwright	Bipolar
Federico Garcia Lorca	Spanish poet/playwright	Depression
Demi Lovato	American singer	Bipolar
Salvador Luria	Italian Nobel Laureate	Depression
Robert Lowell	American poet	Depression
H. P. Lovecraft	American writer	Depression
Rachel Maddow	American broadcaster	Depression
Gustav Mahler	Austrian composer	Depression
Norman Mailer	American writer	Depression
Margaret Manning	American psychologist	Depression

Shirley Manson	Scottish singer	Depression
Ann-Margret	American actor	Depression
Henri Matisse	French artist	Depression
Brian May	British musician	Depression
Sir Paul McCartney	British musician	Depression
Gary McDonald	Australian actor	Depression
Ewan McGregor	Scottish actor	Depression
Sarah McLachlan	Canadian musician	Depression
Kristy McNichol	American actor	Bipolar
Gary McDonald	Australian actor	Depression
John Mellencamp	American musician	Depression
Herman Melville	American writer	Depression
Burgess Meredith	American actor	Bipolar
George Michael	British singer	Depression
Kate Millett	American feminist writer	Bipolar
Spike Milligan	Irish comedian	Bipolar
Dimitri Mihalas	American astronomer	Bipolar
Matthew Mitcham	Australian Olympian	Depression
Claude Monet	French artist	Depression
Marilyn Monroe	American actress	Bipolar
J. P. Morgan	American financier	Bipolar
Alanis Morissette	Canadian singer	Depression
Steven Patrick Morrissey	British singer	Depression
Wolfgang Amadeus Mozart	Viennese composer	Depression
John Mulheren	American financier	Bipolar
Edvard Munch	Norwegian artist	Depression
Robert Munsch	Canadian writer	Bipolar

Bill Murray	American actor	Depression
Les Murray	Australian poet	Depression
Ilie Nastase	Romanian tennis star	Bipolar
Willie Nelson	American singer	Depression
Sir Isaac Newton	British physicist	Bipolar
Friedrich Nietzsche	German philosopher	Bipolar
Florence Nightingale	British nurse	Bipolar
Stevie Nicks	American singer	Depression
Gena Lee Nolin	American actor	Postpartum
Deborah Norville	American journalist	Depression
Conan O'Brien	American comedian	Depression
Graeme O'Bree	Scottish cyclist	Depression
Sinead O'Connor	Irish singer	Bipolar
Rosie O'Donnell	American comedian	Depression
Georgia O'Keeffe	American painter	Depression
Eugene O'Neill	American playwright	Depression
Keith O'Neill	American football player	Bipolar
Ronnie O'Sullivan	British snooker player	Bipolar
Sharon Osbourne	British talk show host	Depression
Donny Osmond	American singer	Depression
Marie Osmond	American singer	Postpartum
Patton Oswalt	American comedian	Depression
Gwyneth Paltrow	American actor	Postpartum
Joe Pantoliano	American actor	Depression
Deepika Padukone	Bollywood actress	Depression
Charles Parker	American jazz composer	Depression
Dorothy Parker	American writer	Depression
Dolly Parton	American singer	Depression

George S. Patton	American general	Depression
Jane Pauley	American journalist	Bipolar
Amanda Peet	American actor	Postpartum
Pierre Péladeau	Canadian publisher	Bipolar
Charley Pell	American football coach	Depression
Walker Percy	American writer	Depression
Murray Pezim	Canadian financier	Bipolar
Ryan Phillippe	American actor	Depression
Mackenzie Phillips	American actress	Depression
Kellie Pickler	American singer	Depression
Chonda Pierce	American comedian	Depression
Jimmy Piersall	American baseball player	Bipolar
Janot Pilinszky	Hungarian poet	Depression
Brad Pitt	American actor	Depression
Valerie Plame	American CIA agent	Postpartum
Edgar Allan Poe	American writer	Bipolar
Jackson Pollock	American painter	Depression
Cole Porter	American composer	Depression
Alma Powell	Wife of US secretary of state	Depression
Susan Powter	American motivational speaker	Depression
Charley Pride	American singer	Bipolar
Sergei Rachmaninoff	Russian composer	Depression
Charlotte Rampling	British actress	Depression
Ayn Rand	Russian writer	Depression
Mac Rebenack	American singer	Bipolar
Burt Reynolds	American actor	Depression

Lou Reed	American singer	Depression
Jerry Remy	American sports broadcaster	Depression
Ann Rice	American writer	Depression
Lisa Rinna	American actor	Postpartum
Joan Rivers	American comedian	Depression
Lynn Rivers	American congresswoman	Bipolar
Barret Robbins	American football player	Bipolar
Paul Robeson	American actor	Depression
Lyndsey Rodrigues	Australian TV presenter	Depression
Norman Rockwell	American artist	Depression
Peter Mark Roget	creator of thesaurus	Depression
Theodore Roosevelt	American president	Bipolar
Roseanne	American comedian	Depression
Ronda Rousey	American UFC fighter	Depression
Raymond Roussin	Archbishop, diocese of Vancouver	Depression
Renee Russo	American actor	Bipolar
J.K. Rowling	British writer	Depression
Winona Ryder	American actor	Depression
J.D. Salinger	American writer	Depression
Yves Saint Laurent	French fashion designer	Depression
Allison Schmitt	American Olympian	Depression
Charles Schulz	American cartoonist	Depression
Robert Schuman	German composer	Bipolar

Jim Shea	American Olympic skeleton racer	Depression
Mary Shelley	British writer	Depression
Brooke Shields	American actor	Postpartum
Sarah Silverman	American comedian	Depression
Lauren Slater	American psychologist	Depression
Michael Slater	Australian cricketer	Depression
Tony Slattery	British comedian	Bipolar
Neil Simon	American playwright	Depression
Paul Simon	American singer	Depression
Joey Slinger	Canadian journalist	Depression
Tim Smith	Australian rugby player	Bipolar
Hope Solo	American Olympian	Depression
Andrew Solomon	American writer	Depression
Britney Spears	American singer	Bipolar
Alonzo Spellman	American football player	Depression
Diana Spencer	Princess of Wales	Depression
Muffin Spencer-Devlin	American golfer	Bipolar
Dusty Springfield	American singer	Bipolar
Rick Springfield	Australian actor/singer	Depression
Bruce Springsteen	American musician	Depression
George Stephanopoulos	American political analyst	Depression
Rod Steiger	American actor	Depression
John Steinbeck	American writer	Depression
Ben Stiller	American actor	Bipolar
Emma Stone	American actor	Depression
Sting	British musician	Depression

Darryl Strawberry	American baseball player	Bipolar
Picabo Street	American Olympic skier	Depression
William Styron	American writer	Depression
Donna Summer	American singer	Depression
Donald Sutherland	Canadian actor	Depression
Shaun Tait	Australian cricketer	Depression
Amy Tam	American writer	Depression
Elizabeth Taylor	American actor	Depression
Holland Taylor	American actor	Depression
James Taylor	American musician	Depression
Lili Taylor	American actor	Bipolar
Pyotr Ilyich Tchaikovsky	Russian composer	Depression
Nikki Teasley	American basketballer	Depression
Nikola Tesla	Austrian/American inventor	Depression
Dylan Thomas	Welsh poet	Depression
Emma Thompson	British actor	Depression
Tracy Thompson	American journalist	Depression
Gene Tierney	American actor	Depression
Leo Tolstoy	Russian writer	Depression
Henri de Toulouse-Lautrec	French artist	Depression
Spencer Tracy	American actor	Depression
Marcus Trescothick	British cricket star	Depression
Margaret Trudeau	Wife of prime minister of Canada	Bipolar
Tanya Tucker	American singer	Depression

Ted Turner	American entrepreneur	Bipolar
Mark Twain	American writer	Depression
Mike Tyson	American boxer	Depression
Dimitrius Underwood	American football player	Depression
Tracy Ullman	British comedian	Bipolar
Jean-Claude Van Damme	Belgian actor	Bipolar
Towns Van Zandt	American musician	Bipolar
Vivian Vance	American actor	Depression
Ben Vereen	American actor	Depression
Alexandrina Victoria	Queen Victoria of UK	Depression
Meredith Vieira	American journalist	Depression
Claus Von Amsberg	Prince of Netherlands	Depression
Ludwig von Beethoven	German composer	Bipolar
Lars von Trier	Danish film director	Depression
Lindsey Vonn	American Olympic skier	Depression
Kurt Vonnegut	American writer	Depression
Tom Waits	American musician	Bipolar
Mike Wallace	American journalist	Depression
David Walliams	British comedian	Bipolar
Arthur Evelyn Waugh	British writer	Depression
Damon Wayans	American comedian	Depression
Mary Foresberg Weiland	American model	Bipolar
Pete Wentz	American musician	Bipolar
Will Wheaton	American actor	Depression
Walt Whitman	American poet	Depression

Serena Williams	American tennis player	Depression
Tennessee Williams	American playwright	Depression
Brian Wilson	American musician	Bipolar
Carnie Wilson	American singer	Postpartum
Owen Wilson	American actor	Depression
Woodrow Wilson	American president	Depression
Oprah Winfrey	American talk show host	Depression
Jonathan Winters	American comedian	Bipolar
Hugo Wolf	Australian composer	Depression
Virginia Woolf	British writer	Depression
Elizabeth Wurtzel	American writer	Depression
Frank Lloyd Wright	American architect	Bipolar
Tammy Wynette	American singer	Depression
Bert Yancey	American golfer	Bipolar
Michael Yardy	British cricketer	Depression
Boris Yeltsin	President of Russian Federation	Depression
Thomas Yorke	British musician	Depression
Robert Young	American actor	Depression
Catherine Zeta-Jones	Welsh actor	Bipolar
Warren Zevon	American musician	Depression

NOTES

I. WHAT IS LATE-LIFE DEPRESSION?

1. Shannon Kolakowski, *When Depression Hurts Your Relationship* (Oakland, Calif.: New Harbinger, 2014).

2. "Depression: A Global Health Concern 2012," *World Health Organization*, www.who.int/mediacentre/events/annual/world_suicide_prevention_day/en/ (accessed May 2, 2015).

3. American Psychiatric Association, *Diagnostic and Statistical Manual of Mental Disorders*, 5th ed. (Washington, D.C.: American Psychiatric Association, 2013).

4. United Nations, "Department of Economic and Social Affairs, Population Division," *World Population of Ageing* (2013).

5. U.S. Census Bureau, *Statistical Abstract of the United States* (Washington, D.C.: U.S. Census Bureau, 2012).

6. Kaare Christensen et al., "Ageing Populations: The Challenges Ahead," *Lancet* 374 (2009): 1196–208.

7. U.S. Census Bureau, *Statistical Abstract of the United States*.

8. Atul Gawande, *Being Mortal: Medicine and What Matters in the End* (London: Profile Books, 2014).

9. Ronald C. Kessler, "Age of Onset of Mental Disorders: A Review of Recent Literature," *Current Opinions in Psychiatry* 20 (2007): 359–64.

10. American Psychiatric Association, *Diagnostic and Statistical Manual*.

11. Warren D. Taylor, "Clinical Practice: Depression in the Elderly," *New England Journal of Medicine* 371 (2014): 1228–36.

12. Sidney Zisook et al., "Effect of Age of Onset on the Course of Major Depressive Disorder," *American Journal of Psychiatry* 164 (2007): 1539–46.

13. Zisook, "Effect of Age."

14. National Alliance on Mental Illness, *Depression in Older Persons Fact Sheet* (Arlington, Va.: National Alliance on Mental Illness, 2009).

15. Melonie Heron, "Deaths: Leading Causes for 2010," *National Vital Statistics Report* 62 (2013): 1–97.

16. Cynthia G. Cahoon, "Depression in Older Adults," *American Journal of Skilled Nursing* 112 (2012): 22–30.

17. "Mental Health and Older Adults," *World Health Organization*, www.who.int/mediacentre/factsheets/fs381/en/ (accessed June 24, 2015).

18. K. D. Kochanek et al., "Deaths: Final Data for 2002," *National Vital Statistics Reports* 12 (2004): 1–115.

19. Carrie A. Levin et al., "Prevalence and Treatment of Diagnosed Depression among Elderly Skilled Nursing Residents," *Journal of the American Medical Directors Association* 8 (2007): 585–94.

20. Lars Vedel Kessing, "Gender Differences in Subtypes of Late-Onset Depression," *International Psychogeriatrics* 8 (2006): 727–38.

21. Joyce T. Bromberg et al., "Racial/Ethnic Differences in the Prevalence of Depressive Symptoms," *American Journal of Public Health* 94 (2004): 1378–85.

22. Johan Mathillas et al., " Risk Factors for Depressive Disorders in Very Old Age: A Population-based Cohort Study with a Five-Year Follow-Up," *Social Psychiatry and Psychiatric Epidemiology* 49 (2014): 831–39.

23. W. Vaughn McCall, *Late Life Depression: An Issue of Psychiatric Clinics* (Cambridge: Elsevier, 2013).

24. Theodore B. Van Itallie, "Subsyndromal Depression in the Elderly: Underdiagnosed and Undertreated," *Metabolism* 54 (2005): 39–44.

25. A. K. Berger et al., "Preclinical Symptoms of Major Depression in Very Old Age: A Prospective Longitudinal Study," *American Journal of Psychiatry* 156 (1999): 1239–41.

26. David C. Steffens et al., "Prevalence of Depression and Its Treatment in an Elderly Population," *Archives of General Psychiatry* 57 (2000): 601–7.

27. "Depression: A Global Health Concern 2012," *World Health Organization*.

28. Alize J. Ferrari et al., "Global Variation in the Prevalence and Incidence of Major Depressive Disorder: A Systematic Review of the Epidemiological Literature," *Psychosomatic Medicine* 43 (2013): 471–81.

29. Walter F. Stewart et al., "Cost of Lost Productive Work Time among U.S. Workers with Depression," *Journal of the American Medical Association* 289 (2003): 3135–44.

30. Ronald C. Kessler, "The Costs of Depression," *Psychiatric Clinics of North America* 35 (2012): 1–14.

31. Helen M. Vasiliadis et al., "The Excess Healthcare Costs Associated with Depression and Anxiety in Elderly Living in the Community," *American Journal of Geriatric Psychiatry* 21 (2013): 536–48.

32. National Alliance for Caregiving, *Caregiving in the U.S. 2009* (Washington, D.C.: Author, 2009).

33. Steven H. Zarit, "Assessment of Family Caregivers: A Research Perspective," in *Caregiver Assessment: Voices and Views from the Field*, vol. 2, edited by Family Caregiver Alliance, 12–37 (San Francisco: Family Caregiver Alliance, 2006).

34. George Engel, "The Need for a New Medical Model: A Challenge for Biomedicine," *Science* 196 (1977): 129–36.

35. Francesco Borrell-Carrió et al., "The Biopsychosocial Model 25 Years Later: Principles Practice and Scientific Inquiry," *Annals of Family Medicine* 2 (2004): 576–82.

36. Mauro Garcia-Toro and Iratxe Aguirre, "Biopsychosocial Model in Depression Revisited," *Medical Hypotheses* 68 (2007): 683–91.

2. GERIATRIC MOOD DISORDERS

1. M. Alpert and A. Rosen, "A Semantic Analysis of the Various Ways That the Terms 'Affect,' 'Emotion,' and 'Mood' Are Used," *Journal of Communication Disorder* 23 (1990): 237–46.

2. Eric Shouse, "Feeling, Emotion, Affect," *M/C Journal* 8 (2005), http://journal.media-culture.org.au/0512/03-shouse.php (accessed April 21, 2015).

3. Shouse, "Feeling, Emotion, Affect."

4. Deborah Serani, *Living with Depression: Why Biology and Biography Matter along the Path to Hope and Healing* (Lanham, Md.: Rowman and Littlefield, 2011).

5. Konstantinos N. Fountoulakis et al., "Unipolar Late-Onset Depression: A Comprehensive Review," *Annals of General Hospital Psychiatry* 2 (2003): 1–14.

6. Gary J. Kennedy, *Geriatric Mental Health Care: A Treatment Guide for the Health Professions* (New York: Guilford, 2000).

7. Deepak Prabhakar and Richard Balon, "Late-Onset Bipolar Disorder: A Case for Careful Appraisal," *Psychiatry* 7 (2010): 34–37.

8. Sohan Rej et al., "Managing Late-Life Bipolar Disorder: Current Issues and Clinical Tips," *Psychiatric Times* (November 27, 2014): 1–6.

9. Anthony R. Carlino, James L. Stinnet, and Deborah R. Kim, "New Onset of Bipolar Disorder in Late Life," *Psychosomatics* 54 (2013): 94–99.

10. Nhi-ha Trinh and Brent P. Forester, "Bipolar Disorder in the Elderly: Differential Diagnosis and Treatment," *Psychiatric Times* (December 1, 2007): 1–2.

11. C. Born et al., "Preliminary Results of a Fine-Grain Analysis of Mood Swings and Treatment Modalities of Bipolar I and II Patients Using the Daily Prospective Life-Chart-Methodology," *Acta Psychiatrica Scandinavica* 120 (2009): 474–80.

12. Jean-Michel Azorin et al., "Late Onset Bipolar Illness: The Geriatric Bipolar Type," *CNS Neurosciences and Therapeutics* 18 (2012): 208–13.

13. Kathleen Merikangas et al., "Lifetime and 12-Month Prevalence of Bipolar Spectrum Disorder in the National Comorbidity Survey Replication," *Archives of General Psychiatry* 64 (2007): 543–52.

14. George S. Alexopoulos and Robert Kelly Jr., "Research Advances in Geriatric Depression," *World Psychiatry* 8 (2006): 140–49.

15. Tomoji Takata, Ken Takaoka, and Maiko Fujigaki, "Catatonia in the Elderly," *International Journal of Psychiatry in Clinical Practice* 9 (2005): 230–37.

16. Takata, Takaoka, and Fujigaki, "Catatonia in the Elderly."

17. George S. Alexopoulos et al., "Clinical Presentation of the Depression–Executive Dysfunction Syndrome of Late Life," *Psychiatry* 10 (2002): 98–106.

18. Joyce M. Gaete and Julien Bogousslavsky, "Post-Stroke Depression," *Expert Review in Neurotherapeutics* 8 (2008): 75–92.

19. Maree L. Hackett and Craig S. Anderson, "Predictors of Depression after Stroke: A Systematic Review of Observational Studies," *Stroke* 36 (2005): 2296–301.

20. Katherine Salter et al., "The Assessment Post Stroke Depression," *Topics in Stroke Rehabilitation* 14 (2007): 1–24

21. George S. Alexopoulos et al., "Vascular Depression Hypothesis," *Archives of General Psychiatry* 54 (1997): 915–22.

22. K. R. Krishnan et al., "Clinical Characteristics of Magnetic Resonance Imaging–Defined Subcortical Ischemic Depression," *Biological Psychiatry* 55 (2004): 390–97.

23. K. R. Krishnan et al., "MRI-Defined Vascular Depression," *American Journal of Psychiatry* 184 (1997): 497–501.

3. DIAGNOSIS FOR DEPRESSION
IN LATER LIFE

1. Bassam Elsawy and Kim E. Higgins, "The Geriatric Assessment," *American Family Physician* 83 (2011): 48–56.

2. Elsawy and Higgins, "The Geriatric Assessment."

3. Hans-Jurgen Heppner et al., "Laboratory Aspects Related to the Detection and Prevention of Frailty," *International Journal of Preventive Medicine* 1 (2010): 149–57.

4. Jean Henny, "Interpretation of Laboratory Results of Elderly Subjects: Effect of Age or Aging," *Annals of Pharmacology Francaise* 67 (2009): 173–81; George S. Alexopoulos and Robert E. Kelly, "Research Advances in Geriatric Depression," *World Psychiatry* 8 (2009): 140–49.

5. Emmet Keeler et al., "The Impact of Functional Status on Life Expectancy of Older Individuals," *Journal of Gerontology* 65 (2010): 727–33.

6. Elsawy and Higgins, "The Geriatric Assessment."

7. Nelson Sousa et al., "The Relation between Functional Performance and Satisfaction with Life in Elderly," *IPLeiria Congresso Internacional de Saúde: Desafios & Inovações em Saúde* (2014), Portugal, May 9–10.

8. Michael B. First et al., *Structured Clinical Interview for DSM-IV-TR Axis I Disorders* (New York: Biometrics Research, New York State Psychiatric Institute, 2002).

9. Marshal F. Folstein et al., "Mini-Mental State: A Practical Method for Grading the Cognitive State of Patients for the Clinician," *Journal of Psychiatric Research* 12 (1975): 189–98.

10. J. R. Copeland et al., "The Geriatric Mental State Examination in the 21st Century," *International Journal of Geriatric Psychiatry* 17 (2002): See comment in PubMed Commons below 729–32.

11. Elizabeth L. Glisky, "Changes in Cognitive Function in Human Aging," in *Brain Aging: Models, Methods, and Mechanisms*, edited by D. R. Riddle, 1–19 (Boca Raton, Fla.: CRC Press, 2007).

12. Nhi-ha Trihn and Brent Forester, "Bipolar Disorder in the Elderly: Differential Diagnosis and Treatment," *Psychiatric Times* (December 1, 2007).

13. Joaquim Cerejeira and Elizabeta B. Mukaetova-Ladinska, "A Clinical Update on Delirium: From Early Recognition to Effective Management," *Nursing Research and Practice* (2011): 1–12.

14. S. A. Castro-Chavira et al., "Genetic Markers in Biological Fluids for Aging-Related Major Neurocognitive Disorder," *Current Alzheimer Research* 12 (2015): 200–209.

15. Henry W. Querfurth and Frank M. LaFerla, "Alzheimer's Disease," *New England Journal of Medicine* 362 (2010): 329–44.

16. Bart Sheehan, "Assessment Scales in Dementia," *Therapeutic Advances in Neurological Disorders* 5 (2012): 349–58.

17. Brent Forester et al., "Geriatric Mania," *Psychiatry* 24 (2004): 43–45.

18. Eric J. Lenz et al., "Comorbid Anxiety Disorders in Depressed Elderly Patients," *American Journal of Psychiatry* 157 (2000): 722–28.

19. Devangere P. Devanand, "Comorbid Psychiatric Disorders in Late Life Depression," *Biological Psychiatry* 52 (2002): 236–42.

20. Devanand, "Comorbid Psychiatric Disorders."

21. David Bruce Matchar and Mugdha Thakur, "Is Genetic Testing for Cytochrome P450 Polymorphisms Ready for Implementation?" *American Family Physician* 76 (2007): 348–51.

22. Greene Shepard et al., "Adverse Drug Reaction Deaths Reported in the United States. Vital Statistics, 1999–2006," *Annals of Pharmacotherapy* 46 (2012): 169–75.

23. Pothitos M. Pitychoutis et al., "Pharmacogenetic Considerations for Late Life Depression Therapy," *Expert Opinion on Drug Metabolism & Toxicology* 9 (2013): 989–99.

24. John Carroll, "Biogenetic Tests Emerge from Their Chrysalis," *Biotechnology Healthcare* 4 (2007): 37–44.

25. Don Asmonga, "Getting to Know GINA: An Overview of the Genetic Information Nondiscrimination Act," *Journal of AHIMA* 79 (2008): 18–22.

26. David A. Mrazek, *Psychiatric Pharmacogenomics* (New York: Oxford University Press, 2010).

4. TRADITIONAL TREATMENTS FOR DEPRESSION IN LATER LIFE

1. Richard K. Morriss and Jan Scott, "Psychological Management of Mood Disorders," *Psychiatry* 8 (2009): 108–12.

2. George S. Alexopoulos and Robert E. Kelly, "Research Advances in Geriatric Depression," *World Psychiatry* 8 (2009): 140–49.

3. Alan S. Bellack and Michel Hersen, *Handbook of Behavior Therapy in the Psychiatric Setting: Critical Issues in Psychiatry* (New York: Springer, 2013).

4. Darcy Cox and Heather D'Oyley, "Cognitive Behavioral Therapy with Older Adults," *Medical Journal* 53 (2011): 348–52.

5. Patricia A. Areán and Barbara Cook, "Psychotherapy and Combined Psychotherapy Pharmacotherapy for Late-Life Depression," *Biological Psychiatry* 52 (2002): 293–303.

6. Forrest Scoggin et al., "Evidence-based Psychotherapies for Depression in Older Adults," *Clinical Psychology* 12 (2005): 222–37.

7. Thomas Lynch et al., "Dialectical Behavior Therapy with Older Adults," *American Journal of Geriatric Psychiatry* 11 (2003): 33–45.

8. Jennifer Francis and Anand Kumar, "Psychological Treatment of Late-Life Depression," *Psychiatric Clinics of North American* 36 (2013): 561–75.

9. Kristen Carreira et al., "A Controlled Evaluation of Monthly Maintenance of Interpersonal Psychotherapy in Late-Life Depression with Varying Levels of Cognition," *International Journal of Geriatric Psychiatry* 23 (2008): 1110–13.

10. Patricia A. Areán, "Psychotherapy," in *Late-Life Mood Disorder*, edited by Helen Lavretsky, Martha Sajatovic, and Charles F. Reynolds III, 390–404 (New York: Oxford University Press, 2013).

11. Scoggin et al., "Evidence-based Psychotherapies."

12. Dimitri N. Kiosses et al., "A Home-delivered Intervention for Depressed, Cognitively Impaired, Disabled Elders," *International Journal of Geriatric Psychiatry* 26 (2011): 256–62.

13. Amanda McGovern et al., "Psychotherapies for Late-Life Depression," *Psychiatric Annals* 44 (2014): 147–52.

14. Patricia A. Areán et al., "Problem-solving Therapy and Supportive Therapy in Older Adults with Major Depression and Executive Dysfunction," *American Journal of Psychiatry* 167 (2010): 1391–98.

15. Ellen Lukens and William McFarlane, "Psychoeducation as Evidence-Based Practice," *Brief Treatment and Crisis Intervention* 4 (2004): 205–25.

16. George S. Alexopoulos and Robert E. Kelley Jr., "Research Advances in Geriatric Depression," *World Psychiatry* 8 (2009): 140–49.

17. Alexopoulos and Kelley, "Research Advances."

18. Bonnie S. Wiese, "Geriatric Depression: The Use of Antidepressants in the Elderly," *BC Medical Journal* 53 (2011): 341–47.

19. David C. Steffens, Charles R. Conway, and C. B. Dombeck, "Severity of Subcortical Gray Matter Hyperintensity Predicts ECT Response in Geriatric Depression," *Journal of ECT* 12 (2001): 45–49.

20. Harold A. Sackeim et al., "Effects of Pulse Width and Electrode Placement on the Efficacy and Cognitive Effects of Electroconvulsive Therapy," *Brain Stimulation* 1 (2008): 71–83.

21. Ricardo E. Jorge, David Moser, and Laura Acion, "Treatment of Vascular Depression Using Repetitive Transcranial Magnetic Stimulation," *Archives of General Psychiatry* 65 (2008): 268–76.

22. Chris Baeken and Rudi Daeradt, "Neurobiological Mechanisms of Repetitive Transcranial Magnetic Stimulation on the Underlying Neuro-circuitry in Unipolar Depression," *Dialogues in Clinical Neuroscience* 13 (2011): 139–45.

23. M. M. Husain, K. Trevino, and L. A. Whitworth, "The Role of Vagus Nerve Stimulation as a Therapy for Treatment-Resistant Depression," *Depression: Mind and Body* 2 (2006): 114–19.

24. Patricio Riva-Posse et al., "The Role of Electroconvulsive and Neuromodulation Therapies in the Treatment of Geriatric Depression," *Psychiatric Clinics of North America* 36 (2013): 607–30.

25. Wayne K. Goodman and Thomas R. Insel, "Deep Brain Stimulation in Psychiatry: Concentrating on the Road Ahead," *Biological Psychiatry* 65 (2009): 263–66.

26. Bruce Luber, Shawn M. McClintock, and Sarah H. Lisanby, " Applications of Transcranial Magnetic Stimulation and Magnetic Seizure Therapy in the Study and Treatment of Disorders Related to Cerebral Aging," *Dialogues Clinical Neuroscience* 15 (2013): 87–98.

5. HOLISTIC APPROACHES TO DEPRESSION IN LATER LIFE

1. Helen Lavretsky, "Complementary and Alternative Medicine Use for Treatment and Prevention of Late-Life Mood and Cognitive Disorders," *Aging Health* 5 (2009): 61–78.

2. Jon Karat, *Coming to Our Senses: Healing Ourselves and the World through Mindfulness* (New York: Hyperion, 2011).

3. David Sousa, *How The Brain Learns* (Thousand Oaks: Sage, 2006).

4. Shaun Smith, *The User's Guide to the Human Mind: Why Our Brains Make Us Unhappy, Anxious, and Neurotic and What We Can Do about It* (Oakland, Calif.: New Harbinger, 2011).

5. Karat, *Coming to Our Senses*.

6. Ritsaert Lieverse et al., "Bright Light Treatment in Elderly Patients with Non-Seasonal Major Depressive Disorder," *JAMA Psychiatry* 68 (2011): 61–70.

7. Paola F. Gasio et al., "Dawn–Dusk Simulation Light Therapy of Disturbed Circadian Rest-Activity in the Elderly," *Experimental Gerontology* 38 (2003): 207–16.

8. Stephen Kaplan, "The Restorative Benefits of Nature: Toward an Integrative Framework," *Journal of Environmental Psychology* 15 (1995): 169–82.

9. Marc G. Berman et al., "The Cognitive Benefits of Interacting with Nature," *Psychological Science* 19 (2008): 1207–12.

10. Raquel Chapin Stephenson, "Promoting Well-Being and Gerotranscendence in an Art Therapy Program with Older Adults," *Journal of the American Art Therapy Association* 30 (2013): 151–58.

11. Sameena Azeemi et al., "A Critical Analysis of Chromotherapy and Its Scientific Evolution," *Evidence-Based Complement Alternative Medicine* 2 (2005): 481–88.

12. Peter Barrett and Lucinda Barrett, "The Potential of Positive Places: Senses, Rain and Spaces," *Intelligent Buildings International* 2 (2010): 46–52.

13. Chryssie Heine and Collette J. Browning, "Mental Health and Dual Sensory Loss in Older Adults: A Systematic Review," *Frontiers in Aging Neuroscience* 6 (2014): 83–90.

14. Roza Naste Krstesk, "Hearing and Visual Impairments as Risk Factors for Late-Life Depression," *Journal of Special Education and Rehabilitation* 13 (2012): 46–59.

15. Rachel S. Herz, "Aromatherapy Facts and Fictions: A Scientific Analysis of Olfactory Effects on Mood, Physiology and Behavior," *International Journal of Neuroscience* 119 (2009): 263–90.

16. Anthony Synnott, "Roses, Coffee and Lovers: The Meanings of Smell," *Compendium of Olfactory Research* 19 (1994): 117–28.

17. Patricia Davis, *Aromatherapy. An A–Z: The Most Comprehensive Guide to Aromatherapy Ever Published* (Essex: C. W. Daniel, 1988).

18. Judith White, *Aromatherapy for Men* (Bloomington, Ind.: Balboa Press, 2011).

19. Cather Harmer et al., "Negative Ion Treatment Increases Positive Emotional Processing in Seasonal Affective Disorder," *Psychological Medicine* 42 (2011): 1605–12.

20. Pierce Howard, *The Owner's Manual for the Brain: Everyday Applications from Mind Brain Research* (Charlotte, N.C.: Bard Press, 2006).

21. Michael Terman and Jiuan Su Terman, "Treatment of Seasonal Affective Disorder with a High-Output Negative Ionizer," *Journal of Alternative and Complementary Medicine* 1 (1995): 87–92.

22. Jolanda Mass et al., "Morbidity Is Related to a Green Living Environment," *Journal of Epidemiology and Community Health* 63 (2009): 967–73.

23. Tom Heath et al., "Human Taste Thresholds Are Modulated by Serotonin and Nonadrenline," *Journal of Neuroscience* 26 (2006): 12664–71.

24. Peter J. Rogers, "A Healthy Body, a Healthy Mind: Long-Term Impact of Diet on Mood and Cognitive Functioning," *Proceedings of the Nutrition Society* 60 (2001): 135–43.

25. Melvyn R. Werbach, "Nutritional Influences on Aggressive Behavior," *Journal of Orthomolecular Medicine* 7 (1992): 45–52.

26. Reeta Hakkarainen et al., "Food and Nutrient Intake in Relation to Mental Well-Being," *Nutrition Journal* 3 (2004): 1–5.

27. Patricia A. Tabloski, "Nutrition and Aging," in *Gerontological Nursing*, edited by Patricia A. Tabloski, 110–46 (Saddle River, N.J.: Prentice Hall, 2006).

28. Larry Christensen and Clare Redig, "Effect of Meal Composition on Mood," *Behavioral Neuroscience* 107 (1993): 346–53.

29. David Mischoulon and Michael F. Raab, "The Role of Folate in Depression and Dementia," *Journal of Clinical Psychiatry* 68 (2007): 28–33.

30. Catherin Rice-Evans and Lester Packer, *Flavonoids in Health and Disease* (New York: Marcel Dekker, 2003).

31. Anirban Chatterjee et al., "Green Tee: A Boon for Periodontal and General Health," *Journal of Indian Society of Peridontology* 16 (2012): 161–67.

32. Carolyn Dean, *The Miracle of Magnesium* (New York: Ballantine, 2006).

33. Joseph Hibbeln, "Fish Consumption and Major Depression," *Lancet* 351 (1998): 1213–17.

34. Patrick Holdford, "Depression: The Nutrition Connection," *Primary Care Mental Health* 1 (2003): 9–16.

35. Yong Ku Kim et al., "Differences in Cytokines between Non-Suicidal Patients and Suicidal Patients in Major Depression," *Progress in Neuropsychopharmacology and Biological Psychiatry* 15 (2008): 356–61.

36. Goren Högberg et al., "Depressed Adolescents in a Case-Series Were Low in Vitamin D and Depression Was Ameliorated by Vitamin D Supplementation," *Acta Paediatrica* 101 (2012): 779–83.

37. James Dowds and Diane Stafford, *The Vitamin D Cure* (Hoboken, N.J.: John Wiley & Sons, 2012).

38. Kai MacDonald and Tina Marie MacDonald, "The Peptide That Binds: A Systematic Review of Oxytocin and Its Prosocial Effects in Humans," *Harvard Review of Psychiatry* 18 (2012): 39–52.

39. Thomas Insel and Larry Young, "The Neurobiology of Attachment," *National Review of Neuroscience* 2 (2001): 129–36.

40. Wayne Drevets, "Orbitofrontal Cortex Function and Structure of Depression," *Annals of the New York Academy of Sciences* 1121 (2007): 499–527.

41. Joseph H. Flaherty and Ryutaro Takahashi, "The Use of Complementary and Alternative Medical Therapies among Older Persons around the World," *Clinical Geriatric Medicine* 20 (2004): 179–200.

42. Raphael Leo and Jesus Salvador Ligot, "A Systematic Review of Randomized Controlled Trials of Acupuncture in the Treatment of Depression," *Journal of Affective Disorders* 97 (2007): 13–22.

43. Yasuhiro Honda et al., "A Study on the Acute Effects of Self-Acupressure on Mood and Its Usability," *Kurume University Psychological Research* 11 (2012): 8–14.

44. E. Paul Cherniack and Ariella R. Cherniack, "The Benefit of Pets and Animal-Assisted Therapy to the Health of Older Individuals," *Current Gerontology and Geriatrics Research* 2014 (2014): 1–10.

45. Peggy Nepps et al., "Animal-Assisted Therapy: Effects on Stress, Mood, and Pain," *Journal of Lancaster General Hospital* 6 (2011): 1–4.

46. B. Jones, *The Psychology of Human/Companion Animal Bond: An Annotated Bibliography* (Philadelphia: University of Pennsylvania Press, 1985).

47. Florence Nightingale, *Notes on Nursing: What It Is and What It's Not* (New York: Dover, 1969).

48. Cherniack and Cherniack, "The Benefit of Pets and Animal-Assisted Therapy."

49. Yasuyuki Fukukawa et al., "Age Differences in the Effect of Physical Activity on Depressive Symptoms," *Psychology of Aging* 19 (2004): 346–51.

50. Neela K. Patel et al., "The Effects of Yoga on Physical Functioning and Health Related Quality of Life in Older Adults: A Systematic Review and Meta-Analysis," *Journal of Alternative Complementary Medicine* 8 (2012): 902–17.

51. W. Jack Rajeski and Shannon L. Mihalko, "Physical Activity and Quality of Life in Older Adults," *Journals of Gerontology* 56 (2001): 23–36.

52. Karen L. Hill, "Promoting Exercise Compliance," *Women and Therapy* 25 (2002): 75–90.

53. Amanda Aboush et al., "Ballroom Dance Lessons for Geriatric Depression: An Exploratory Study," *Arts in Psychotherapy* 33 (2006): 89–97.

54. Mahyar Mokhtari et al., "The Effect of 12-Week Pilates Exercises on Depression and Balance Associated with Falling in the Elderly," *Social and Behavioral Science* 70 (2013): 1714–23.

55. Daisuki Sato et al., "The Water Exercise Improves Health-Related Quality of Life of Frail Elderly People at a Day Service Facility," *Quality of Life Research* 16 (2007): 1577–85.

56. Iris Chi et al., "Tai Chi and Reduction of Depressive Symptoms for Older Adults: A Meta-Analysis of Randomized Trials," *Geriatric Gerontology* 13 (2013): 3–12.

57. Susan Salvo, *Massage Therapy: Principles and Practice* (St. Louis, Mo.: Elsevier, 2012).

58. Melodee Harris and Kim Culpepper Richards, "The Physiological and Psychological Effects of Slow-Stroke Back Massage and Hand Massage on Relaxation in Older People," *Journal of Clinical Nursing* 97 (2010): 917–26.

59. Kevin Kunz and Barbara Kuna, "Understanding the Science and Art of Reflexology," *Alternative and Complementary Therapies* (April/May 1995): 183–86.

60. Pamela Miles, *Reiki: A Comprehensive Guide* (New York: Tarcher Books, 2008).

61. Lisa Gill, "More Hospitals Offer Alternative Therapies for Mind, Body, and Spirit," *USA Today*, September 15, 2008, http://usatoday30.usatoday.com/news/health/2008-09-14-alternative-therapies_N.htm (accessed July 8, 2015).

62. Nancy Richardson et al., "Effects of Reiki on Anxiety, Depression, Pain, and Physiological Factors on Community-Dwelling Adults," *Research in Gerontological Nursing* 3 (2010): 187–99.

63. Sasha Carr and Sandra Choron, *The Caregiver's Essential Handbook: More than 1200 Tips to Care for and Comfort the Seniors in Your Life* (New York: McGraw Hill, 2003).

64. K. L. Chou, "Combined Effect of Vision and Hearing Impairment on Depression in Older Adults: Evidence from the English Longitudinal Study of Ageing," *Journal of Affective Disorders* 106 (2008): 191–96.

65. K. Tambs, "Moderate Effects of Hearing Loss on Mental Health and Subjective Well-Being: Results from the Nord-Trondelag Hearing Loss Study," *Psychosomatic Medicine* 66 (2004): 776–82.

66. John Sloboda, "Empirical Studies of Emotional Response to Music," in *Cognitive Bases of Musical Communication*, edited by Mari Reiss Jones and Susan Holleran, 33–46 (Washington, D.C.: American Psychological Association, 1991).

67. M. F. Chan et al., "Effect of Music on Depression Levels and Physiological Responses in Community-Based Older Adults," *International Journal of Mental Health and Nursing* 18 (2009): 285–94.

68. Carol Krumhansl and Justin Zupnick, "Cascading Reminiscence Bumps in Popular Music," *Psychological Science* 24 (2013): 2057–68.

69. Patrik N. Juslin and John Sloboda, *Handbook of Music and Emotion: Theory, Research, and Applications* (New York: Oxford University Press, 2011).

70. John Sloboda, *Exploring the Musical Mind: Cognition, Emotions, Ability, Function* (New York: Oxford University Press, 2005).

71. Thomas Schafer et al., "The Psychological Functions of Listening to Music," *Frontiers in Psychology* 4 (2013): 511–38.

72. Helane Wahbeh, Carlos Calabrese, and Heather Zwickey, "Binaural Beat Technology in Humans: A Pilot Study to Assess Psychologic and Physiologic Effects," *Journal of Alternative and Complementary Medicine* 13 (2007): 25–32.

73. Thomas W. Meeks et al., "Complementary and Alternative Treatments for Late-Life Depression, Anxiety, and Sleep Disturbance: A Review of Randomized Controlled Trials," *Journal of Clinical Psychiatry* 68 (2007): 1461–71.

74. Elliott Salamon et al., "Sound Therapy Induced Relaxation: Down Regulating Stress Processes and Pathologies," *Medical Science Monitor* 9 (2003): RA96–RA101.

75. Olav Skille, *Manual of Vibroacoustics* (Levanger, Norway: ISVA, 1991).

76. Sylvie Mozziconacci, "Pitch Variations and Emotions in Speech," *International Congress of Phonetic Science* 95 (1995): 178–82.

77. Leslie Seltzer et al., "Instant Messages vs. Speech: Why We Still Need to Hear Each Other," *Evolution and Human Behavior* 33 (2012): 42–45.

78. Anne LeClaire, *Listening below the Noise: The Transformational Power of Silence* (New York: Harper Perennial, 2010).

6. HOW TO MAINTAIN SUCCESS IN TREATMENT

1. Philip Gorwood et al., "Treatment Response in Major Depression: Effects of Personality Treatment Dysfunction and Prior Depression," *British Journal of Psychiatry* 196 (2010): 139–42.

2. Mark Zimmerman et al., "How Should Remission from Depression Be Defined? The Depressive Patient's Perspective," *American Journal of Psychiatry* 163 (2006): 148–50.

3. Eugene S. Paykel, "Partial Remission, Residual Symptoms," *Dialogues in Clinical Neuroscience* 10 (2008): 431–37.

4. Roger S. McIntyre and Claire O'Donovan, "The Human Cost of Not Achieving Full Remission in Depression," *Canadian Journal of Psychiatry* 49 (2004): 10S–16S.

5. Martin B. Keller, "Issues in Treatment-Resistant Depression," *Journal of Clinical Psychiatry* 66 (2005): 5–12.

6. Keller, "Issues in Treatment-Resistant Depression."

7. Deidre Bonner and Richard Howard, "Clinical Characteristics of Treatment-Resistant Depression in the Elderly," *International Journal of Geriatric Psychiatry* 10 (1995): 1023–27.

8. Erin Miller et al., "Treatment-Resistant Depression in Later Life," in *Treatment-Resistant Depression: A Roadmap for Effective Care*, edited by John F. Greden and Michelle B. Riba, 115–36 (Arlington: American Psychiatric Association, 2011).

9. Tracy Greer et al., "Defining and Measuring Functional Recovery in Depression," *CNS Drugs* 24 (2010): 267–84.

10. C. Steven Richards and Michael G. Perri, *Relapse Prevention for Depression* (Washington: American Psychological Association, 2010).

11. Stephanie L. Burcusa and William Iacono, "Risk for Recurrence in Depression," *Clinical Psychology Review* 27 (2008): 959–85.

12. Burcusa and Iacono, "Risk for Recurrence."

13. Jay D. Amsterdam and Justine Shults, "Does Tachyphylaxis Occur after Repeated Antidepressant Exposure in Patients with Bipolar II Major Depressive Episode?" *Journal of Affective Disorders* 115 (2010): 234–40; William E. Evans and Howard McLeod, "Pharmacogenomics: Drug Disposition, Drug Targets and Side Effects," *New England Journal of Medicine* 348 (2003): 538–49.

14. Ross J. Baldessarini et al., "Illness Risk Following Rapid versus Gradual Discontinuation of Antidepressants," *American Journal of Psychiatry* 167 (2010): 934–41.

15. Robert Kohn et al., "The Treatment Gap in Mental Health Care," *Bulletin of the World Health Organization* 82 (2004): 858–72.

16. Kohn et al., "The Treatment Gap."

17. Otto F. Wahl, *Media Madness: Public Images of Mental Illness* (New Brunswick, N.J.: Rutgers University Press, 1995).

18. Jocelyn Angus and Patricia Reeve, "Ageism: A Threat to 'Aging Well' in the 21st Century," *Journal of Applied Gerontology* 25 (2006): 137–52.

19. Bruce G. Link et al., "Stigma as a Barrier to Recovery: The Consequences of Stigma for the Self-Esteem of People with Mental Illnesses," *Psychiatric Services* 52 (2001): 1621–56.

20. Mental Health Commission of Canada, "Eliminating Stigma: A Focus on Seniors' Mental Health," *Mental Health Strategy for Canada* (September 2014): 1–9.

21. Patrick Corrigan, "Stigmatizing Attitudes about Mental Illness and Allocation of Resources to Mental Health Services," *Community Mental Health Journal* 40 (2004): 297–307.

22. Gerhard Falk, *Stigma: How We Treat Outsiders* (New York: Prometheus Books, 2001).

23. Jessie Gruman, *AfterShock: What to Do When the Doctor Gives You— Or Someone You Love—a Devastating Diagnosis* (New York: Walker Books, 2007).

24. Ami Schattner et al., "The Hazards of Diagnosis," *QJM* 103 (2010): 583–87.

25. S. Gilbody et al., "Collaborative Care for Depression," *Archives of Internal Medicine* 166 (2006): 2314–21.

26. Katharine M. McDonald et al., "Care Coordination," in *Closing the Quality Gap: A Critical Analysis of Quality Improvement Strategies*, vol. 7 (Rockville, Md.: Agency for Health Care Research and Quality, 2007).

27. Anilkrishna Thota et al., "Collaborative Care to Improve the Management of Depressive Disorders: A Community Guide, Systematic Review and Meta-Analysis," *American Journal of Preventive Medicine* 42 (2012): 525–38.

28. Jeannie Haggerty et al., "Continuity of Care: A Multidisciplinary Review," *BMJ* 327 (2003): 1219–21.

29. Haggerty et al., "Continuity of Care."

7. SUICIDE IN LATER LIFE

1. José Manoel Bertolote and Alexandra Fleischmann, "Suicide and Psychiatric Diagnosis: A Worldwide Perspective," *World Psychiatry* 1 (2002): 181–85.

2. World Health Organization, *Preventing Suicide: A Global Imperative* (Geneva: World Health Organization, 2014).

3. World Health Organization, *Preventing Suicide*.

4. World Health Organization, *Preventing Suicide*.

5. World Health Organization, *Preventing Suicide*.

6. Kimberely Van Oordean and Yeates Cornwell, "Suicides in Late Life," *Current Psychiatry Reports* 13 (2011): 234–41.

7. Centers for Disease Control and Prevention, National Center for Injury Prevention and Control, *Web-based Injury Statistics Query and Reporting System* (WISQARS) [online], 2010, [cited July 28, 2015], www.cdc.gov/injury/wisqars/index.html.

8. Yeates Conwell and Caitlin Thompson, "Suicide Behavior in Elders," *Psychiatric Clinics of North America* 31 (2008): 333–56.

9. Conwell and Thompson, "Suicide Behavior in Elders."

10. Conwell and Thompson, "Suicide Behavior in Elders."

11. Stefan Wiktorsson et al., "Attempted Suicide in the Elderly: Characteristics of Suicide Attempters 70 Years or Older and a General Population Comparison Group," *American Journal of Geriatric Psychiatry* 18 (2010): 57–67.

12. J. B. Luoma et al., "Contact with Mental Health and Primary Care Providers before Suicide: A Review of the Evidence," *American Journal of Psychiatry* 159 (2002): 909–21.

13. Richard Lester and Bijou Yang, "Recalculating the Economic Cost of Suicide," *Death Studies* 31 (2006): 351–61.

14. Douglas Jacobs and Marci Klein, "The Expanding Role of Psychological Autopsies," in *Suicidology: Essays in Honor of Edwin S. Shneidman*, edited by Antoon A. Leenaars (Northvale, N.J.: Aronson, 1993).

15. Yeates Conwell, "Suicide Later in Life: Challenges and Priorities for Prevention," *American Journal of Preventative Medicine* 47 (2014): S244–50.

16. Conwell and Thompson, "Suicide Behavior in Elders.

17. Conwell and Thompson, "Suicide Behavior in Elders.

18. Conwell and Thompson, "Suicide Behavior in Elders.

19. Gary Kennedy, *Suicide and Depression in Late Life: Critical Issues in Treatment, Research, and Public Policy* (New York: Wiley, 1996); John F. McCarthy et al., "Suicide Mortality Following Nursing Home Discharge in the Department of Veterans Affairs Health System," *American Journal of Public Health* 103 (2013): 2261–66.

20. Lydia Li and Yeates Conwell, "Pain and Self Injury in Elderly Men and Women Receiving Home Care," *Journal of American Geriatrics* 58 (2010): 2160–65.

21. Juliet Holt-Lunstand, Timothy B. Smith, and J. Bradley Layton, "Social Relationships and Mortality Risk: A Meta-Analytic Review," *PloS Medicine* 7 (2010): e1000316.

22. Conwell and Thompson, "Suicide Behavior in Elders."

23. Camila Haw et al., "Dementia and Suicidal Behavior: A Review of the Literature," *International Psychogeriatrics* 21 (2009): 440–53.

24. Thomas Joiner, *Why People Die by Suicide* (Cambridge, Mass.: Harvard University Press, 2005).

25. Roy Baumeister and Mark Leary, "The Need to Belong: Desire for Interpersonal Attachments as a Fundamental Human Motivation," *Psychological Bulletin* 117 (1995): 497–529.

26. Kimberly A. Van Orden et al., "Perceived Burdensomeness as an Indicator of Suicidal Symptoms," *Cognitive Therapy and Research* 30 (2006): 457–57.

27. M. David Rudd et al., "Warning Signs for Suicide: Theory, Research, and Clinical Applications," *Suicide and Life-Threatening Behavior* 36 (2006): 255–62.

28. Rudd et al., "Warning Signs for Suicide."

29. Ildri Kjølsethl and Øivind Ekeberg, "When Elderly People Give Warning of Suicide," *International Psychogeriatrics* 24 (2012): 1393–401.

30. American Association of Suicidology, *Know the Warning Signs*, 2006, www.suicidology.org/web/guest/stats-and-tools/warning-signs (accessed August 1, 2015).

8. WHAT TO EXPECT SHOULD YOU NEED HOSPITALIZATION

1. Sungkyu Lee, Aileen B. Rothbard, and Elizabeth L. Noll, "Length of Inpatient Stay of Persons with Serious Mental Illness: Effects of Hospital and Regional Characteristics," *Psychiatric Services* 63 (2012): 889–95.

2. Deborah Barnes et al., "Acute Care for Elders Units Produced Shorter Hospital Stays at Lower Cost while Maintaining Patients' Functional Status," *Health Affairs* 31 (2012): 1227–36.

3. Penelope A. Pollitt and Daniel W. O'Connor, "What Was Good about Admissions to an Aged Psychiatry Ward? The Subject Experiences of Patients with Depression," *International Psychogeriatrics* 20 (2008): 628–40.

4. Thomas W. Kallert, Matthias Glockner, and Matthias Schutzwohl, "Involuntary vs. Voluntary Hospital Admission," *European Archives of Psychiatry and Clinical Neuroscience* 258 (2008): 195–209.

5. Pollitt and O'Connor, "What Was Good about Admissions."

6. Pollitt and O'Connor, "What Was Good about Admissions."

7. Iris Sher et al., "Effects of Caregiver's Perceived Stigma and Causal Beliefs on Patient's Adherence to Antidepressant Treatment," *Psychiatric Services* 56 (2005): 564–69.

8. Walid K. Abdul-Hamid et al., "Older People with Enduring Mental Illness: A Needs Assessment Tool," *Psychiatrist* 33 (2009): 91–95.

9. Andrea M. Sephar et al., "Seamless Care: Safe Patient Transfers from Hospital to Home," *Advances in Patient Safety* 1 (2005): 79–98.

10. Tomasso Dazzi et al., "Does Asking about Suicide and Related Behaviours Induce Suicidal Ideation? What Is the Evidence?" *Psychological Medicine* 44 (2014): 3361–63.

11. Evangelos C. Karademas, "Self-efficacy, Social Support and Well-being: The Mediating Role of Optimism," *Personality and Individual Differences* 40 (2006): 1281–90.

12. James D. Tew, "Post-Hospitalization Transitional Care Needs of Depressed Elderly Patients: Models for Improvement," *Current Opinion in Psychiatry* 18 (2005): 673–77.

13. Gina R. Kruse and Barbara M. Rohland, "Factors Associated with Attendance at a First Appointment after Discharge from a Psychiatric Hospital," *Psychiatric Services* 53 (2002): 473–76.

14. Lissa Rankin, *Mind over Medicine* (Carlsbad: Hay House, 2014).

15. Pollitt and O'Connor, "What Was Good about Admissions."

9. CONSCIOUS AGING WITH DEPRESSION IN LATER LIFE

1. Harry R. Moody. "Conscious Aging: A Strategy for Positive Change in Later Life," in *Mental Wellness in Aging: Strengths-Based Approaches*, edited by Judah L. Ronch and Joseph A. Goldfield, 139–59 (Baltimore: Health Professionals Press, 2003).

2. Ron Pevny, *Conscious Living, Conscious Aging: Embrace and Savor Your Next Chapter* (New York: Atria Books, 2014).

3. Matteo Tosato et al., "The Aging Process and Potential Interventions to Extend Life Expectancy," *Clinical Interventions in Aging* 2 (2007): 401–12.

4. Ake Wahlin et al., "How Do Health and Biological Age Influence Chronological Age and Sex Differences in Cognitive Aging: Moderating, Mediating, or Both?" *Psychology and Aging* 21 (2006): 318–32.

5. Michael Roisen, *RealAge: Are You as Young as You Can Be?* (New York: William Morrow, 1999).

6. Karen Anne Mather et al., "Is Telomere Length a Biomarker of Aging? A Review," *Journal of Gerontology* 66A (2011): 202–13.

7. Veryan Codd et al., "Identification of Seven Loci Affecting Mean Telomere Length and Their Association with Disease," *Nature Genetics* 45 (2013): 422–27.

8. Davis C. Hendricks and Jon Hendricks, "Concepts of Time and Temporal Construction among the Aged, with Implications for Research," in *Time, Roles, and Self in Old Age*, edited by Jaber F. Gubrium, 13–49 (New York: Human Sciences Press, 1936).

9. Lissy F. Jarvik, "Thought on the Psychobiology of Aging," *American Psychologist* 30 (1975): 576–83.

10. Benny Barak and Leon G. Schiffman, "Cognitive Age: A Nonchronological Age Variable," in *Advances in Consumer Research*, vol. 8, edited by Kent B. Monroe, 602–6 (Ann Arbor, Mich.: Association for Consumer Research, 1981).

11. R. A. McFarland, "The Need for Functional Age Measurement in Industrial Psychology," Industrial Gerontology 19 (1973): 1–19 .

12. Janet Lawrence, "The Effect of Perceived Age on Initial Impressions and Normative Role Expectations," *International Journal of Aging and Human Development* 5 (1975): 369–91.

13. Zena Smith Blau, "Changes in Status and Age Identification," *American Sociological Review* 21 (1956): 198–203.

14. Erik H. Erikson, "Life Cycle," *International Encyclopedia of the Social Sciences* 9 (1968): 286–92.

15. Michael J. Lowis et al., "Ego Integrity and Life Satisfaction in Retired Males," *Counselling Psychology in Africa* 2 (1997): 12–23.

16. Ruthellen Josselson, "Relationship as a Path to Integrity, Wisdom, and Meaning," in *The Psychology of Mature Spirituality: Integrity, Wisdom, Transcendence*, edited by Polly Young-Eisendrath and Melvin Miller, 68–80 (Philadelphia: Routledge, 2000).

17. Paul T. Wong, "Positive Psychology 2.0: Towards a Balanced Interactive Model of the Good Life," *Canadian Psychology* 52 (2011): 69–81.

18. Sofia von Humboldt, Isabel Leal, and Filipa Pimenta, "What Predicts Older Adults' Adjustment to Aging in Later Life? The Impact of Sense of Coherence, Subjective Well-Being, and Sociodemographic, Lifestyle, and Health-Related Factors," *Educational Gerontology* 40 (2014): 641–54.

19. Becca R. Levy et al., "Longevity Increased by Positive Self-Perceptions of Aging," *Journal of Personality and Social Psychology* 83 (2002): 261–70; Robin L. West and Erin C. Hastings, "Self-regulation and Recall: Growth Curve Modeling of Intervention Outcomes for Older Adults," *Psychology and Aging* 26 (2011): 803–12.

20. Wong, "Positive Psychology 2.0."

21. Viktor Frankl, *The Doctor and the Soul* (New York: Bantam Books, 1971).

22. John W. Rowe and Robert L. Kahn, "Successful Aging," *Gerontologist* 37 (1997): 433–40.

23. Marilyn Schlitz, Tina Amorok, and Marc Micozzi, *Consciousness and Healing: Integral Approaches to Mind-Body Medicine* (London: Churchill Livingston, 2004).

24. Marilyn Mandala Schlitz et al., "Conscious Aging and Worldview Transformation," *Journal of Transpersonal Psychology* 43 (2011): 223–39.

25. Schlitz et al., "Conscious Aging."

26. Schlitz et al., "Conscious Aging."

27. Norman Doige, *The Brain That Changes Itself: Stories of Personal Triumph from the Frontiers of Brain Science* (New York: Penguin Books, 2007).

28. Schlitz et al., "Conscious Aging."

29. Schlitz et al., "Conscious Aging."

30. Schlitz et al., "Conscious Aging."

31. Schlitz et al., "Conscious Aging."

32. Paul T. Wong, "Meaning Management Theory and Death Acceptance," in *Existential and Spiritual Issues in Death Attitudes*, edited by A. Tomer, E. Grafton, and Paul T. Wong, 65–87 (New York: Erlbaum, 2008).

33. Moody, "Conscious Aging."

34. Julian Seifter and Besty Seifter, *After the Diagnosis: Transcending Chronic Illness* (New York: Simon & Schuster, 2010).

35. Philip Berman, *The Courage to Grow Old* (New York: Ballantine Books, 1983), 303.

36. Scott Miller, "Blurring the Lines, Expanding the Vision," in *Mental Wellness in Aging: Strengths-Based Approaches*, edited by Judah L. Ronch and Joseph A Goldfield, 13–15 (Baltimore: Health Professionals Press, 2003).

10. LONG-TERM CARE AND LATE-LIFE DEPRESSION

1. Centers for Disease Control, "Long-Term Care Services in the United States: 2013 Overview," *Vital and Health Statistics* 37 (2013): 1–107.

2. "What Is Home Health Care?" *Eldercare*, www.eldercare.gov/elder-care.net/public/resources/factsheets/home_health_care.aspx (accessed August 21, 2015).

3. Sheryl Zimmerman et al., "Assisted Living and Skilled Nursing Homes: Apples and Oranges?" *Gerontologist* 43 (2003): 107–17.

4. "What Is Home Health Care?" *Eldercare*.

5. Centers for Disease Control, "Long-Term Care Services."

6. Lee Hyer, "Depression in Long-Term Care," *Clinical Psychology: Science and Practice* 12 (2008): 280–99.

7. Mary Naylor and Stacen A. Keating, "Transitional Care: Moving Patients from One Care Setting to Another," *American Journal of Nursing* 108 (2008): 58–63.

8. Richard Schulz et al., "Effects of a Psychosocial Intervention on Caregivers of Recently Placed Nursing Home Residents: A Randomized Controlled Trial," *Clinical Gerontologist* 37 (2014): 347–67.

9. Office of the Inspector General Report, "Care in Skilled Nursing Facilities Harmed Nearly One-Third of Medicare Residents in August 2011," www.medicareadvocacy.org/oig-report-care-in-skilled-nursing-facilities-harmed-nearly-one-third-of-medicare-residents-in-august-2011 (accessed August 18, 2015).

10. Office of the Inspector General Report, "Care in Skilled Nursing Facilities."

11. Office of the Inspector General Report, "Care in Skilled Nursing Facilities."

12. Mugdha Thankur and Dan G. Blazer, "Depression in Long-Term Care," *Journal of the American Medical Directors Association* 9 (2008): 82–87.

13. Centers for Disease Control, "Long-Term Care Services."

14. Jane Zarren, "Today's Continuing Care Retirement Communities," *American Seniors Housing Association* (July 2010): 1–32.

15. U.S. Government Accountability Office, *Continuing Care Retirement Communities Can Provide Benefits, but Not without Some Risk* (Washington, D.C.: Government Accountability Office, 2010).

16. Tetyana Pylypiv Shippee, "'But I Am Not Moving': Residents' Perspectives on Transitions within a Continuing Care Retirement Community," *Gerontologist* 49 (2009): 418–27.

17. Shiho Sugihara, "Place Attachment and Social Support at Continuing Care Retirement Communities," *Environment and Behaviors* 32 (2000): 400–409.

18. Richard Rosner, *Geriatric Psychiatry and the Law* (New York: Springer, 2011).

19. Melissa M. Garrido et al., "Quality of Life and Cost of Care at the End of Life: The Role of Advance Directives," *Journal of Pain and Symptom Management* 49 (2014): 825–35.

20. Lawrence Wissow et al., "Promoting Advance Directives among Elderly Primary Care Patients," *Journal of General Internal Medicine* 19 (2004): 944–51.

21. Seth Feuerstein et al., "The Last Will and Testament and the Psychiatrist," *Psychiatry* 3 (2006): 18–29.

22. Jeffrey W. Swanson et al., "Psychiatric Advance Directives: An Alternative to Coercive Treatment," *Psychiatry* 63 (2000): 160–72.

23. "Psychiatric Advance Directives: An Overview," *National Alliance on Mental Illness*, https://www2.nami.org/Template.cfm?Section=Issue_Spotlights&template=/ContentManagemet/ContentDisplay.cfm&ContentID=137779 (accessed August 19, 2015).

24. "Overview of Psychiatric Advance Directives in the United States," *National Resource Center of Psychiatric Directives*, www.nrc-pad.org/images/stories/PDFs/overview%20of%20pads%20in%20the%20us.pdf (accessed August 28, 2015).

25. Rebecca L. Sudore and Terri R. Fried, "Redefining the Planning in Advance Care Planning: Preparing for End-of-Life Decision Making," *Annals of Internal Medicine* 153 (2010): 256–61.

I I. I5 LATE-LIFE DEPRESSION MYTHS EVERYONE SHOULD KNOW

1. Jan Harold Brunvand, *The Vanishing Hitchhiker: American Urban Legends and Their Meanings* (New York: W.W. Norton, 2003).

2. Peter Sheridan Dodds and Duncan J. Watts, "A Generalized Model of Social and Biological Contagion," *Journal of Theoretical Biology* 232 (2005): 587–604.

3. Diane Maron, "Fact or Fiction: If You Shave Your Hair, Will It Come Back Thicker?" *Scientific American*, www.scientificamerican.com/article/fact-or-fiction-if-you-shave-or-wax-your-hair-will-come-back-thicker/ (accessed September 1, 2015).

4. "Knuckles and Joints: Does Cracking Your Knuckles Cause Arthritis?" *Medical News Today*, www.medicalnewstoday.com/articles/259603.php (accessed September 1, 2015).

5. Chris Higgins, "Napoleon Wasn't Short, Vikings Didn't Wear Horned Helmets, and Three Other Historical Misconceptions," *Metal Floss*, http://mentalfloss.com/article/32125/napoleon-wasnt-short-vikings-didnt-wear-horned-helmets-and-3-more-historical (accessed September 1, 2015).

6. Theodore Millon, *Masters of the Mind: Exploring the Story of Mental Illness from Ancient Times to the New Millennium* (Hoboken, N.J.: John Wiley and Sons, 2004).

7. Patrick Corrigan, David Roe, and Hector W. H. Tsang, *Challenging the Stigma of Mental Illness: Lessons for Therapists and Advocates* (Hoboken, N.J.: Wiley Blackwell, 2011).

8. Anne Lise Holm, Anne Lyberg, and Elisabeth Severinsson, "Living with Stigma: Depressed Elderly Persons' Experiences of Physical Health Problems," *Nursing Research and Practice* 2014 (2014): 1–8.

9. Simon Jones, Louise Howard, and Graham Thornicroft, "'Diagnostic Overshadowing': Worse Physical Health Care for People with Mental Illness," *Acta Psychiatrica Scandinavica* 118 (2008): 169–71.

10. Ann Jacoby, "Felt versus Enacted Stigma: A Concept Revisited. Evidence from Study of People with Epilepsy in Remission," *Social Science and Medicine* 38 (1994): 269–74.

11. Marc Corbiere et al., "Strategies to Fight Stigma toward People with Mental Disorders: Perspective from Different Stakeholders," *Scientific World Journal* 2012 (2012): 1–10.

12. Patrick Corrigan, "Stigmatizing Attitudes about Mental Illness and Allocation of Resources to Mental Health Services," *Community Mental Health Journal* 40 (2004): 297–307.

13. Adrienne Van Nieuwenhuizen et al., "Emergency Department Staff Views and Experiences on Diagnostic Overshadowing Related to People with Mental Illness," *Epidemiology and Psychiatric Sciences* 22 (2013): 255–62.

14. Ann Jacoby, "Felt Versus Enacted Stigma."

15. Robert M. Anderson and Martha M. Funnell, "Patient Empowerment: Myths and Misconceptions," *Patient Education and Counseling* 79 (2010): 277–82.

GLOSSARY

acoustic sound therapy: the use of soundscapes to enhance well-being.

advanced directives: set of legal plans that outline your wishes.

affect regulation: techniques to help manage the swings of moods.

affective disorders: alternative phrase used for mood disorders.

ageism: stereotyping or prejudice toward aging or elderly adults.

amygdala: brain structure responsible for emotion and motivation.

animal-assisted therapy: holistic treatment that uses pets to ease depression and other mental illnesses. *See also* pet therapy.

antidepressant discontinuation syndrome: negative experience that results from reducing dosage of, or coming off, antidepressant medication too quickly.

antidepressant tachyphylaxis: when your body no longer functions to counteract or control serotonin, norepinephrine, or other neurotransmitters.

appoggiatura: note that clashes with melody that creates an emotional response.

aromatherapy: the practice of using aromas to promote physical and emotional well-being.

augmentation: pharmacological approach of adding a supplemental medication to boost the effectiveness of current antidepressant medication.

basal ganglia: structure located deep within the brain that is involved with movement, thinking, and mood regulation.

binaural beats: sounds or music that ease you into a meditative state.

bipolar: moods that fluctuate between the lows of depression and the highs of mania.

bright light therapy: holistic therapy for depression in which direct sunlight or artificial lights are used to regulate melatonin production.

centenarians: adult aged 100 years or older.

chromotherapy: the ancient practice of using color to heal.

chronicity: length and intensity of a depressive or manic episode.

cingulate gyrus: important component of the limbic system that regulates emotions.

circadian rhythm: regularity of daily rhythms, influenced by neurochemistry, light, and darkness.

comorbidity: having more than one medical or psychiatric disorder.

conscious aging: mindful approach toward aging with insight and wisdom.

cortisol: stress hormone released from the adrenal gland.

cycling: a rapid mood swing that can occur monthly, weekly or hourly.

cytokines: proteins that increase inflammation in the body.

dawn–dusk simulation light therapy: holistic light treatment that mimics the rising and setting of the sun.

deep brain stimulation: neurosurgical procedure for depression that stimulates deep brain regions through implanted electrodes.

Diagnostic and Statistical Manual of Mental Disorders (DSM): manual for diagnosis of mental disorders as classified by the American Psychiatric Association.

diagnostic overshadowing: the experience of a health professional wrongly attributing new physical symptoms to a preexisting mental illness.

Diathesis–Stress model: method that examines the interactions that occur between a person's biology, social environment, and unique temperament, to explain the development of a mood disorder.

discontinuation syndrome: *See* antidepressant discontinuation syndrome.

docosahexaenic acid (DHA): omega-3 fatty acid essential for health brain growth.

dopamine: inhibitory neurotransmitter that is involved in regulating mood.

double depression: presence of major depressive disorder and dysthymia in a person.

drug therapy: another term often used for pharmacotherapy.

dual sensory loss: hearing and vision loss experienced at the same time in seniors.

dysthymic disorder: clinical depressive disorder less severe in intensity than major depressive disorder but longer in its duration.

early onset: depression that occurs in childhood, teen, or young adulthood.

endorphins: neurotransmitters that reduce pain and influence emotions.

etiology: the cause or origin of a disorder.

filial piety: the practice of respecting one's elders and ancestors.

flight into health: temporary improvement or denial of problems when confronted with treatment.

frailty: clinical syndrome that places seniors at risk for coping with everyday stressors.

gaps in treatment: issues that prevent you from having consistent treatment of your depression.

gene: unit of DNA that carries a specific genetic code.

geriatric: the population of individuals aged 65 years or older.

geriatric depression: category of depression that occurs in adults aged 65 years or older. *See also* late-life depression.

geriatric massage: form of massage that is designed specifically for the elderly.

geriatrician: physician who specializes in the care of elderly patients.

gerontology: the field of science devoted to studying aging.

geropsychology: the field of psychology that studies health and well-being in the aged population.

green space: areas that incorporate plants, trees, and park-like settings.

hippocampus: brain structure involved in emotional regulation, learning, and memory.

hypomania: less intensive form of mania.

hypothalamus: walnut-sized structure that functions as a major relay station for communication in the brain.

International Classification of Diseases: manual for diagnosis of medical and psychiatric disorders as classified by the World Health Organization.

late-life depression: category of depression that occurs in seniors aged 65 years or older. *See also* geriatric depression.

late-onset bipolar illness (LOBI): clinical term used for adults aged 50 and over who experience a first-time bipolar illness.

late onset depression: depression that occurs after the age of 65 years.

life cycle: the stages of life human beings move through across the lifespan.

limbic system: series of brain structures involving emotions, memory, awareness, and homeostasis.

major depressive disorder: clinical mood disorder involving unshakable sadness, despair, and fatigue.

medial prefrontal cortex: brain structure in the prefrontal cortex involving cognitions and emotions.

melatonin: hormone that regulates circadian rhythm.

mood: feeling or emotional state.

mood disorder: chronic disturbance of mood that disrupts daily life.

mood swing: cycling between highs and lows of affective states.

negative ion therapy: air cleaners that produce negative ions that relieve stress, improve concentration, and boost energy.

neurobiological: having to do with the biological study of the nervous system and brain behavior.

neurotransmitter: chemical that helps communication between neurons.

nonagenarians: adults who are 90 years old or more.

opioids: natural morphine-like brain chemicals that ease pain.

orbitofrontal cortex: brain structure associated with the processing of emotions.

oxytocin: feel-good hormone secreted by the pituitary gland.

partial remission: not fully achieving a symptom-free state.

personalized medicine: medical model emphasizing the unique genetic makeup of a person.

pet therapy: the use of animals to assist in reducing depressive and anxiety symptoms. *See also* animal-assisted therapy.

pharmacotherapy: form of therapy that uses medication as a means to treat disease.

pineal gland: brain structure that functions as the body's time clock.

psychogeriatric units: specifically designed inpatient programs for older adults.

psychopharmacology: *See* pharmacotherapy.

recovery: experience of being symptom-free for at least four months after achieving remission.

recurrence: another depressive episode after recovery has been attained.

relapse: full return of depressive symptoms after remission but before recovery.

reminiscence bump: the experience of listening to music that brings forth emotions, memories, and nostalgia.

remission: experience of being symptom-free.

residual symptoms: not reaching remission, with some symptoms still existing.

resilience: ability to overcome difficulties and function in a state of well-being.

response: improvement from the initial onset of illness.

risk factors: variables that increase the chance of developing mental or physical illness.

sandwich generation: adult who is raising children and caring for an aged parent.

self-actualization: desire to find fulfillment and acceptance in oneself.

serotonin: neurotransmitter that regulates behavioral and emotional expression.

skilled nursing facility: another term used for skilled nursing home.

social contagion: psychological phenomenon responsible for stigmatizing and myth-making beliefs.

soft bipolar disorder: term used to describe atypical bipolar II and bipolar spectrum disorders.

somatic complaints: physical aches and pains.

stigma: social disapproval or marginalizing of a person with mental illness.

stigma by association: form of stigma that results from one's connection to someone with mental illness. *See also* associative stigma and courtesy stigma.

subclinical: symptoms that fall just below the criteria for a clinical disorder.

suicidality: range of self-harm and suicidal behaviors.

talk therapy: term used to describe psychotherapy.

thwarted belongingness: lack of meaningful connections to others.

transitional care: plan of action that facilitates your safety and treatment from hospital to home.

treatment lag: issues that stall or delay your healing from late-life depression.

treatment-resistant depression (TRD): depression that does not respond well to traditional therapies and medications.

triggers: feelings, thoughts, or experiences that cause trauma.

unipolar: moods that are rooted in a depressive state.

vibroacoustic therapy: holistic treatment that utilizes sound and music and vibration.

warning signs: behaviors that indicate an immediate risk for suicide.

well-being: finding an optimal quality of life in spite of living with a chronic illness.

INDEX

AAT. *See* animal-assisted therapy
acceptance: of LLD, 154–155; of
    mortality, 152, 154
acoustic sound therapy, 82
activities of daily living (ADL), 33
acupressure, 76
acupuncture, 76
adaptation, with conscious aging, 151
ADDM. *See* adjustment disorder with
    depressed mood
Adele, 81
adjustment disorder with depressed mood
    (ADDM), 24
ADL. *See* activities of daily living
Administration on Aging
    recommendations: for assisted living,
    164–165; for home health care,
    162–163
admission, to hospital, 128–130
ADRs. *See* adverse drug reactions
Adult Suicide Ideation Questionnaire
    (ASIQ), 36
advanced directives, 170–171, 171; LADs,
    171, 173–175; MADs, 171, 172–173;
    PADs, 171, 171–172
adverse drug reactions (ADRs), 39
AES. *See* Apathy Evaluation Scale
affect, 15, 15–16
affective disorders, 3
African Americans, late onset of
    depression in, 6

age, of depression onset, 4–5
age interactions antidepressant response,
    39
ageism, 94–95, 96, 144–145
agencies, collaborative care with, 97–98,
    99
aging: attaining well-being, 148–151; case
    study: Dawn, 156–160; conscious,
    143–144, 151–154; definition of,
    144–145; in different cultures, 144;
    filial piety, 144; life stages, 148; LLD
    and acceptance with, 154–155;
    negative beliefs about, 144–145;
    successful, 151; summary of, 156
aging measures, 145; biological, 145–146;
    chronologic, 146, 147–148; functional,
    146–147; physiological, 145;
    psychological, 147–148
Alzheimer's disease, 24, 34–36, 167
American Association of Retired Persons,
    169
American Association of Suicidology, 116
American Hospital Association, 79
amygdala, 70
ancient grains, 72
animal-assisted therapy (AAT), 76–77
antidepressant discontinuation syndrome,
    93
antidepressant tachyphylaxis (AT), 92
Apathy Evaluation Scale (AES), 36
appoggiatura, 81

aromatherapy, 70
ASIQ. *See* Adult Suicide Ideation
    Questionnaire
assisted living, 164, 165; Administration
    on Aging recommendations for,
    164–165; Medicare and, 164
AT. *See* antidepressant tachyphylaxis
attention: cognition screening for, 34;
    with conscious aging, 151–152, 152
audio books, 82
augmentation, of medicinal agent, 91
awareness, of stigma, 95, 95–96

bad mood, 16
basal ganglia, 58
BD-I. *See* bipolar disorder I
BD-II. *See* bipolar disorder II
BD-NOS. *See* bipolar disorder not
    otherwise specified
Beck Depression Scale (BDS), 36
behave, with depression, 3
Behavior Rating Inventory of Executive
    Function (BRIEF), 34–36
behavior therapy for older adults (BT-
    OA), 50
binaural beats, 82
biological age, 145–146
bipolar depression, 17, 21, 23–24;
    frequent episodes of, 21; LOBI, 21,
    23; mood swing with, 21; symptoms of,
    21–23
bipolar disorder, soft, 23
bipolar disorder I (BD-I), 23, 24
bipolar disorder II (BD-II), 23, 24
bipolar disorder not otherwise specified
    (BD-NOS), 24
BRIEF. *See* Behavior Rating Inventory of
    Executive Function
bright light therapy, 67
Brunvand, Jan, 181
BT-OA. *See* behavior therapy for older
    adults

CAM. *See* complimentary alternative
    medicine
capability for suicide, 112, 113
care: continuity of, 97–98; coordination
    of, 97; transitional, 133. *See also*
    collaborative care; long-term care,

LLD and
caregivers, 11; during hospitalization,
    131–133; tips for, 132–133
CASE. *See* Clinical Assessment Scales for
    the Elderly
catatonic depression, 25
categories, of geriatric mood disorders,
    17, 17–26
Caucasians, late onset of depression in, 6
CB. *See* cognitive bibliotherapy
CBT-OA. *See* cognitive-behavioral
    therapy for older adults
CCRCs. *See* Continuing Care Retirement
    Communities
CD. *See* cyclothymic disorder
CDC report. *See* Centers for Disease
    Control
CDR. *See* Clinical Dementia Rating
centenarians, 3
Centers for Disease Control (CDC)
    report, 108, 162, 164, 165
changes, in skilled nursing homes,
    165–166
chromotherapy, 68, 70
chronic illness, depression as, 1, 2
chronologic age, 146, 147–148
cingulate gyrus, 74
circadian rhythm, 67
Clinical Assessment Scales for the Elderly
    (CASE), 36
Clinical Dementia Rating (CDR), 34–36
clinical interview, 34
clothing, during hospitalization, 129
cognition screening: for attention and
    memory, 34; for delirium, 34–36; for
    dementia, 34–36; for polypharmacy,
    34–36
cognitive-behavioral therapy for older
    adults (CBT-OA), 50–51
cognitive bibliotherapy (CB), 51
collaborative care: with independent
    senior, 95, 97, 98; with many agencies,
    97–98, 99
communication, with home transition,
    134–136
comorbidity, 36
complimentary alternative medicine
    (CAM), 65

conscious aging, 143–144, 151; accepting mortality, 152, 154; adaptation with, 151; attention, 151–152, 152; guidance, 152, 153; integration, 152, 153; intention, 152; living deeply, 152, 153–154; moving from "I" to "We", 152, 153; repetition, 152, 153. *See also* aging

conscious childbirthing, 143

conscious dying, 143

conscious eldering, 143

consciousness, 151

conscious uncoupling, 143

context, of stigma, 95, 96

Continuing Care Retirement Communities (CCRCs), 168; description of, 168–169; Medicare and, 169; questions for, 169–170; services offered by, 170; standards of, 169

continuity of care, 97–98

co-occurring issues, 36

Cornell Scale for Depression in Dementia (CSDD), 36

Corrigan, Patrick, 183

cortisol, 75

costs: of depression, 8–9; of home health care, 161–162

CSDD. *See* Cornell Scale for Depression in Dementia

cultures, of aging, 144

cyclothymic disorder (CD), 23–24

cytochrome P450, 39, 39–43, 43

cytokines, 75

dawn-dusk simulation light therapy, 67

DBS. *See* deep brain stimulation

DBT. *See* dialectical behavior therapy

DD. *See* dysthymic disorders

death anxiety, 150

deep brain stimulation (DBS), 58

Deep Theta Music (Halpern), 83

delirium, 34–36

dementia, 24, 34–36

Dementia Rating Scale (DRS-2), 34–36

Department of Health and Human Services, 166–167

depressed mood, 16

depression: catatonic, 25; as chronic illness, 1, 2; cost of, 8–9; definition of, 2–3; double, 1; etiology of, 5; feel, think, behave with, 3; geriatric, 5, 89, 93, 131–132; negative beliefs about, 185; personal experiences with, 2; symptoms of, 4; treatment-resistant, 56; types of, 54; work productivity and, 8. *See also* bipolar depression; late-life depression; late-life depression myths; neurobiological depression; onset, of depression; subclinical depression; unipolar depression

depression-executive dysfunction syndrome, 25

depression in later life: case study: Davina, 43–47; diagnosis for, 31; genetic testing for, 38–43; geriatric assessment, 31–32, 36–38; mental health specialist, 33–36; physician evaluation, 32–33; summary of, 43

depression in later life, holistic approaches to, 65; case study: Uncle Rey, 84–88; five senses relating to, 66–84; summary of, 84

depression in later life, treatments for, 49; case study: Wendy, 59–63; medical, 54, 54–59; psychotherapy, 49–53; summary of, 59

depressive disorder not otherwise specified (D-NOS), 20

DHA. *See* docosahexaenoic acid

Diagnostic and Statistical Manual of Mental Disorders (DSM), 16, 90

diagnostic overshadowing, 184

diagnostic trauma. *See* stigma and diagnostic trauma

dialectical behavior therapy (DBT), 51

Diathesis-Stress model, 9–10, 10

discharge plan, 133

discontinuation syndrome, 93

disease screening and testing, 32–33

disorders. *See specific disorders*

D-NOS. *See* depressive disorder not otherwise specified

docosahexaenoic acid (DHA), 74

dopamine, 25

double depression, 1

DRS-2. *See* Dementia Rating Scale

drug therapy, 55
DSM. *See* Diagnostic and Statistical
    Manual of Mental Disorders
dual sensory loss, 69
durable power of attorney, 174
dysthymic disorders (DD), 1, 20

early onset, of depression, 4, 5, 6
ECT. *See* electroconvulsive therapy
Ego Integrity *versus* Despair, 148
electroconvulsive therapy (ECT), 56–57,
    58, 94
EM. *See* extensive metabolizer
emotion, 15, 16
endorphins, 74
Erickson, Erik, 148, 149
etiology, of depression, 5
exercise, 77–78
extensive metabolizer (EM), 41

factors. *See* risk factors, for late onset de-
    pression; risks, for suicide in later life
family members: during hospitalization,
    131–133; tips for, 132–133
feel, with depression, 3
feeling, 15–16
filial piety, 144
flight into health, 135
folate, 72–73
Frankl, Victor, 150
frequent episodes, of bipolar depression,
    21
functional ability: ADL, 33; IADL, 33
functional age, 146–147
functional impairments, 110–111

gamma-aminobutyric acid (GABA), 25
Gattefossé, René Maurice, 70
GDS. *See* Geriatric Depression Scale
genetic illiteracy, 39–40
Genetic Information Non-Discrimination
    Act of 2008 (GINA), 40
genetics, LLD and, 10
genetic testing, for depression in later life,
    38–43
geriatric assessment, 31–32, 36–38
geriatric depression, 5, 89, 93, 131–132
Geriatric Depression Scale (GDS), 36
Geriatric Hopelessness Scale (GHS), 36

geriatrician, 4
Geriatric Mental State Schedule (GMSS),
    34
geriatric mood disorders, 15–17; bipolar
    depression, 17, 21–24; case study:
    Joan, 27–30; categories of, 17, 17–26;
    neurobiological depression, 17, 25–26;
    summary of, 26; unipolar depression,
    17, 17–20. *See also* other mood
    disorders
geriatric population, with LLD, 3–4
geriatric therapy, 78
gerontology, 3–4
geropsychology, 4
GHS. *See* Geriatric Hopelessness Scale
GINA. *See* Genetic Information Non-
    Discrimination Act of 2008
Global Burden of Disease Study (2010), 8
GMSS. *See* Geriatric Mental State
    Schedule
golden years, 148
good mood, 16
Government Accountability Office, U.S.,
    169
green space, 71
Gruman, Jessie, 96
guidance, with conscious aging, 152, 153

HA. *See* depression in later life, holistic
    approaches to
Halpern, Steve, 83
healthcare proxy, 173
healthcare system, LLD's impact on, 8
hearing loss, 81
high-efficiency particulate arrestance
    (HEPA) air cleaner, 71
high-flavonoid foods, 73
hippocampus, 70
Hispanics, late onset of depression in, 6
holistic approaches (HA). *See* depression
    in later life, holistic approaches to
home health care, 161; Administration on
    Aging recommendations for, 162–163;
    chemistry with, 163; costs of, 161–162;
    insurance for, 162, 163; Meals on
    Wheels, 162; Medicare and, 162, 163;
    PACE, 162
hospitalization, 127; admission, 128–130;
    case study: Ruby, 137–141; clothing

during, 129; daily routine of, 130; discharge plan, 133; family members or caregivers, 131–133; inpatient hospital treatments, 130–131; intake at, 129; involuntary, 128–129; in psychogeriatric units, 127–128; setting of, 127–128; summary of, 136–137; transitional care, 133; transitioning back home, 133–136; voluntary, 128
hypomania, 23
hypothalamus, 66–67

IADL. *See* instrumental activities of daily care
ICD. *See* International Statistical Classification of Diseases and Health Related Problems
IM. *See* intermediate metabolizer
independent senior, 97
inpatient hospitalization, 57–58; treatments during, 130–131
institutional stigma, 184, 185
Instructive PADs, 172
instrumental activities of daily care (IADL), 33
insurance, for home health care, 162, 163
intake, at hospital, 129
integration, with conscious aging, 152, 153
intensive short-term dynamic psychotherapy (ISTDP), 51
intention, with conscious aging, 152
intermediate metabolizer (IM), 40–41
International Statistical Classification of Diseases and Health Related Problems (ICD), 16–17
interpersonal psychotherapy (IPT), 51–52
interpersonal theory of suicide, 111; capability for suicide, 112, 113; perceived burdensomeness, 112, 112–113; thwarted belongingness, 111–112, 112
involuntary hospitalization, 128–129
IPT. *See* interpersonal psychotherapy
IS PATH WARM, 116–117
ISTDP. *See* intensive short-term dynamic psychotherapy
"I" to "We," with conscious aging, 152, 153

Joiner, Thomas, 111
Joint Commission for the Accreditation of Healthcare Organizations, 162

Kutner, Luis, 171

LADs. *See* legal advanced directives
language, stigma relating to, 95
last will and testament, 174–175
late-life depression (LLD), 1–2; and acceptance, 154–155; case study: Sully, 11–14; Diathesis-Stress model, 9–10, 10; genetics and, 10; geriatric population, 3–4; healthcare system impacted by, 8; negative consequences of, 8–9; onset of, 5; statistics for, 6, 6–7; summary of, 11. *See also* long-term care, LLD and
late-life depression myths, 181; case study: big and little Joe, 189–192; social contagion, 182; and stigma, 182–185; types of, 185–188
late onset, of depression, 4–5, 6; of African American, Caucasian, and Hispanic ancestry, 6; risk factors for, 6–7
late-onset bipolar illness (LOBI), 21, 23, 56
lazy medicine, 184
legal advanced directives (LADs), 171, 173; durable power of attorney, 174; last will and testament, 174
lethal catatonia, 25
life cycle, 148, 149
life review psychotherapy (LRP), 52
life stages: of aging, 148; Erickson on, 148, 149; golden years, 148; life cycle, 148, 149
light therapies: bright, 67; dawn-dusk simulation, 67
limbic brain, 69–70
living deeply, with conscious aging, 152, 153–154
living will, 173
LLD. *See* late-life depression
LOBI. *See* late-onset bipolar illness
long-term care, LLD and, 161; advanced directives, 170–175; assisted living, 164–165; case notes: Reuben and

Marta, 175–179; CCRCs, 168–170; home health care, 161–163; skilled nursing homes, 165–168; summary of, 175

LRP. *See* life review psychotherapy

L-theanine, 73

Ma, Yo-Yo, 81

MADs. *See* medical advanced directives

magnesium, 73–74

magnetic seizure therapy (MST), 58–59

major depressive disorder (MDD), 20

major depressive episode, 1

major psychiatric illness, 109

mania, 23

massage therapy, 78–79

McFarland, Robert, 146–147

MDD. *See* major depressive disorder

Meals on Wheels, 162

medial prefrontal cortex, 58

Medicaid, 162, 164, 165, 167, 169, 174

medical advanced directives (MADs), 171, 172, 173; healthcare proxy, 173; living will, 173; witnessing provisions, 173

medical conditions, 24

medical history, 32

medical treatments, 54, 54–59

Medicare, 41–42, 174; assisted living and, 164; CCRCs and, 169; home health care and, 162, 163; skilled nursing homes and, 165, 167

medications, 91

medicinal agent, augmentation of, 91

medicine: CAM, 65; lazy, 184; personalized, 38

melatonin, 66–67

memory, cognition screening for, 34

mental health specialist, 33; clinical interview with, 34; cognition screening by, 34–36; co-occurring issues assessed by, 36; mental status assessed by, 34; mood assessment by, 36

mental status assessment, 34

metabolizer, 40; EM, 41; IM, 40–41; PM, 40; UM, 41

Mini-Cognition Test, 34–36

Mini-Mental State Exam (MMSE), 34

mood, 15, 16; assessment of, 36; bad, 16; depressed, 16; good, 16

mood disorders, 2, 3, 11; due to medical conditions, 24; not otherwise specified, 25. *See also* geriatric mood disorders; other mood disorders

mood swing, 21

mortality, acceptance of, 152, 154

MST. *See* magnetic seizure therapy

music, 81–82

myths. *See* late-life depression myths

National Alliance on Caregiving, 8–9

National Alliance on Mental Health, 172

National Resource Center of Psychiatric Directives, 172

negative beliefs: about aging, 144–145; about depression, 185

negative consequences, of LLD, 8–9

negative ion therapy, 71

negatives, about skilled nursing homes, 166–167

neurobiological depression, 17, 25; catatonic depression, 25; depression-executive dysfunction syndrome, 25; PSD, 26; V-Dep, 26

neurobiology, 95, 107

neurochemistry, 10

neurocognitive disorder, 34–36

neurotransmitters, 56

Nightingale, Florence, 77

nonagenarians, 146

nursing homes. *See* skilled nursing homes

omega-3-fatty acids, 74

onset, of depression: age of, 4–5; early, 4, 5, 6; LLD, 5. *See also* late onset

opioids, 75

orbitofrontal cortex, 76

other mood disorders, 17, 24; ADDM, 24; mood disorder due to medical conditions, 24; mood disorder not otherwise specified, 25; substance-induced mood disorder, 25

oxytocin, 75

PACE. *See* Program of All-Inclusive Care for the Elderly

PADs. *See* psychiatric advanced directives

pain. *See* physical illness and pain
Parkinson's disease, 24, 58
partial remission, 90
PATH. *See* problem-adaptive therapy
PE. *See* psychoeducation
perceived burdensomeness, 112, 112–113
personal experiences, with depression, 2
personality traits and coping style, 109–110
personalized medicine, 38
pet-assisted therapy, 76–77
pharmacotherapy, 55–56
physical health exam, 32
physical illness and pain, 110
physician evaluation, 32; disease screening during, 32–33; functional ability with, 33; medical history taken during, 32; physical health with, 32; polypharmacy during, 32
physiological age, 145
pineal gland, 66–67
PM. *See* poor metabolizer
polypharmacy, 32, 34–36
poor metabolizer (PM), 40
post-stroke depression (PSD), 26
problem-adaptive therapy (PATH), 52
problem-solving therapy (PST), 52–53
problem-solving therapy for executive dysfunction (PST-ED), 53
Program of All-Inclusive Care for the Elderly (PACE), 162
protective factors, for risk minimization, 114–115
proteins, 74
Proxy PADs, 172
PSD. *See* post-stroke depression
PST. *See* problem-solving therapy
PST-ED. *See* problem-solving therapy for executive dysfunction
psychiatric advanced directives (PADs), 171, 171–172
psychoeducation (PE), 53
psychogeriatric units, 127–128
psychological age, 147–148
psychological autopsy, 109
psychotherapy treatments, 49; BT-OA, 50; CB, 51; CBT-OA, 50–51; DBT, 51; IPT, 51–52; ISTDP, 51; LRP, 52; PATH, 52; PE, 53; PST, 52–53; PST-

ED, 53; schools of, 49; SP, 53; talk therapy, 49
public stigma, 183, 185

questions: for CCRCs, 169–170; for skilled nursing homes, 167–168

RealAge (Roizen and Roach), 145–146
recognition, of suicide risks, 109–111
recovery, 91, 97
recurrence. *See* relapse, recurrence and
reflexology, 79
Reiki, 79–80
relapse, recurrence and, 92–94
relational process, stigma as, 185
reminiscence bump, 81
reminiscence therapy, 52
remission, 90, 97
repetition, with, 152, 153
repetitive transcranial magnetic stimulation (rTMS), 56–57, 58, 94
residual symptoms, 90
resiliency, 150
response level, of treatment, 89–90
risk factors, for late onset depression, 6–7
risks, for suicide in later life: factors for, 113–114; functional impairments, 110–111; major psychiatric illness, 109; personality traits and coping style, 109–110; physical illness and pain, 110; protective factors for minimization of, 114–115; recognition of, 109–111; social disconnectedness, 110
Roach, Keith, 145–146
Roizen, Michael, 145–146
routine: with home transition, 135–136; during hospitalization, 130
rTMS. *See* repetitive transcranial magnetic stimulation

sandwich generation, 137
schools, of psychotherapy treatments, 49
screening. *See* cognition screening; disease screening and testing
self-actualization, 153–154
self-stigma, 183, 184, 185
seniors, 96; independent, 95, 97, 98; stigma and, 183–185

senses, holistic approach relating to, 66; sight, 66–69; smell, 69–72; sound, 81–84; taste, 72–75; touch, 75–80
serotonin syndrome, 40, 92
services, with CCRCs, 170
setting, of hospital, 127–128
shower, 80
sight, 66–69
silence, 83–84
skilled nursing homes, 165, 168; changes in, 165–166; Medicare and, 165, 167; negatives about, 166–167; questions for, 167–168; transitional programs at, 166
smell, 69–72
social contagion, 182
social disconnectedness, 110
Social Security, 164
soft bipolar disorder, 23
solution-focused therapy, 52
somatic complaints, 19
"Someone Like You" (Adele), 81
sound, 81–84
SP. See supportive psychotherapy
standards, of CCRCs, 169
statistics: for LLD, 6, 6–7; for subclinical depression, 7–8; for suicide in later life, 108–109
stigma: institutional, 184, 185; of LLD, 182–185; public, 183, 185; as relational process, 185; self, 183, 184, 185; seniors and, 183–185; understanding of, 182–183
stigma and diagnostic trauma, 94; ageism relating to, 94–95, 96; awareness of, 95, 95–96; context of, 95, 96; language relating to, 95; seeing the senior, 95, 96; treatment success for, 94–96
Structured Clinical Interview Form, 34
subclinical depression, 7; statistics for, 7–8; symptoms of, 7
substance-induced mood disorder, 25
success. See treatment success
successful aging, 151
suicidality: definition of, 117; levels of, 117–119; understanding of, 117–119
suicide: attempt at, 1; prevention plan for, 120–121; protective factors relating to, 114–115. See also risks, for suicide in

later life
suicide in later life, 107; capability for, 112, 113; case study: my father, 121–125; interpersonal theory of, 111–113; statistics for, 108–109; summary of, 120–121; warning signs of, 113–114, 115–117, 116
supportive psychotherapy (SP), 53
symptoms: of bipolar depression, 21–23; of depression, 4; residual, 90; of subclinical depression, 7; of unipolar depression, 18–19
syndromes. See specific syndromes

talk therapy, 1–2, 49
taste, 72; ancient grains, 72; folate, 72–73; high-flavonoid foods, 73; L-theanine, 73; magnesium, 73–74; omega-3-fatty acids, 74; proteins, 74; vitamin B12, 74–75; vitamin D, 75
telomeres, 145–146
therapies: acoustic sound, 82; animal-assisted, 76–77; chromotherapy, 68, 70; drug, 55; geriatric, 78; massage, 78–79; negative ion, 71; pet-assisted, 76; pharmacotherapy, 55–56; reminiscence, 52; solution-focused, 52; talk, 1–2; vibroacoustic, 82–83. See also electroconvulsive therapy; light therapies; magnetic seizure therapy; psychotherapy treatments
therapy goals, 89; recovery, 91, 97; remission, 90, 97; response, 89–90
think, with depression, 3
thwarted belongingness, 111–112, 112
touch, 75–76; AAT, 76–77; acupressure, 76; acupuncture, 76; exercise, 77–78; massage therapy, 78–79; reflexology, 79; Reiki, 79–80; shower, 80
transitional care, 133
transitional programs, at skilled nursing homes, 166
transitioning back home, 133; communication with, 134–136; flight into health, 135; routine with, 135–136
TRD. See treatment-resistant depression
treatment lag, 94
treatment-resistant depression (TRD), 56, 90–91

treatments: gaps in, 94; inpatient hospitalization, 130–131; medical, 54, 54–59; response level of, 89–90. *See also* depression in later life, treatments for; psychotherapy treatments

treatment success, 89; case study: Yvonne, 101–105; continuity of care, 97–98; relapse and recurrence, 92–94; stigma and diagnostic trauma, 94–96; summary of, 100–101; therapy goals, 89–91; why *vs.* what, 98–100

triggers, 98

"Two Physician Certificate", 129

ultrarapid metabolizer (UM), 41

understanding: of stigma, 182–183; of suicidality, 117–119

unipolar depression, 17, 19; DD, 20; D-NOS, 20; MDD, 20; symptoms of, 18–19

universal life energy. *See* Reiki

vagus nerve stimulation (VNS), 58

Valnet, Jean, 70

vascular depression (V-Dep), 26

VBT. *See* vibroacoustic therapy

V-Dep. *See* vascular depression

vibroacoustic therapy (VBT), 82–83

vitamin B12, 74–75

vitamin D, 75

VNS. *See* vagus nerve stimulation

voluntary hospitalization, 128

warning signs, of suicide in later life, 113–114, 115–117, 116

Wechsler Memory Scales (WMS), 34–36

well-being attainment, 148–151

why *vs.* what, with treatment, 98–100

Williams, Robin, 111

witnessing provisions, 173

WMS. *See* Wechsler Memory Scales

work productivity, depression and, 8

World Health Organization, 3, 6, 8, 183

ABOUT THE AUTHOR

Deborah Serani is a psychologist in private practice in New York. She is the author of the award-winning books *Living with Depression: Why Biology and Biography Matter along the Path to Hope and Healing* and *Depression and Your Child: A Guide for Parents and Caregivers*. Dr. Serani is a columnist for *Esperanza Magazine* and *Psychology Today*, and is a professor at Adelphi University. She is a go-to media expert, with interviews found at ABC News, CNN, HuffPost Live, the *New York Times*, the *Chicago Tribune, Scientific American Mind, USA Today*, CBS, NPR radio shows, and many more. She has also worked as a technical advisor for the NBC television show *Law & Order: Special Victims Unit*.